ISBN 978-1-331-42436-9
PIBN 10188261

Hall on Insurance Adjustments

FIRST REVISED EDITION

By
THRASHER HALL
Adjuster

The Rough Notes Co.
Publishers
Indianapolis, Indiana

INTRODUCTION

TO

"HALL ON INSURANCE ADJUSTMENTS"

FIRST REVISED EDITION

This work was issued from the press in 1907, and at once became popular with adjusters of fire insurance losses. Its noted author had long maintained a high reputation as a skilled and accurate adjuster and, being widely known, his work soon became popular with adjusters of fire insurance losses and it was regarded as an authoritative work in all the forty-eight states in the Union; hence the necessity of its revision much sooner than was anticipated. The conflicting nature of insurance codes of laws of so many states, new laws enacted by their legislatures and rules made by state officials imposed a herculean task upon its author in his work of revision in order to adapt it to the exact requirements of the present day—wholly up-to-date, and wholly accounting for the great delay of more than a year in publishing the revision after it was commenced.

The merit of the work has been greatly enhanced by the time taken by the author in making his revision as of to-day, at the expense of much new matter, necessarily considerably enlarging the book. It is with much confidence that the publishers are putting forth the first revised edition of Thrasher Hall's work, as we believe that Mr. Hall has exhausted his powers of research upon it and would not allow it to be published until it satisfied him.

On behalf of the Publishers.

INDEX
TITLE TO CHAPTERS

———

"HALL ON INSURANCE ADJUSTMENTS"

CHAPTER I.

DIRECT LOSS.

"Direct" Defined.

The word "direct" in a policy of insurance has been construed to mean merely "immediate" or "proximate," as distinguished from "remote."

Ermentraut et al. v. Girard F. & M. Ins. Co., 63 Minn. 305, 65 N. W. 635, 30 L. R. A. 346, 25 Ins. L. J. 81 (Annotated in 56 Am. St. 481).

What Is Direct Loss?

Where the contract of insurance was against loss by fire on goods which were being transported by a steamboat which came in collision with another boat, causing a fire, and the boat was sunk before the goods insured were injured by fire. Held, That, if means and appliances were at hand by which the sinking of the boat could have been avoided, and the intervention of a new agency, namely, that of fire, prevented their use, then the fire was the proximate and immediate cause of the loss, and that it was a question for the jury to decide, from all the circumstances of the case, what was the proximate cause of the loss sustained by the plaintiff, and whether it was the result of the fire.

New York & Boston Dispatch Express Co. v. Traders Ins. Co., 132 Mass. 377 (Annotated in 42 Am. R. Ext. Anno. 440, Notes).

Where it clearly appeared that the boat would have been destroyed by fire had it not been sunk, and the evidence clearly showed that ignition or combustion had begun before the boat was sunk, this taken in connection with the evidences of fire which were discovered, before the boat was sunk, the smoke issuing from the hold, with the deck so hot that pitch oozed from its seams, made it reasonably certain that a fire had broken out in the vessel before it was sunk, and which was the proximate cause of the loss.

Singleton v. Phoenix Ins. Co., 132 N. Y. 298, 30 N. E. 839.

In an action to recover for a general average loss, sustained by the sinking of the Propeller Potomac, it was held, that in order to render the insurance company liable upon the policy, the loss complained of must have been occasioned by one of the risks assumed by it.

Wex v. Boatmen's F. Ins. Co. (N. Y.), 11 St. Rep. 713.

Windstorm or Lightning.

Where the defendant had insured the plaintiff's property against loss by fire. The contract of insurance containing no exception exempting the defendant from liability for fire occasioned by storm or lightning. *Held*, That if the property was destroyed by that element, no difference whether occasioned by windstorm or lightning, the loss in question was one included in the risk for which the defendant was liable.

Farrell v. Farmers Mut. F. Ins. Co., 66 Mo. App. 153.

Testimony by Wool Merchants.

Where in an action upon a fire insurance policy to recover for loss and damage to a large quantity of wool, it was alleged, was caused by fire. It was held that wool merchants and manufacturers, who having had years of experience in their business, were competent to give opinions based upon facts falling within their experience, such as the effect of water on a large mass of wool and the probability of spontaneous combustion in it.

Sun Ins. Office of London, England v. Western Woolen Mill Co., 72 Kan. 41, 82 Pac. 513.

Testimony by Chemist.

In an action upon a fire insurance policy to recover for loss and damage to a large quantity of wool, it was alleged, was caused by fire, where the question was as to whether spon taneous combustion occurred. It was held not error to refuse to permit an expert chemist to define "fire," "ignition," ignition point," the relation between "fire" and "flame," and kindred terms, of which the meaning is commonly understood by all well-informed persons.

Sun Ins. Office of London, England v. Western Woolen Mill Co., 72 Kan. 41, 82 Pac. 513.

Expert Testimony and Scientific Works

In an action upon a fire insurance policy to recover for loss and damage to a large quantity of wool, it was alleged, was caused by fire, it was held that where scientific works of well-known authority and the opinions of experts are widely at variance upon the question whether spontaneous combustion is possible in a certain substance, courts will not assume as a matter

of law and fact which theory is true, but will leave its deter
mination to the jury.

Sun Ins. Office of London, England v. Western Woolen Mill Co.,
72 Kan. 41, 82 Pac. 513.

Instruction as to "A Total Loss."

Where the merits of the appeal was as to whether the loss
was "a total loss" by fire within the meaning of Section 5897,
or "a partial loss" only and falling within Section 5899 (Rev.
Stat. of Mo. 1889), and to ascertain the fact the Court instructed
the jury as follows: "By a total loss is meant that the building
had lost its identity and specific character as a building and
become so far disintegrated that it can not be properly designated as a building, although some part of it may remain standing." *Held*, The instruction was proper.

O'Keefe v. Liverpool, London & Globe Ins. Co., 140 Mo. 558, 41
S. W. 922, 26 Ins. L. J. 888.

Necessity for Instruction Defining Fire.

Where in an action upon a fire insurance policy to recover
for loss and damage to a large quantity of wool, it was alleged,
was caused by fire. It was held not error to refuse to give an
instruction that "wool can not set fire to itself," nor to define
"fire," nor to instruct that "no degree of heat, short of ignition,
producing an actual burning, is covered by the policy," where
the court of its own motion charged the jury that the definition
of the word "fire" was unnecessary, and that "it would make no
difference, if there was fire, whether it was in the form of flame
or merely smoldering, but there must be in fact the presence
of fire."

Sun Ins. Office of London, England v. Western Woolen Mill Co.,
72 Kan. 41, 82 Pac. 513.

Destruction of Building Leaving Walls Standing.

Where building "A" was destroyed by fire, leaving some of
the walls standing, and two or three days thereafter one of the
gables fell, damaging building "B." *Held*, That the insurance
company was liable.

Johnston v. Ins. Co., 7 Sess. Cas. (Scotland) 52, 1 Bennett, 259.

The company is liable for such a loss where the walls fell
seven days after the fire.

Russell v. German F. Ins. Co., 100 Minn. 528, 111 N. W. 400.

Building Removed from Foundation by Windstorm.

Where in an action upon a fire insurance policy it appeared

from the evidence that the building was not blown down by the storm, but merely removed a few feet from its foundation and left sufficiently intact as to be still subject to identification as the building covered by the risk, by a reference to the description in the policy, and one or more of the agencies of the storm, wind, or electricity caused fire to be communicated to the building, either from that in the stove contained therein, or in any other way, whereby such building became a loss. The contract of insurance contained no exception exempting the defendant from liability for fire occasioned by storm or lightning. *Held*, That the loss in question was one included in the risk and for which the insurer was liable.

Farrell v. Farmers Mut. F. Ins. Co., 66 Mo. App. 153.

Loss of Goods in Building Blown up by Municipality.

Insurers against loss by fire were held liable for goods destroyed in the blowing up of a building with gunpowder by direction of municipal authorities to prevent the spread of fire.

City Ins. Co. v. Corlies (N. Y.), 21 Wend. 367, 1 Bennett, 753.

Prohibition of Repair of Building by Ordinance.

Where a policy covered a building located within the fire limits of a city, and the building was of a class the repair of which was, under certain conditions, prohibited by the city ordinance. *Held*, That the insurers were liable for a total loss (value of the building) where the city ordinances would not permit the same to be repaired.

Larkins v. Glens Fall Ins. Co., 80 Minn. 527, 83 N. W. 409, 29 Ins. L. J. 527.

To the same effect.

Brady v. Northwestern Ins. Co., 11 Mich. 425, 4 Bennett 663; Hamburg-Bremen Fire Ins. Co. v. Garlington, 66 Tex. 103, 18 S. W. 337, 15 Ins. L. J. 509.

Building Condemned and Repair Prohibited.

Where the building insured was condemned by the proper authorities and an attempt to repair the same was prohibited by them. *Held*, The insured could claim a total loss, although the building when insured was not sound.

Monteleone v. Royal Ins. Co. of Liverpool and London, 47 La. Ann. 1563, 18 So. 472, 24 Ins. L. J. 531.

Contract of Insurance and Election to Repair Made After Adoption of Ordinance.

Where the contract of insurance and the election of the

insurance company to repair a wooden building under the same, were both made after the adoption of a city ordinance, the parties contracted with reference to the law as it existed at the time, and the question whether the city authorities would permit the building to be repaired in wood was therefore a risk the insurers assumed at the issuing of the policy, and which they reassumed at the making of the election.

Fire Association v. Rosenthal, 108 Pa. St. 474, 1 Atl. 303, 15 Ins. L. J. 658.

Exemption Clause Written Out of Policy by Valued Policy Law.

Where a policy contained the following exemption clause: "This company shall not be liable, beyond the actual value destroyed by fire, for loss occasioned by ordinance or law regulating construction or repair of buildings." *Held*, That by virtue of the valued policy law of Mississippi (Section 2592 of the Code of 1906) the clause of exemption from liability was written out of the policy.

Palatine Ins. Co. v. Nunn, 99 Miss. 493, 55 So. 44, 40 Ins. L. J. 1447.
To same effect is
Dinneen v. American Ins.Co. (Neb. S. C.), 152 N. W. 307.

Increased Cost of Repairs Under Building Laws.

In an action upon Massachusetts Standard form policies for a balance alleged to be due upon a partial loss by fire, it was held that the referees had the right, in determining the amount of damages to which the plaintiffs were entitled, to take into consideration the increased cost of repairing by reason of the building laws.

Hewins v. London Assurance Corporation et al., 184 Mass. 177, 68 N. E. 62.

Change in Physical Condition of Building Caused Wholly by Fire.

Where the building laws were the same at the time of the fire as at the time the policies were issued, and the only change in the situation was in the physical condition of the building, and that change was caused wholly by the fire, and the sole operating cause of the change in the building was the fire. *Held*, In the absence of any provision in the policy expressly excluding from the damages the part arising out of that condition, that part was not to be excluded, but was to be regarded as primarily the result of the fire, or as "loss or damage by fire."

Hewins v. London Assurance Corporation et al., 184 Mass. 177, 68 N. E. 62.

Ordinance Requiring Walls of Increased Thickness.

Where an ordinance was passed during the life of the policy requiring walls of an increased thickness. *Held*, That there was no good reason why the insurance company would not be held liable for the actual loss incurred, up to the extent of the amount designated in the policy, provided the proportional amount of the loss falling upon the company reached that sum.

Pennsylvania, etc. v. Philadelphia, etc., 201 Pa. St. 497, 51 Atl. rep. 351.

Stock Destroyed by Fire Caused by Lightning.

Where in an action upon a policy of insurance upon live stock against lightning. The barn had been destroyed by fire, and the stock burned in it, and the main issue was whether the barn was struck by lightning, and thereby set on fire. *Held*, That if the stock was destroyed by fire which was immediately caused by the lightning, or by the lightning itself, the defendant was liable.

Hapeman v. Citizens Mut. F. Ins. Co., 126 Mich. 191, 85 N. W. 454, 30 Ins. L. J. 452.

"Ice Clause" Applied to Boat Detailed by Gale.

Where in an action upon a marine policy, which was issued upon a cargo of hay laden on a canal boat, it appeared that while the boat was proceeding down a river a heavy gale separated her from the steam tugs which had her in tow and drove her to shore, and her detention there until ice formed around her was due to a consequence of the gale, stranding. The policy contained the following ice clause: "It is understood and agreed that if any boats the cargo of which are covered by this policy are prevented or detained by ice, or the closing of navigation, from terminating the trip, then in such case the policy shall cease to attach upon said cargo, and this company shall return the premium for the unexpired portion of said trip." *Held*, That as the efficient cause of the detention was the loss of the motive-power through the stress of the storm, and the ice acted only as an obstacle to its restoration, the insurers were liable.

Brown et al. v. St. Nicholas Ins. Co., 61 N. Y. 332.

Loss Due to Moisture from Water in Extinguishing Fire.

Where a policy of fire insurance in the standard form covered property (a stock of fish) in a warehouse, and the property insured was at the time of the fire in an annex. The question was as to whether the loss of the fish in the annex was due directly to the fire. It appeared from the evidence that there was no fire in the annex, and that no part of plaintiff's property in the annex was injured by heat or fire, and it was conceded by plaintiff that the fish were destroyed by moisture. But it claimed that this moisture came directly from water used in extinguishing the fire in the warehouse, which got into the annex. In an action upon the policy, it was held that the policy covered the property, and that the evidence was sufficient to sustain the finding of the jury that the loss was directly due to the fire.

Boak Fish Co. v. Manchester F. Assur. Co., 84 Minn. 419, 87 N. W. 932, 31 Ins. L. J. 253.

Removal of Stove Pipe as Breach of Condition that Pipe Be Secured.

Where in an action upon a policy of insurance against loss or damage by fire, upon the dwelling house and household furniture of the plaintiff, it appeared that plaintiff's wife had taken down a stove in a second story room, but neglected to remove the stove in the room underneath, afterwards placed a bed in the room over the hole through which the stove pipe passed. Several days thereafter a fire was built in the stove in the room underneath the bed, which set bed on fire and destroyed the house. Policy provided that stoves and pipes should be well secured. *Held*, The insurance company was liable.

Mickey v. Burlington Ins. Co., 35 Iowa 174, 5 Bennett 439, 2 Ins. L. J. 15, (Annotated in 14 Am. R. Ext. Anno. 494, Notes).

Burning of Building After Destruction of Minor Portion.

Where in an action upon a policy of insurance it appeared that a portion of the building had fallen, leaving the larger portion—more than three-fourths of it standing, and afterwards it burned. The policy contained the following condition: "XII. If a building shall fall, except as the result of a fire, all insurance by this company on it, or its contents, shall immediately cease and determine." *Held*, The building was not a fallen building within the meaning of the thirteenth condition of the policy.

Breuner v. L. & L. & G. Ins. Co., 51 Cal. 101, 6 Ins. L. J. 475 (Annotated in 21 Am. R. Ext. Anno. 703, Notes).

Where the policy contained a clause that, if the building or any part thereof fall except as the result of fire, all insurance by this policy on such building or its contents shall immediately

cease," and before the fire destroyed the insured building, it
had been visited by a cyclone, and the roof of the two front
upper rooms had been blown away, the rafters, ceiling, and
parts of walls remaining. *Held,* That the insurance company
was not exempt under the policy, as its terms did not contemplate the fall of fragmentary portions of the building, but "some
functional portion of the structure."

London & L. Ins. Co. v. Crunk, 91 Tenn. 376, 23 S. W. 140.

(B) What Is Not Direct Loss?

Where in an action on a policy of insurance effected with
the defendant "against all the damage which the plaintiffs should
suffer by fire," on their "stock and utensils in their regular built
sugar house." It appeared that the loss to the sugar by the heat
of the usual fires employed for refining had been increased by
the mismanagement of the insured, who inadvertently kept the
top of the chimney closed, and it was held not a loss within
the meaning of the policy.

Austin et al. v. Drewe, 6 Taunt. 436, 1 Bennett 102.

It is suggested that insurance adjusters read the full decision
of the court in Austin et al. v. Drewe. It was the first and
leading case on this subject and is frequently quoted. A very
full report of it may be had in 1 Bennett 102.

Loss From Smoke and Soot From Defective Stove Pipe.

The insurer was held not liable for loss or damage occasioned by smoke and soot escaping from a defective stove pipe
and emanating from a fire intentionally built in a stove and
kept confined therein; or for damages caused by the water used
in cooling a portion of the ceiling heated by the pipe, where in
the proofs of loss it was not claimed that anything was actually
ignited by this heat, and it did not appear that the use of the
water was necessary to prevent ignition.

Cannon v. Phoenix Ins. Co., 110 Ga. 566, 35 S. E. 775, 29 Ins. L. J.
1023, citing: Austin v. Drewe, 6 Taunt. 436 and Gibbons v.
Savings Inst., 30 Ill. App. 263.

But where the assured's servant burned some rubbish and
cannel coal in the furnace causing a loss from smoke and soot
it was held the insurance company was liable for the loss that
it was not a friendly fire, the furnace was for heating purposes
and not meant to burn rubbish.

O'Connor v. Queen Ins. Co., 140 Wis. 388, 122 N. W. 1038, Annotated in 25 L. R. A. (N. S.) 501, and 17 Am. & Eng. Anno. Cas.
1118.

Smoke From Lamp.

Where in an action upon a policy insuring the plaintiff against loss or damage by fire or lightning, etc. It appeared upon the trial that all the damage was caused by smoke from a lamp left lighted in plaintiff's office. *Held*, That a lighted lamp was not a "fire" within the meaning of the policy, and that it was not contemplated by the parties to the contract of insurance that the policy would cover damages arising from a smoking lamp.

Fitzgerald v. German Am. Ins. Co., 30 Miscl. (N. Y.) 72, 62 N. Y. Supp. 824.

Hop-House.

Where the insurance issued by the defendant to plaintiff was specified to be "on his frame shingle roof hop-house, while drying hops," and the defendant agreed to make good to plaintiff all loss or damage which should happen "by fire to the property so specified, from the 15th day of August, to the 15th day of October, 1875. The hop-house was destroyed by fire after the plaintiff had ceased drying hops. *Held*,, That as the fire happened after the plaintiff had ceased drying hops, the defendant was not liable.

Langworthy v. O. & O. Ins. Co., 85 N. Y. 632, 10 Ins. L. J. 546.

Lightning.

Where a policy insured against loss by lightning, an electric discharge causing a concussion or shock of such violence as to jar and injure the walls of plaintiff's building, was not within the contemplation of such policy.

Kattleman v. Fire Ass'n, 79 Mo. App. 447.

Where an insurance policy contained a lightning clause which limited the liability of the company to the direct loss caused by lightning, and expressly excluded damage by cyclone, tornado or windstorm. *Held*, There could be no recovery for loss by windstorm, although the windstorm completed the work of destruction of the building, as the jury must be required to limit the recovery of plaintiff to the direct loss or damage caused by lightning.

Beaks v. Phoenix Ins. Co., 143 N. Y. 402, 24 Ins. L. J. 73, 38 N. E. 453 (Annotated in 26 L. R. A. 267).

Where in an action upon a policy to recover for loss alleged to have been caused by lightning. The property insured was a gristmill and sawmill. During a severe storm a sharp flash of lightning was seen, followed immediately by a loud report near by and in the vicinity of the mill, and soon thereafter a noise was heard, as of the falling and crashing of a building, and in the following morning the water in the river was quite high, and the building lay in broken disorganized heaps of material at various points, the timbers were broken and splintered, but there were no marks of fire on any of the remaining portions of the building. *Held*, That as there were no marks of fire anywhere, such as are customarily found when lightning has come in contact with dry wood, there was no justification in the evidence for the finding that the buildings were destroyed by the latter cause, and since the evidence established clearly that the undermining of the buildings by water caused the loss complained of.

     Clark v. Farmers Mut. Fire Ins. Co., 111 Wis. 65, 86 N. W. 549, 14 Deitch 86.

     Where in an action upon a policy of insurance, which insured the plaintiff against "all direct loss or damage by fire" on his store and office furniture and fixtures contained in a three-story, brick, tin-roof building, it appeared that the building and its contents were damaged by fire, the plaintiff was permitted to let his personal property remain in the building, and twenty-five days after such fire and after a new roof was put on the building, the building fell, destroying plaintiff's property. *Held*, That there was no error in granting a non-suit, since it did not appear that the fire was the proximate, or, in any sense of the term, the "direct" cause of the loss; but the evidence tended to show that the efficient and predominating cause was the pouring and damming up of the water against the wall from the heavy rains which fell subsequent to the fire.

     Cuesta v. Royal Ins. Co., 98 Ga. 720, 27 S. E. Rep. 172.

     Where in an action upon two policies of fire insurance upon wool, against all direct loss or damage by fire, it appeared that the wool insured had become entirely submerged by water, caused by an unusual flood, and remained so for eight days, and after subsidence of the water, it was found to be wet and covered with mud, very much heated, and there was smoke in the rooms where the wool was and an odor of burned wool, but there was no flame to be seen, and no visible fire, and whatever damage was done to the wool had been caused by the action of water thereon. *Held*, That, since it appeared from the evidence that the internal development of heat never at any time became so rapid as to produce a flame or a glow, nor any visible heat or light in or about the wool, the plaintiff had not shown any direct loss by fire within the meaning of the word "fire," as used in the policies, and as that word is known to the public generally.

Western Woolen Mills Co. v. Northern Assurance Co., 139, Fed. 637.
(Annotated in 72 C. C. A. 1).

An insurance policy covering against direct loss by fire, does not contemplate a loss to steam boiler caused by assured or his servants negligently leaving the boiler with insufficient water, so that any loss that was done to it must of necessity have been caused by the fire or heat used for heating it, which fire was in its usual or accustomed place and therefore not a hostile one.

McGraw v. Home Ins. Co. (Kan. S. C.) 28 Ins. Digest 18, 144 Pac. 821.

"This company shall not be liable beyond the actual value destroyed by fire, for loss occasioned by ordinance of law regulating construction or repair of buildings." Insurance, $2,500; value of building was $3,500; loss, $1,400. The insured was prohibited from reconstructing building by the ordinances of the city governing the repair and construction of buildings within the fire limits of the city of Jackson, in which it was located. It is thoroughly well settled that in such cases, where the loss by fire is partial, but the injury by fire has rendered the building unfit for use for the purpose for which it was constructed and there are ordinances or there is a law prohibiting its reconstruction, the loss in such cases is total. This is very clearly set forth in Sandberg v. St. Paul and S. R. R. Co., 80 Minn. 442, 83 N. W. 411. The sole question before us in this, the only material contention in the case, is whether or not this clause in the contract of insurance was written out by virtue of the provisions of our valued policy law, §2592 of Code of 1906. The question is not one at all free from difficulty and we have given it the most careful consideration. The authority chiefly relied on by the learned counsel for appellant is the case of Hewins v. London Assurance Corp., 184 Mass. 178, 68 N. E. 62, and that case clearly holds that the defense here would be good, the contract stipulation referred to being valid, in a state where there is no valued policy law substantially like ours.

We have found one case, New Orleans R. E. M. & S. Co. v.

Teutonia Ins. Co., La. 54 S. 466, which does squarely hold, on
a valued policy law substantially like ours, though not identical
in its phraseology, that the very clause here relied on is written
out of the policy by the valued policy law.

Palatine Ins. Co. v. Nunn, 99 Miss. 493, 55 So. 44. To same effect
is Dinneen v. American Ins. Co. (Neb. S. C.), 152 N. W. 307.

Recovery on account of the increased cost of repairing,
by reason of the building laws, of a building partially destroyed,
is excluded by a policy providing that loss or damage shall in
no event exceed what it would cost the insured to repair or replace the same with material of like kind and quality, and the
insurer shall not be liable beyond the actual value destroyed by
fire for loss occasioned by law regulating construction or repair
of buildings. This, too, notwithstanding the fact that under the
Massachusetts standard policy it is a total loss, but where a
company issued a policy on property in Masachusetts, which
policy provided that in case of loss or damage, "loss shall in no
event exceed what it would cost the insured to repair or replace
the same with material of like kind and quality" and that the
company should not be liable beyond the actual value destroyed
by fire for loss occasioned by ordinance or law regulating construction or repair of buildings. * * * The standard policy
law does not provide any rule of interpretation as do the valued
policy laws of other states, nor does it say that another form of
policy shall be void. On the contrary, it provides for a fine for a
company issuing a different policy, but also declares it to be
binding on the company. Its legal effect is not changed. The
illegal policy is not changed by law so as to conform to the
legal. The assured may sue upon it, but it must be construed
as it reads. No statute is incorporated in it. The penalty suffered by the company is a fine and not a liability to be held on
a contract different from that made by it.

Hewins v. London Assur. Corp etl al., 184 Mass. 178, 68 N. E. 62.

Some time since I asked the following question of "Rough
Notes": If a New York Standard form of policy covered meats
in cold storage warehouse "A" against direct loss by fire, and
building "B" located across the street was a refrigerating plant
supplying through pipes the cold air for storage warehouse "A,"
the same owner owning and operating both buildings, would the
insurance company be liable for a loss to stock of meats in
building "A" by reason of the destruction by fire of building
"B"? Mr. Deitch answered, the company would not be liable

and I think his answer is correct. Yet, a large list of companies paid the Dold Packing Company at Kansas City for just such a loss a few years ago, not one of them contested it, I presume on account of the claim against each company being so small, though the aggregate against all was considerable.

If such a loss be one of the perils insured against, why would not the insurer be liable if assured chilled his meats by natural ice from his ice house across the street, carried across on chutes, if such icehouse be destroyed by fire and it be impossible to procure any other ice?

If the insurer be liable for such losses, at what distance from the property insured must the cold storage plant be, before liability of the insurer for loss will cease in consequence of its destruction by fire? Here in St. Louis (and I presume in other cities) we have a corporation which has a large cold storage plant, furnishing chilled air to cold storage warehouses, restaurants, hotels, etc., throughout the city, by means of pipes under the streets and if such losses as I have mentioned are covered under a fire policy, then the losses which may occur in any or all of such places at any time by the burning of the cold storage plant is one for which the insurer is liable.

Loss by Negligence of Another.

He who by his negligence or misconduct creates or suffers a fire upon his own premises, which, burning his own property, spreads thence to the immediately adjacent premises and destroys the property of another, is liable to the latter for the damages sustained by him. (The cases of Ryan v. N. Y. C. R. R. Co., 35 N. Y. 210, and Pa. R. R. Co. v. Kerr, 62 Pa. 353, distinguished.)

Webb. v. R., W. & O. R. R. Co., 49 N. Y. 420.

Loss of Blankets Used to Protect Building From Fire.

A fire happening in the neighborhood, the insured, with the approbation of the insurer, procured blankets and spread them (wet) on the outside of the building, whereby it and its contents were saved, but the blankets were rendered worthless. *Held*, loss of blankets not covered by policy, but that it was a subject of general average, to which the insurer and insured should contribute in the proportion to the amount which they respectively had at risk in the store and contents, but that other neighboring property upon which the insurer had risks which

would have been in danger if the store had burned, were too re-
motely affected to be liable to contribution.

Wells v. Boston Ins. Co., 6 Pick (23 Mass.) 182.

Loss by Negligence of Assured's Agent.

Underwriters are answerable for any loss occasioned by the
negligence of those in charge of the property insured by them.
But the negligence must be unaffected by any fruad or design
on the part of the insured.

Henderson v. Western M. & F. Ins. Co., 10 Robinson (La.) 164.

Loss by Wilful Burning of Assured's Property by His Wife.

A policy of fire insurance covers a loss occasioned by the
wife of the insured; and her acts and declarations at, and dur
ing the fire are not evidence against the husband, unless done
by his consent, nor are they part of the res gestae.

Walker v. Phoenix Ins. Co., 62 Mo. App. 209.

To same effect is

Plinsky v. Germania F. Ins. Co., 32 Fed. 47;
Feibelman v. Manchester F. Assur. Co., 108 Ala. 180, 19 So. 540;
Perry v. Mechanics M. Ins. Co., 11 Fed. 485.

Loss by Carelessness of Assured's Son.

Where the loss was caused by the assured's son filling a
stove in the building destroyed, with combustible materials, and
thus recklessly causing the loss, the company will not be
relieved from liability, where the act was unaffected by fraud or
design on the part of the assured.

Malin v. Mercantile T. M. Ins. Co., 105 Mo. App. 625.

Loss by Negligence of Another.

The negligent burning of a house, and the spreading of the
fire to a neighboring house, and the burning thereof, does not
give the owner of the last house a cause of action against the
owner in which the fire originated. The damages are too remote.

Ryan v. N. Y. Central R. R. Co., 35 N. Y. 210.

Loss by Negligence of Another.

A railroad company, which has negligently set a fire to in-
flamable material which it has allowed to accumulate on its right
of way, is not liable to the owner of lands not abutting on its
premises, for damages caused by fire communicated through the
abutting and intervening woodlands of a third person, over

which the railroad had no control and without which the fire could not have extended.

Hoffman v. King, 160 N. Y. 618, 55 N. E. 401.

Assured Must Protect Property at Fire.

The assured is bound diligently to labor in saving the property by fire; but the insertion of a clause in the policy requiring such labor and effort, does not impose any additional duty upon him.

Cincinnati M. Ins. Co. v. May, 20 Ohio 211.

Loss by Assured's Recklessness.

Where an act of Congress passed to secure steamboats against fire, in order to secure the lives of passengers; provides that turpentine, etc., on such vessels shall be secured in metallic containers at a secure distance from any fire. The act of plaintiff in placing a barrel of turpentine near the furnace and used it to increase the head of steam so as to give greater speed to his boat; whereby it was set on fire; he cannot recover the insurance on his boat. The only question for the jury to determine is, was the turpentine used in the manner shown, if it was he cannot recover on his insurance.

Citizens Ins. Co. v. Marsh, 41 Pa. St. 386.

What is not General Average Loss.

The scuttling of a ship by the municipal authorities of a port, without the direction of her master or other commanding officer, to extinguish a fire in her hold, is not a general average loss.

Ralli v. Troop, 157 U. S. 386.

Damage by Fire Engine on Way to Fire.

Where a fire engine on its way to a fire was deflected from its course, collided with and damaged plaintiff's building. Held, such loss is not a direct fire loss within the meaning of a fire insurance policy.

Foster v. Fidelity F. Ins. Co., 24 Pac. Supt. Ct. 585.

Damage by Smoking Lamp.

Smoke and soot from a lamp whose flame accidentally flared up two or three feet above the lamp chimney, is not a direct fire loss as used in an insurance policy.

Samuels v. Continental Ins. Co., 2 Pa. Dist. Ct. 397.

Damage by Soot and Smoke from Ignition of Accumulated Soot in Chimney.

A distinction should be made between a fire intentionally started and maintained for a useful purpose in connection with the occupation of a building, and a fire which starts from such a fire, without human agency, in a place where fires are never lighted nor maintained, although such ignition may naturally be expected to occur occasionally as an incident to the maintenance of necessary fires.

Way v. Abington M. F. Ins. Co., 166 Mass. 67, 43 N. E. 1032.

Profits not Insured.

The liability upon a policy insuring a turn pike company against loss by fire of a bridge, is to be measured by the pecuniary value of the injury to the bridge, not by the loss of tolls suffered before the bridge could be rebuilt.

Such turn pike company has no insurable interest in a public county bridge on the line of its road but free to all travel, even though it contributed to its cost, erection and maintenance.

Farmers M. Ins. Co. v. New H. T. Co., 122 Pa. St. 37, 15 Atl. 563

Company is Liable for Loss by Fire Where Assured's Insane Wife Burns the Property.

Where the assured was for the time being entrusted with the care of his insane wife and she burned his insured property, the insurer will be held liable for the loss unless it can show actual design or such a degree of negligence and carelessness on the part of the husband, as will evince a corrupt design or a fraudulent purpose on his part.

Gove v. Farmers M. F. Ins. Co., 48 N. H. 41.

Loss by Assured or His Servant's Negligence.

In relation to insurance against fire, the doctrine seems to have prevailed for a great length of time that it covers losses occasioned by the mere faults and negligence of the assured and his servants unaffected by any fraud or design. Ins. Co. v. Lawrence, 10 Pet. 507; see also, Mickey v. Burlington Ins. Co., 35 Ia. 174, and cases there cited. Hence the action of the assured's president in burning rubbish, which fire spread to and burned the assured's building, is not such an increase of risk as to avoid the policy, where there was no design to burn the building.

Des Moines Ice Co. v. Niagara Ins. Co., 99 Ia. 193, 68 N. W. 600.

Smoke and Soot from Coal Oil Stove.

The question whether the smoke proceeded from a fire outside the place where, under the contract of insurance, it was intended to burn was for the jury under the evidence in this case. It was submitted to them in a charge of which the defendant has no reason to complain. If the smoke that did the damage proceeded from a fire "out of place," it is no answer to say that this originated in a fire in the place fitted and intended for it.

Collins v. Delaware Ins. Co., 9 Pa. Supr. Ct. 576.

CHAPTER II.

CASH VALUE—MEASURE OF DAMAGE.

"This company shall not be liable beyond the actual cash value of the property at the time the loss occurs, * * * with proper deduction for depreciation however caused, and shall in no event exceed what it would then cost the assured to repair or replace the same with material of like kind and quality."

Assured being a manufacturer, can not recover more than the sum it would cost him to replace the property destroyed.

Standard Sew. Mch. Co. v. Royal Ins. Co. (Pa. S. C.), 51 Atl. Rep. 345, 15 Deitch 29.

Cash value means what it would cost the insured in actual cash to replace the goods, at the time and place of fire.

Niagara F. Ins. Co. v. Heflin (Ky. C. A.), 60 S. W. Rep. 393, 30 Ins. L. J. 326;

Equitable F. Ins. Co. v. Quinn, 11 Low. Can. 170;

Fisher v. Crescent Ins. Co. (U. S. C. C.), (W. Dist. N. C.), 17 Ins. L. J. 712;

Western Assurance Co. v. Studebaker, 124 Ind. 176, 20 Ins. L. J. 64;

Grubbs v. North Carolina Home Ins. Co. (S. C. of N. C.), 108 N. C. 472, 20 Ins. L. J. 784;

Queen v. McCoin (Ky. C. A.), 49 S. W. Rep. 800, 12 Deitch 67;

Post Printing & Publishing Co. v. Ins. Co. of N. A. (Pa. S. C.), 42 Atl. Rep. 192;

Hedger v. Ins. Co., 12 Ins. L. J. 926, 17 Fed. 498;

Marchessen v. Merchants Ins. Co., 1 Rob. (La.) 438, 2 Bennett 166;

Fowler v. Old N. C. S. Ins. Co., 74 N. C. 81;

Burgess v. Alliance Ins. Co., 10 Allen (Mass.) 221, 5 Bennett 46;

Boyd v. Royal Ins. Co., 111 N. C. 372, 16 S. E. 389;

Hedger v. Ins. Co. (U. S. C. C.), 12 Ins. L. J. 926;

Mack v. Lancashire Ins. Co. (U. S. C. C.), 19 Ins. L. J. 68.

And this, too, regardless of cost of reproduction.

Hartford F. Ins. Co. v. Cannon et al. (Tex. C. C. A.), 46 S. W. Rep. 851; 11 Finch 109;

Mitchell v. St. Paul German F. Ins. Co. (Mich. S. C.), 52 N. W. Rep. 1017; 21 Ins. L. J. 1003.

The policy provided that the company should not be liable "beyond the actual cash value of the property at the time any loss or damage occurs, * * * and shall in no event exceed what it would then cost the insured to repair or replace the same with material of like kind and quality." Plaintiff contended that, as the goods burned could not be immediately replaced at the scene of the fire with goods of like kind and quality, it is entitled to recover the cash market value of the goods, which is what the goods could have been sold for in San Antonio to dealers at wholesale, in quantities of a single article or in car-load lots, or in less than car-load lots, in plaintiff's ordinary course of business. The contention of defendant is that the value is to be determined by what it would cost to replace said goods from other markets with goods of like kind and quality within a reasonable time, which could be done, and was done in this instance, within 30 days. *Held,* That the expression, "What it would then cost the assured" evidently was not intended to mean what it would cost to replace immediately or instanter upon the destruction of the goods by fire, but what it would cost to replace the burned articles from the markets where such goods were usually manufactured or could be purchased within a reasonable time. The goods were replaced within 30 days after the fire at a sum less than that claimed by plaintiff. This was within a reasonable time, and fixed the sum of plaintiff's recovery.

> Texas Moline Plow Co. v. Niagara Fire Ins. Co. (Tex. C. C. A.):
> 87 Southwestern Reporter (June 7, 1905), 192

If the insured is liable to the government for tax on whisky, such tax forms part of the cash value for which the insurer is liable.

> Hedger v. Ins. Co. (U. S. C. C.), 12 Ins. L. J. 926;
> Queen v. McCoin (Ky. C. A.), 49 S. W. Rep. 800, 12 Deitch 67;
> Security Ins. Co. v. Farrell (Ill. S. C.), 2 Ins. L. J. 302.
> (Though in this case—2 Ins. L. J. 302—it was held assured was not liable and in that case it necessarily follows that insurer is not.)

)

The aim should be to arrive as nearly as possible at the value of the building as it stood on the day of the fire, taking into consideration cost to rebuild or replace, and difference in value between new building and the condition it was in at the time of the fire.

> Stenzel v. Pennsylvania F. Ins. Co. et al. (La. S. C.), 35 S. W. Rep. 271;
> Hilton v. Phoenix Ass'n Co. (Me. S. J. C.), 42 Atl. Rep. 412; 28 Ins. L. J. 309.

Linotype machines cost manufacturer $1.000 each. They were sold to publisher for $3,000. The contract between the two provides that title is to remain in manufacturer. *Held,* That such an agreement is constructively fraudulent, and a mere attempt to maintain a secret lien, and the title is really in the publishing company, which is entitled to recover $3,000, the cost to them of replacing the machines.

Post Printing and Publishing Co. v. Ins. Co. of N. A. (Pa. S. C.), 42 Atl. Rep. 192.

ASSESSORS VALUE—ASSURED'S TAX RETURNS.

The assessed value is not the measure of damage. Where the destroyed building was in a small village it had an intrinsic but no market value, therefore, estimates of cost to rebuild must be relied on.

German M. Ins. Co. v. Niewiede, 11 Ind. App. 634, 39 N. E. 534; Helm v. Anchor F. Ins. Co., 109 N. W. 605; Knickerbocker Ins. Co. v. McGinness, 87 Ill. 70.

CASH VALUE OF WHISKY.

The policy contains the fellowing provision: "This company shall not be liable beyond the actual cash value of the property at the time any loss or damage occurs, and the loss or damage shall be ascertained, or estimated, according to such actual cash value, with proper deduction for depreciation, however caused, and shall in no event exceed what it would then cost the insured to repair or replace the same with material of like kind and quantity." This provision of the contract furnishes the measure of damages and raises the important question in the case. The policy is the contract between the parties, and must be given an interpretation which will carry out their intention. If the language of the policy is doubtful or obscure, it will be construed most unfavorable to the insurer. Merrick v. Germania Fire Insurance Co., 54 Pa. 277. A contract of insurance must have a reasonable interpretation such as was prob ably in the contemplation of the parties when it was made; and when the words of a policy are, without violence, suscepti ble of two interpretations, that which will sustain a claim to the indemnity it was the object of the assured to obtain should be preferred. Humphreys v. National Benefit Association, 139 Pa. 214, 20 Atl. 1047, 11 L. R. A. 564.

The property covered by this policy is of a peculiar character, but the intention of both parties was to protect the insured against its loss by fire, and the policy must be construed so as to effect that purpose. It not like a machine, a house, or property of that character. There is no difficulty whatever in ascertaining the cost of repairing or replacing such property as of the date it is injured or destroyed. Proof is readily accessible which will enable the insured to establish "what it would then cost to repair or replace the same with material of like kind and quantity." A moment's reflection will show that this is not true of whisky which has been destroyed. From the uncontradicted evidence it appears, and therefore it must be taken as a fact, that the age of whisky materially affects its character and quality, and hence is an important factor in ascertaining or determining its value. It also appears in the case that this, like other brands of whisky, has a distinctive character and quality of its own, and that no brand of whisky can be substituted in the market for another brand.

Now, under the clause of the policy above quoted, how should the plaintiffs' loss be measured? The whisky insured by the several policies issued to the plaintiffs was of different inspections. There were 6,910 barrels destroyed. The most of it was manufactured about six months prior to the fire; some in 1903 and 1904, and some in 1898 and 1899. The defendant company is not liable beyond the actual "cash value." What is that value? That is fixed by the uncontradicted testimony of a number of witnesses. It ranges from 50 cents to $1.05 per gallon, according to its age. This was the cash value of the A. Overhold & Co. whisky in the wholesale liquor market on November 19, 1905, when it was destroyed. As appears in the evidence, there was whisky of that brand of the different inspections on the market at that date. It must be conceded, we think, that, if the cash value of the whisky at the date of the loss is the only practical standard for measuring the plaintiffs' damages, the court and jury must accept the value fixed by the plaintiffs' witnesses. It will be observed, however, that the policy provides that the cash value of the whisky "shall in no case exceed what it would then cost the insured to repair or replace the same with material of like kind and quality." The defendant company contends that the loss could not be estimated at more than it would have cost the insured to replace the whisky. In other words, the position of the defendants is that, under this provision of the contract, the plaintiffs' right of recovery is limited to the cost of material, the expense of manufacturing the whisky, the charges for carrying it in bond, insurance, and interest on the amount invested in the whisky. This provision of the policy is simply a limitation on the former provision, which fixes the loss at the cash value of the property. In estimating the loss, the insured is entitled to the cash value of the property destroyed, provided it does not exceed what it would cost to replace it with material of like kind and quality at the date it was consumed. How shall this cost be ascertained? It is doubtless true that the cost of manufacturing a gallon of whisky is easily ascertained. But that does not meet the requirements of this case. The plaintiffs are not restricted to the simple cost of reproducing the whisky. They are entitled to have the whisky which was destroyed replaced as of the date of the loss with the same material of like kind and quality. The whisky consumed by the fire was, as we have seen, of different inspections. It had age which gave it character and quality. It was of the A. Overholt & Co. brand, dissimilar in character and quality from other brands, and for which there is no substitute. The cost of whisky of like character, quality and age is the measure of the plaintiffs' right of recovery. It is manifest that this cost can not be ascertained by simply taking into consideration the cost of the elements suggested by the learned counsel for the defendant company. It omits from the calculation the effect which age has on that particular brand of whisky, which is a most important factor in determining its cost. Nor can any witness, as is apparent, definitely estimate what the age of each of the several inspections in this case will add to the actual cost of the material entering into the particular brand of whisky. It is an important element entering into its value, but the precise extent to which its value is increased cannot be fixed by testimony. There is, therefore, but one way to ascertain the cost of replacing the whisky at the date it was destroyed, considering the brand, character, quality and age of the whisky; and that is to ascertain by competent evidence its actual cash value on the day of the fire. By that method of computing the cost the whisky destroyed will be replaced "with material of like kind and quality" as of the date it was consumed, and that is therefore the measure of the plaintiffs' damages.

The rule adopted in ascertaining the cost of replacing the insured property in Standard Sewing Machine Company v. Royal Insurance Company, 201 Pa. 645, 51 Atl. 354, is not applicable here, for the reasons above stated. To enforce it under the circumstances of this case would deprive the plaintiffs of the protection against loss of their property by fire which the policy stipulates. In the sewing machine case there was no difficulty in applying the rule. Here, owing to the peculiar character of the property insured, the cost of replacing it must be determined by its value at the date of loss.

The judgment of the court below is affirmed.

Frick v. United Firemen's Ins. Co., 67 Atl. 743, 218 Pa. 489.

The court affirmed the cases of Frick v. Svea F. & L. Ins. Cos. and twenty-three other companies at same time on same grounds.

To same effect is Mechanics Ins Co. v. Hoover, 182 Fed. 590, aff'g 173 Fed. 888.

CASH VALUE AS APPLIED TO MANUFACTURERS' STOCK.

Houghton , J. The plaintiff is a manufacturer of straw hats, and the defendant issued to him a policy of insurance, insuring him against loss by fire to his manufactured and unmanufactured stock in the sum of $2,000. On February 11, 1906, while such policy was in force, a fire occurred by which the plaintiff's factory and contents were destroyed. A portion of the property so destroyed consisted of a quantity of hats which had been finished, bargained for, cased for shipment, and marked with the buyers' names prior to the fire. The delivery and shipment of these goods would have commenced the morning after the fire occurred, and would have continued for four months following. The stipulated facts concede that it would have required four months to reproduce the hats in the condition they were at the time of the fire and that plaintiff's factory could not be rebuilt in time to reproduce the goods for the coming season's trade, and that after diligent effort the plaintiff was unable to procure any other mill to reproduce the goods and was unable to replace them by purchase in the market. The policy was the standard form, and contained the following provision with respect to ascertaining the loss:

"This company shall not be liable beyond the actual cash value of the property at the time any loss or damage occurs, and the loss or damage shall be ascertained or estimated according to such actual cash value, with proper deductions for depreciation, however caused, and shall in no event exceed what it would then cost the insured to repair or replace the same with material of like kind and quality."

It is stipulated that the actual cost of manufacture to the plaintiff of that portion of the hats for which defendant is liable was $1,841.95, and that the actual selling price at which plaintiff had made sales on which he was about to make delivery was $1,966.79. There would be no difficulty in deciding the question, and doubtless no controversy, except for the clause of the con-tract providing that the loss or damage "shall in no event exceed what it would then cost the insured to repair or replace the same with material of like kind and quality."

Without this clause the actual cash value must be conceded to be the measure of damage. Whatever may be the rule with respect to ordinary manufactured articles, and whether under ordinary circumstances the cost of manufacture under this clause would be the measure of loss, we are of the opinion, under the facts as stipulated, that the plaintiff is entitled to recover the actual cash value, and it not limited to the cost of manufacture. Straw hats are not an ordinary staple. Their value depends upon style and finish, and they must be produced for the summer market. In order to reach the retailer in time for the summer trade, they must be manufactured in the fall and winter, so they may come to the hands of the retailer in the spring and early summer. It is conceded the plaintiff could not repair his factory or obtain another in which to reproduce the hats lost by fire in time for the season's trade, nor could he go upon the market and replace them by purchase. Under the stipulated facts it is impossible to apply the clause of the contract respecting repair or replacement. The plaintiff could neither buy them nor could he again manufacture them in time to be of any value. It cannot be ascertained what it would cost the insured to "repair or replace" the hats "with material of like kind and quality," because they could be neither repaired nor replaced. There is no other mode, therefore, under the contract of ascertaining the plaintiff's loss, except by taking "the actual cash value" of the property destroyed, which is conceded to be the price at which they were contracted to be sold.

In Frick v. United F. Ins. Co., 218 Pa. 409, 67 Atl. 743, a quantity of whisky of various ages was destroyed by fire, and the policy of insurance contained the same clause as that of the policy under consideration. The question involved was whether the measure of loss was the cost of manufacture or cash value. Because of the fact that it was impossible to produce whisky of the precise quality and mellowness of that destroyed, which condition added largely to its value, it was concluded that the only practical method of ascertaining the loss was to take the actual cash value. In its decision the court was careful to distinguish it from its former decision in Standard Sewing Machine Co. v. Royal Ins. Co., 201 Pa. 645, 51 Atl. 354, where it had limited the loss to the cost of manufacture, deeming the peculiar situation a controlling feature. A like peculiar situation exists under the stipulated facts in this case, and the goods being im-

possible of replacement, the plaintiff is entitled to recover the
actual cash value, and is not limited to the cost of manufacture.

Judgment is ordered for the plaintiff in the sum of $1,966.79,
with interest from the 28th day of March, 1906, with costs.

Laughlin and Scott, JJ., concur.

McLaughlin, J. (dissenting).   The contract in question was
one of indemnity only.   13 Am. & Eng. Enc. of Law (2d Ed.) p.
101.   Profits may be recovered only when insured as such.   Id.
105; Niblo v. North Am. Fire Co., 1 Sandf. 551; Buffalo El. Co.
v. Prussian Nat. Ins. Co., 64 App. Div. 182, 187, 71 N. Y. Supp.
918, affirmed 171 N. Y. 25, 63 N. E. 810.   Upon the facts the
plaintiff would be indemnified by the payment to him of
$1,841.95, and any greater sum necessarily includes profits.   He
was a manufacturer, and his actual loss was obviously what he
had expended upon the goods destroyed, and not what he would
have realized had he sold them, since his profits would be included in the selling price.   Standard Sewing Machine Co. v.
Insurance Co., 201 Pa. 645, 51 Atl. 354; Scottish Union Ins. Co.
v. Keene, 85 Md. 263, 37 Atl. 33; Mumford v. Hallett, 1 Johns.
433; Harris v. The Eagle Fire Co., 5 Johns. 368.

It is doubtless true that "actual cash value" is frequently to
be construed as equivalent to market value; but that term is used
in the policy to limit the liability of the insurer, and the provision that the loss "shall, in no event, 'exceed what it would
then cost the insured to repair or replace the same with material of like kind and quality" shows it was never intended by
the use of such words to insure the manufacturer's profits.   The
value of an article is ordinarily fixed by its market value, but in
the case before us the amount which would indemnify the plaintiff is conceded, and to allow him anything more is simply to allow him the profits which he would have realized, had the fire
not occurred.

I am, therefore, of the opinion that upon the agreed facts
the plaintiff is entitled to judgment for the sum of $1,841.95,
with interest from the 28th day of March, 1906.

Phillips v. Home Ins. Co., 112 N. Y. Supp. 769.

HOUSEHOLD GOODS.

The measure of recovery for loss on household goods cannot be based on what a junk shop or second-hand dealer would
have given for them, nor what they would have brought at
forced sale.   Nor is it limited to their market value, since their

value to the owner and the cost of replacing them would exceed their market value.

Sun Fire Office v. Ayers, 37 Neb. 184, 55 N. W. 635;
Birmingham & Co. v. Huitoh, 157 Ala. 630, 47 So. 576.

But the company may prove the value by showing the assured offered to sell it for a certain price.

Joy v. Security F. Ins. Co., 83 Ia. 12, 48 N. W. 1049.

FREIGHT.

Freight is a part of the cost of the goods.

Case v. Mfrs. F. & M. Ins. Co., 82 Cal. 263, 22 Pac. 1083.

MANUFACTURER'S MEASURE OF LOSS.

The measure of the loss on stock of a manufacturer is the fair market value at the place of its destruction.

Parrish v. Virginia F. & M. Ins. Co., 20 Ins. L. J. 95;
Grubbs v. North Carolina H. Ins. Co., 108 N. C. 472, 20 Ins. L. J. 784.

PARTY WALLS.

The owner of a one-half interest in a party wall has an insurable interest in the easement of the other half.

Nelson v. Continental Ins. Co., 182 Fed. 783.

The owner of such a half interest may recover the full value of the entire wall if it is a loss.

Citizens Ins. Co. v. Lochridge, 132 Ky. 1, 116 S. W. 303, 38 Ins. L. J. 491, annotated in 20 L. R. A. (N. S.) 226;
Kinzer v. National M. Ins. Co., 88 Kan. 93, 127 Pac. 762, annotated in 44 L. R. A. (N. S.) 121.

But see

Northwestern M. L. Ins. Co. v. Rochester Ger. Ins. Co., 88 Minn. 48, 88 N. W. 272.

The following was written in the year 1905, long before the decisions in the whisky cases were decided (see first edition "Hall on Insurance Adjustments") and is applicable to those decisions and all others rendered since 1905.

I apprehend, after carefully reading the foregoing decisions, that most of the courts will uphold the wording of the policy, which means nothing more nor less than the cash market value of the cost to replace or reproduce the article new, on the day and at the place it was damaged or destroyed, less whatever difference in value there may be between new and the condition in which the destroyed article was at the time of its destruction. At least that is the interpretation I place on the language of the courts, after carefully reading the decisions, especially the cases of Stenzel v. Pennsylvania, Hilton v. Phoenix, Grubbs et al. v. Ins. Co. and Mack v. Ins. Co., and, as was said in these decisions, cash value does not necesarily mean prime cash cost, plus freight, nor does it mean cost of (original) production; the cash value on the day of the fire might be much less and it might be much more than the goods cost. If the goods have declined in price, the insurance company is entitled to that decline. If prices have advanced, the assured is entitled to the benefit of such advance. In both cases the insurance company is entitled to any depreciation it can show has taken place in the goods from shop wear, change in styles or for any other valid reason.

There may be great difference between cost of production and cost of reproduction, not only for the reason that cost of labor and material fluctuates, but other conditions may intervene, as, for instance, a manufacturer's factory may burn and he be thereby placed in a position where he can not reproduce the destroyed goods. In such case, if his goods have a known cash market value, such as flour, lumber or whisky, then the measure of damage for which the company would be liable is the sum a similar grade of goods would have cost him delivered at the time and place of fire.

If the property destroyed be whisky, the chances are it can not be reproduced by the assured, even though his distillery may not have been harmed, for the reason that the longer he has had it the more valuable it is. New whisky has to be aged. The same principle holds good with it that was expressed by the court in Western Assurance Co. v. Studebaker, 124 Ind. 176, 20 Ins. L. J. 64, in sustaining the objection of plaintiff to the introduction of evidence showing what the contract was between plaintiff and a party in another State for green lumber used in their business. The court said: "These contracts are for green lumber to be manufactured and delivered in future. The lumber destroyed was seasoned, dry lumber. It was, therefore, proper to show what first-class poplar lumber, dry and of the sam dimensions, was worth in the market at the time and place of the fire." If there was no market at such time and place, then it might probably be proper to show what it was worth in the nearest market, with cost of transportation to scene of the loss added.

.. Suppose, too, that a manufacturer has contracted for the

sale of his entire output, and has only a certain time in which to deliver a certain quantity of goods. In case of fire, his loss will be what it costs him to go on the market and buy the goods, and that will be the measure of damage for which the insurer is liable for those goods that were destroyed by the fire. The contract does not insure the goods themselves; it insures their owner against loss on same.

An insurance policy is a personal contract.

Wilcox v. Hill, 44 Mass. 66.

CHAPTER III.
NOTICE OF LOSS.

"If fire occur the insured shall give immediate notice of any loss thereby, in writing, to this company."

The requirement of immediate notice of loss contained in a New York standard policy is satisfied by a notice given within a reasonable time. (In this case, 53 days after the fire, where, however, the policy was in the safe in the building which was burned and could not be obtained until about the time the notice was given), taking into consideration the situation of the insured and all the circumstances by which he is surrounded, and if he uses due diligence in discovering the policy, and serving the notice of loss, this is sufficient.

Solomon v. Continental Ins. Co., 160 N. Y. 595.

Citing:

O'Brien v. Phoenix Ins. Co., 76 N. Y. 459; Carpenter v. German Amer. Ins. Co., 135 N. Y. 298; Griffey v. N. Y. Central Ins. Co., 100 N. Y. 417; N. Y. Cent. Ins. Co. v. Nat. Protection Ins. Co., 20 Barb. 468; Inman v. Western Ins. Co., 12 Wend. 452; Bennett v. Lycoming County M. Ins. Co., 67 N. Y. 274; Matthews v. American Central Ins. Co., 154 N. Y. 458; McNally v. Phoenix Ins. Co., 137 N. Y. 389; Trustees Amherst College v. Ritch, 151 N. Y. 282; Paltrovitch v. Phoenix Ins. Co., 143 N. Y. 73; Sergeant v. Liverpool and London and Globe Ins. Co., 155 N. Y. 349.

It is for the jury to determine whether, in view of all the circumstances, the insured acted with due diligence and without unnecessary delay in giving notice forthwith.

Griffey v. N. Y. Central Ins. Co., 100 N. Y. 417; affirming 30 Hun. 299;

O'Brien v. Phoenix Ins. Co., 76 N. Y. 459.

Eleven days after fire is not forthwith:

Trask v. Ins. Co., 5 Casey 198.

Eighteen days after fire is not forthwith:

Edwards v. Lycoming Co. Mut. Fire Ins. Co. (Pa. S. C.), 3 Ins. L. J. 534.

Standard form policy requiring immediate notice is not complied with by giving notice thirty-three days after fire.

Quinlan v. Providence-Washington Ins. Co. (N. Y.), 39 St. Rep., 820; affirmed in 133 N. Y. 356.

Fourteen days after the fire, unaccompanied by any fact or circumstances excusing delay is not such immediate notice.

La Force v. Williamsburgh City Fire Ins. Co., 43 Mo. App. 518.

Failure to notify insurer within the term prescribed unless waived, will avoid the policy.

Blossom v. Lycoming Fire Ins. Co., 64 N. Y. 162;
Burnham v. Royal Ins. Co., 75 Mo. App. 394.

Requirement of notice forthwith is not complied with by serving proofs of loss seven weeks after fire.

Brown v. London Assurance Corp. (N. Y.), 40 Hun. 101.

Where assured has failed to notify insurer of the loss, thereby forfeiting his claim under the policy, the insurer does not waive his rights to claim forfeiture by refusing to pay loss on other grounds.

Blossom v. Lycoming Fire Ins. Co., 64 N. Y. 162;
Brown v. London Assurance Corp. (N. Y.), 40 Hun. 101.

Notice may be given the local agent who wrote the policy.

Kendall v. Holland Purchase Ins. Co. (N. Y.), 2 S. C. 375; affirmed
in 58 N. Y. 682;
Germania F. Ins. Co. v. Curran (Kan. S. C.), 1 Ins. L. J. 191.

A notice of loss sent by the local agent who informs the insured that it is sent, though not purporting to be sent in behalf of insured, if received by the company, is sufficient.

Loeb v. American Central Ins. Co., 99 Mo. 50, 21 Ins. L. J. 889.

Where policy makes the notice of loss a condition precedent to recovery, no suit can be maintained without proof of such notice.

Washington M. Ins. Co. v. Heckenath (N. Y.), 7 Leg. & Ins. Rep.
357.

Forthwith means in reasonable time, or with reasonable diligence, dependent on the circumstances of the case.

Bennet v. Lycoming Mo. Mut. Ins. Co., 67 N. Y. 274.

It means due diligence, four days after the fire is sufficient.

St. Louis Ins. Co. v. Kyle, 11 Mo. 278.

In case of an infant, the guardian appointed after the loss may give the requisite notice.

O'Brien v. Phoenix Ins. Co., 76 N. Y. 459.

Knowledge by a fire insurance company's agent of the loss by fire does not relieve the insured from the duty of giving notice.

Smith v. Haverhill Ins. Co., 83 Mass. 297.

Verbal notice given by assured to insurance company's agent who wrote the policy is not such notice as the policy requires.

Ermentraut v. Girard F. and M. Ins. Co. (Minn. S. C.), 25 Ins. L. J. 87.

Where a fire insurance policy requires notice of loss forthwith, it means with all reasonable diligence under the circumstances of the particular case.

Central City Ins. Co. v. Oates, 86 Ala. 558, 18 Ins. L. J. 761.

CHAPTER IV.

PROOFS OF LOSS AND REQUIREMENTS OF ASSURED.

"If fire occur, the insured shall * * * protect the property from further damage, forthwith separate the damaged and undamaged personal property, put it in the best possible order, make a complete inventory of the same, stating the quantity and cost of each article and the amount claimed thereon; and, within sixty days after the fire, unless such time is extended in writing by this company, shall render a statement to this company, signed and sworn to by said insured, stating the knowledge and belief of the insured as to the time and origin of the fire; the interest of the insured and of all others in the property; the cash value of each item thereof and the amount of loss thereon; all incumbrances thereon; all other insurance, whether valid or not, covering any of said property; and a copy of all the descriptions and schedules in all policies; any changes in the title, use, occupation, location, possession, or exposures of said property since the issuing of this policy; by whom and for what purpose any building herein described and the several parts thereof were occupied at the time of fire; and shall furnish, if required, verified plans and specifications of any building, fixtures, or machinery destroyed or damaged; and shall also, if required, furnish a certificate of the magistrate or notary public (not interested in the claim as a creditor or otherwise, nor related to the insured), living nearest the place of fire, stating that he has examined the circumstances and believes the insured has honestly sustained loss to the amount that such magistrate or notary public shall certify."—New York Standard Policy.

"The insured shall forthwith separate the damaged and undamaged personal property, put it in the best possible order and make a complete inventory of same."

Oshkosh Match Co. v. Manchester Assur. Co., 92 Wis. 510; Thornton v. Security Ins. Co., 117 Fed. 773; 32 Ins. L. J. 557; Astrich v. German Amer. Ins. Co., 33 Ins. L. J. 308; affirmed (U. S. C. C. A. 3d Dist.), 33 Ins. L. J. 925.

The assured took an inventory and at the end of it stated the claim for loss as follows:

	Inventory	Loss
33 1/3 % on dry goods, underwear, etc.	$6,061	$2,020.53
25 % on furniture and fixtures.....	650	162.50
15 % on boots, shoes and rubbers..	1,050	157.50
15 % on groceries, spices, etc.......	2,850	427.50

Total Loss $2,768.03

In this inventory are found some items of a collective character, such as "a lot of goods in show windows," "contents of a small show case," "lot of shirt bosoms, handkerchiefs, fly netting, etc." The point taken is that policy requires each article to be given, its quantity and cost and the amount claimed thereon separately. *Held*, This stipulation is not to be construed most strictly against the insured. Its object is to secure a full statement of the loss he claims, so that company may have notice and the neccessary opportunity to test its correctness.

Boyle v. Hamburg-Bremen F. Ins. Co. (Pa. S. C.), 24 Ins. L. J. 699.

If unable to give cost of each article, the number of such articles of each kind may be given with the average price.

Clement's Digest, Rule 5, p. 15, citing Peoples F. Ins. Co. v. Pulver, 127 Ill. 246; 20 N. E. Rep. 18.

The expense of putting in order and of inventorying must be borne by the assured.

Clement's Digest, Rule 4, p. 15.
Hebner v. Palatine Ins. Co., 157 Ill. 144; 41 N. E. Rep. 627.

The expense of the insured in saving and protecting the property and putting it in the best possible order is one incidental to the loss, and, until the case of Hebner v. Palatine Ins. Co., and Fire Ins. Assn' v. Wickham et al., I never heard of an adjuster taking the position that his company was not liable for such loss. The fact that the policy requires the assured to do certain acts in the preservation of his property is all the more reason for reimbursing him for the expense. If goods of an unknown value were among the debris of a building, and the insured, by hard work, succeeds in saving them at an expense of $5,000 and they sell for $7,500, the salvage has, according to this Illinois decision, two values, one of $7,500 to the insurance companies, but only $2,500 to the insured, but fortunately for the insured, the insurance companies do not take such an unreasonable and unfair view of the matter in adjusting losses with their claimants and policyholders, and if they were inclined to settle losses according to the Illinois decision, I am of the belief that other States would follow the doctrine laid down by the U. S. S. C. in the case of Fire Ins. Ass'n, (Ltd.), v. Wickham et al., 21 Ins. L. J. 193, in which they say:

In this case there are two distinct and separate claims of similar amounts, namely, $15,364.78, one of which was for the direct loss by fire to the property insured, and the other was for incidental cost of saving and protecting it from further damage. The plaintiff assumed on the face of the receipts (which were in usual form one for payment of loss, the other for payment of return premium, both providing for cancellation and surrender of the policy) to settle with the plaintiff for both of these claims for the exact amount of one of them. In other words, they assumed to settle for a moiety of the entire claim, a claim, the legality and justness of which was so far beyond dispute that it could hardly fail to be recognized by the adjusters for the companies * * *. The appraisement (which provided that it was "of binding effect only as far as regards the actual cash value of or damage to such property insured." It was further added that "the property on which loss or damage is to be estimated and appraised is the hull of the propeller St. Paul, including tackle, awnings, furniture, engine and boiler connections and appurtenances thereto belonging," with a further memorandum following the signature of Wickham, but preceding those of the companies that this agreement does not apply to or cover any question that may arise for saving boat and cargo") the actions of the parties and the statement of the adjusters that they had no authority whatever for considering the claim for raising and saving the steamer, as the companies were not liable for such expenses, all show that this claim was not intended to be included in the receipts.

Judgment for plaintiff in court below was here affirmed.

In both these cases, Hebner v. Palatine and Fire Ins. Ass'n v. Wickham, the property insured was a boat and the risk assumed was against fire only.

But the insured is not required to put the goods in order (or to make inventory) when the value is trifling and no proof is offered that by so doing the value would be enhanced.

Clement's Digest, Rule 4, p. 15.

Citing:

Wright v. Hartford Fire Ins. Co., 36 Wis. 522.

Where goods (merchandise) are totally destroyed, an itemized inventory is not required.

Clement's Digest, Rule 6, p. 15.

Citing:

Davis v. Grand Rapids Ins. Co., 15 Misc. 263; 36 N. Y. Supp. 792;
    affirmed 157 N. Y. 685, no opinion.
Johnston v. Farmers Ins. Co., 106 Mich. 96; 64 N. W. Rep. 5.

Nor where they are so damaged as to render the making of such an inventory impracticable.

Clement's Digest, Rule 6, p. 15.

Citing:

Powers D. G. Co. v. Imperial Ins. Co., 48 Minn. 380.

A clause in a fire policy requiring an itemized statement of the cash value of each article and the amount of loss thereon, applies only to the goods saved from the fire and not to those which were burned.

Davis v. Grand Rapids Ins. Co., 36 N. Y. Supp. 792, affirmed in
    157 N. Y. 685, no opinion.

Where the books and papers of the insured and all means of making an accurate inventory were consumed with the insured merchandise, a statement on oath, showing this fact, and that the property insured and destroyed was, at least,⎜ of the value of the sum named is sufficient.

Bumstead v. Dividend Mut. Ins. Co., 12 N. Y. 81;
Hoffman v. Ætna Ins. Co., 1 Rob. 501; S. C. 19 Abb. Pr. 325;
Mortimer v. N. Y. Fire Ins. Co., 2 U. S. Law Mag. 452.

The furnishing of preliminary proofs of loss, unless waived, is condition precedent to recovery.

Underwood v. Farmers Joint Stock Ins. Co., 57 N. Y. 500;
Irving v. Excelsior F. Ins. Co., (N. Y.), 1 Bos. 507;
Burnham v. Royal Ins. Co., 75 Mo. App. 394;
Kingsley v. N. E. Ins. Co., 62 Mass. 393;
Wellcome v. Peoples Ins. Co., 68 Mass. 480;
Shawmut S. R. Co. v. Peoples Ins. Co., 78 Mass. 535;
Home Ins. Co. v. Duke (Ind. S. C.), 3 Ins. L. J. 365;
Ins. Co. v. Hathaway, 43 Kans. 399;
Ins. Co. v. Seyferth, 29 Ill. App. 513;
Leigh v. Ins. Co., 37 Mo. App. 542;
Lee v. Ins. Co., 73 Tex. 641.

And they must be furnished within the time required by the policy.

McDermott v. Lycoming F. Ins. Co. (N. Y.), 12 J. and S. 221;
Smith v. Haverhill Ins. Co., 83 Mass. 297;
Eastern R. R. v. Relief Ins. Co., 98 Mass. 420.

Where proofs are served 60 days after the fire has terminated or abated to such an extent that an inspection of the damaged property may be had, it is a sufficient requirement of the policy that proofs must be furnished within 60 days after the fire.

National Wall Paper Co. v. Associated Mfrs. Mut. F. Ins. Co.,
    175 N. Y. 226.

The requirement in the policy that proofs be furnished within 60 days after the fire, is not complied with by depositing such proofs in the mail on the 60th day after the loss, where it does not reach its destination within the limited time.

Peabody v. Satterlee, 166 N. Y. 174, reversing (S. C.) 36 App. Div. 426; 30 Ins. L. J. 885.

A statement in the proofs of loss, that the property belonged to the assured, and that no other person or persons had any interest therein, is equivalent to a statement that there were no incumbrances on the property.

Davis v. Grand Rapids Ins. Co., N. Y. S. C. 5, App. Div. 36; affirmed in 157 N. Y. 685 (no opinion.)

Where several policies are issued to one person, upon the same property, a single proof of loss referring to all the policies is sufficient.

Dakin v. L. and L. and G. Ins. Co., 13 Hun. 122; S. C. 77 N. Y. 600.

Preliminary proofs may be signed by a member of a co-partnership in the absence of any provision in the policy requiring the names of the individual members of the firm to be given.

Kerelsen v. Sun Fire Office, 122 N. Y. 545; affirming S. C. 16 St. Rep. 239.

The retention of proofs of loss for more than twenty-three days without objection operates as a waiver of defects therein.

Davis v. Grand Rapids Ins. Co., N. Y. S. C., 5 App. Div. 36; affirmed in 157 N. Y. 685 (no opinion.)

Where proofs of loss are kept without objection that they were not served by the proper party, the insurer can not make defense that they were not served by the "insured."

De Witt v. Agricultural Ins. Co., 89 Hun. 229; S. C. 71 St. Rep. 556; Affirmed in 157 N. Y. 353.

Where the insured in his proofs of loss makes a statement of what he had been "informed" was the origin of the fire, and no question of surprise was raised on the trial, he is not estopped or precluded from showing that, in fact, the fire originated from some other cause.

White v. Royal Ins. Co., 149 N. Y. 485; affirming S. C. 8 Misc. 613.

The preliminary proofs are not evidence of the loss on the trial.

> Yonkers and N. Y. F. Ins. Co. v. Hoffman F. Ins. Co., (N. Y.), 6 Rob. 316;
> Sexton v. Montgomery Co. Mut. Ins. Co., 9 Barb. 191.

Unless made so by the terms of the policy.

> Sexton v. Montgomery Co. Mut. Ins. Co., 9 Barb. 191.

The furnishing of preliminary proofs according to the conditions of the policy must be averred in the declaration; or it will be bad on demurrer.

> Inman v. Western Fire Ins. Co., 12 Wend. 452, (N. Y.);
> Furlong v. Agricultural Ins. Co., 28 Abb. N. C. 444; S. C. (N. Y.), 45 St. Rep. 856.

A denial of liability waives proofs and suit may be brought at once.

> Hicks v. British America Assur. Co., 8 (N. Y. S. C.) App. Div. 444; S. C. 43 N. Y. Supp. 623.
> Flaherty v. Continental Ins. Co., 20 App. Div. 275; (N. Y.) S. C. 46 N. Y. Supp. 934;
> Ins. Co. v. Richardson (Neb. S. C.), 24 Ins. L. J. 690;
> Ins. Co. v. Journal Pub. Co. (Wash. S. C.), 20 Ins. L. J. 395;
> Ins. Co. v. Carey (Ill. S. C.), 6 Ins. L. J. 493.
> Ins. Co. v. Maguire, 57 Ill. 342;
> Cobb v. Ins. Co., 11 Kans. 93;
> Ins. Co. v. Gracey (Cal. S. C.), 20 Ins. L. J. 28;
> Donohoe v. Ins. Co. (Vt. S. C.), 13 Ins. L. J. 116.

The trustee in bankruptcy of an absconding bankrupt may, by direction of the court, make proofs of loss under policies of insurance held by the bankrupt.

> Sims v. Union Assur. Soc. (U. S. C. C. Ga.), 129 Fed. Rep. 804.

Mortgagee may make proofs.

> Nickerson v. Nickerson et al. (Me. S. J. C.), 12 Atl. Rep. 880.
> Bull v. North British and Merc. Ins. Co. (Ont. S. C. of J.), 9 Can. Law Times 26;
> Armstrong v. Agricultural Ins. Co. (N. Y. S. C.), 31 N. Y. St. Rep. 201.

The case of Peabody v. Satterlee, 30 Ins. L. J. 885, does not pass upon the question as to who may make proofs. The attorney for the assured in that case made proofs which were returned by the company, with the request that the insured make the proofs. The fact that the assured accepted the rejected proofs made by his lawyer, and made new proofs in his own name, waived any right that he might have had to claim that the proofs were in order, hence, the court did not pass upon this question.

A proof of loss is an entirely ex parte statement of facts

concerning the property, the loss and the insurance, intended only to afford information as a basis of settlement, if satisfactory, and if not, a basis for investigation. This statement made in behalf of the insured, by an agent fully conversant with all the facts, and having charge of the property, serves these purposes as well as if made by the insured himself. Accordingly, it has been generally held, when the principal is absent, and the facts are within the knowledge of the agent, a proof so made is sufficient.

Fireman's Fund Ins. Co. v. Sims (Ga. S. C.), 42 S. E. Rep. 269;
Lumbermen's Ins. Co. v. Bell (Ill.), 45 N. E. Rep. 130;
German F. Ins. Co. v. Grunert (Ill.);
Sims v. State Ins. Co., 4 Am. Rep. 311;
Pearlstine v. Westchester F. Ins. Co. (S. C. S. C.), 34 I. L. J. 39;
Sims v. Union Assur. Soc. (U. S. C. C. Ga.), 129 Fed. Rep. 804.

But see cases under examination under oath, which places it within the power of the adjuster to practically nullify the ruling of the courts allowing a third party to make proofs for the insured.

Objections to proofs of loss must be specific and not general.

Hartford F. Ins. Co. v. Meyer (Neb. S. C.), 46 N. W. Rep. 292;
Bean v. Travelers Ins. Co. (Cal. S. C.), 29 Pac. Rep. 1113;
Dwelling House Ins. Co. v. Gould (Pa. S. C.), 19 Atl. Rep. 793;
Paltrovitch v. Phoenix Ins. Co., 143 N. Y. 73; S. C. 60 St. Rep. 462;
    affirming S. C. 68 Hun. 304.

It is the duty of the company immediately to notify the assured wherein his proofs are defective.

Dwelling House Ins. Co. v. Gould (Pa. S. C.), 19 Atl. Rep. 793.

Company must object to defects in reasonable time.

Union Ins. Co. v. Barwick (Neb. S. C.), (Mar. 18, 1893), 6 Finch
    Digest 57;
Nease v. Aetna Ins. Co. (W. Va. C. A.), 9 S. E. Rep. 233;
Peet v. Dakota F. and M. Ins. Co. (Dakota S. C.), 20 Ins. L. J. 253.

Company must object to defects promptly.

Kernochan v. N. Y. Bowery F. Ins. Co., 17 N. Y. 428;
Biddleford Savings Bank v. Dwelling House Ins. Co. (Me. S. C.),
    18 Atl. Rep. 298.

Retention of proofs of loss without objection for:
Twenty-three days is waiver of defects.

Paltrovitch v. Phoenix Ins. Co., 143 N. Y. 73; S. C. 60 St. Rep. 462;
    affirming S. C. 68 Hun. 304.

Thirty days is waiver of defects.

Peoples F. Ins. Co. v. Pulver (Ill. S. C.), 20 N. E. Rep. 18;
Carpenter v. Allemannia F. Ins. Co. (Pa. S. C.), 26 Atl. Rep. 781.

Thirty-eight days is waiver of defects.

Keeney v. Home Ins. Co., 71 N. Y. 396.

Forty-five days is waiver of defects.

Jones v. Howard Ins. Co., 117 N. Y. 103.

Forty-eight days is waiver of defects.

Capitol Ins. Co. v. Wallace (Kan. S. C.), 22 Ins. L. J. 397.

The failure of the insurance company to object to proofs of loss after notice, in other words by undue length of silence after presentation; or its refusal to pay on grounds other than defective proofs, will waive proofs. But none of the courts hold that its mere silence after receipt of notice of loss will waive proofs.

Central City Ins. Co. v. Oates, 86 Ala. 558, 18 Ins. L. J. 761.

CHAPTER V.

NOTARY PUBLIC'S OR MAGISTRATE'S CERTIFICATE.

The production of such certificate when required, unless the insurer has waived it or prevented the obtaining it, is a condition precedent to recovery.

DeLand v. Aetna Ins. Co., 68 Mo. App. 277;
Johnson v. Phoenix Ins. Co., 112 Mass. 49;
Dolliver v. St. Joseph Ins. Co., 131 Mass. 39;
Fink v. Lancashire Ins. Co., 60 Mo. App. 673;
Hubbard v. North British and M. Ins. Co., 57 Mo. App. 1;
Cornell v. Hope Ins. Co., 3 Martin (La.) 223;
Columbian Ins. Co. v. Lawrence, 10 Pet. 507;
Leadbetter v. Aetna Ins. Co., 13 Me. 265.

The clause requiring notary public or magistrate most contiguous to the fire, will be liberally construed, the magistrate's proximity to the place is all that can be required.

Turley v. North American F. Ins. Co. (N. Y. S. C.), 25 Wend. 374.

His certificate that he is not concerned in the loss is sufficient until disproved.

Cornell v. LeRoy (N. Y. S. C.), 9 Wend. 163.

Where the policy requires the certificate within 60 days after fire, no recovery can be had unless it is furnished.

Gottlieb v. Dutchess Mut. Ins. Co. (N. Y. S. C.), 89 Hun. 36; S. C. 69 St. Rep. 250.

The requirement as to nearest magistrate must be strictly complied with, when the nearest not only does not refuse to act, but actually gives a certificate which does not meet the requirement.

Noonan v. Hartford F. Ins. Co., 21 Mo. 81.

The capricious refusal of the nearest magistrate to give the certificate will not prevent a recovery if the certificate of another magistrate is obtained

Leigh v. Springfield F. and M. Ins. Co., 37 Mo. App. 542.

Where the nearest notary refuses certificate, that of next nearest notary is a compliance with the policy.

Lang v. Eagle F. Ins. Co., 12 App. Div. 39; S. C. 42 N. Y. Supp. 539.
Walker v. Phoenix Ins. Co., 62 Mo. App. 209.

49

Not concerned in the loss as a creditor means that he shall not have a specific interest by way of lien, and does not dis-qualify a magistrate who is a general creditor.

Dolliver v. St. Joseph Ins. Co., 131 Mass. 39.

Where the insurer furnishes blank proof of loss containing form for a certificate, and rejects two sets of proofs because they each fail to contain such certificate, it will defeat recovery on the policy, unless it is otherwise waived.

Sullivan v. Germania F. Ins. Co., 89 Mo. App. 106.

If the certificate be so drawn as to mean the same thing without using the exact words of the policy, it is sufficient.

Aetna F. Ins. Co. v. Tyler (N. Y. S. C.), 16 Wend. 385

Assured complies with the requirement if he goes to the nearest de jure magistrate.

Walker v. Phoenix Ins. Co., 62 Mo. App. 209.

Without requirement assured did furnish certificate, which insurer objected to on the ground that it did not mention the damage. *Held,* This did not amount to a requirement for such certificate. (Ætna Ins. Co. v. Bank, 62 Fed. Rep. 222, distinguished).

Swearinger v. Pacific F. Ins. Co., 66 Mo. App. 90.

An objection to proof because certificate was not furnished is not good unless such certificate has been requested before-hand. (Cases reviewed and distinguished).

Burnett v. American Central Ins. Co., 68 Mo. App. 343.

Retention for 23 days of certificate of notary not nearest fire waives company's right to reject proofs on that ground.

Paltrovitch v. Phoenix Ins. Co., 143 N. Y. 73; S. C. 60 St. Rep. 462; affirming S. C. 68 Hun. 304.

Where company rejects certificate on the ground that there is a nearer notary, it should give the name and address of such notary to enable the insured to comply with its demands.

Paltrovitch v. Phoenix Ins. Co., 143 N. Y. 73; S. C. 60 St. Rep. 462; affirming S. C. 68 Hun. 304.

Where proofs of loss not containing certificates were re-jected and nearly a year afterwards proofs of loss and certificate were served and suit commenced the same day, it was held suit was not prematurely brought.

McNally v. Phoenix Ins. Co., 137 N. Y. 389; S. C. 50 St. Rep. 680; reversing S. C. 42 St. Rep. 21.

Where nearest notary's certificate was not secured, but no defect in this respect was pointed out until after commencement of action, the objection was too late.

Barnum v. Merchant's F. Ins. Co., 98 N. Y. 188; Smith v. Home Ins. Co. (N. Y. S. C.), 47 Hun. 30.

CHAPTER VI

EXAMINATION UNDER OATH, AND THE PRODUCTION OF BOOKS, INVOICES, ETC.

"The insured, as often as required, shall exhibit to any person designated by this company all that remains of any property herein described, and submit to examinations under oath by any person named by this company, and subscribe the same; and, as often as required, shall produce for examination all books of account, bills, invoices, and other vouchers or certified copies thereof, if originals be lost, at such reasonable place as may be designated by this company or its representative, and shall permit extracts and copies thereof to be made."

The trustee in bankruptcy of an absconding bankrupt may, by direction of the court, make proofs of loss under policies of insurance held by the bankrupt.

Sims v. Union Assur. Soc. (U. S. C. C. Ga.), 129 Fed. Rep. 804.

A proof of loss is an entirely ex parte statement of facts concerning the property, the loss and the insurance, intended only to afford information as a basis of settlement if satisfactory, and if not, a basis for investigation. This statement, made in behalf of the insured by an agent fully conversant with all the facts, and having charge of the property, serves these purposes as well as if made by the insured himself. Accordingly, it has been generally held, when the principal is absent and the facts are within the knowledge of the agent, a proof so made is sufficient.

Fireman's Fund Ins. Co. v. Sims (Ga. S. C.), 42 S. E. Rep. 269;
Lumbermen's Ins. Co. v. Bell (Ill.), 45 N. E. Rep. 130.
German F. Ins. Co. v. Grunert (Ill.),
Sims v. State Ins. Co., 4 Am. Rep. 311.
Pearlstine v. Westchester F. Ins. Co. (S. C. S. C.), 34 Ins. L. J. 39;
Sims v. Union Assur. Soc. (U. S. C. C. Ga.), 129 Fed. Rep. 804;
Burns v. Michigan Mfrs. Mut. F. Co. (Mich. S. C., May, 1902), 31 Ins. L. J. 663.

But the provision for examination under oath stands upon an entirely different footing from that requiring proofs of loss; the manifest purpose of this stipulation is to afford a method of detecting imposition and fraud. In demanding examination, the insurer indicates dissatisfaction with the formal ex parte statement of proof. In such case, the insured has agreed his conscience may be searched by questions put to him face to face, where there is no opportunity for studied concealment. He, and not his agent, has an interest in the claim for the insurance and, therefore, a motive for fraud. To hold that a person to whom an insurance policy was issued could substitute an agent for himself to undergo such an examination would be to disregard not only the letter, but the spirit of the actual contract, and make another for the parties. We know of no authority which holds that an agent may be substituted for such an examination.

Pearlstine v. Westchester F. Ins. Co. (S. C. S. C.), 34 Ins. L. J. 39;

Citing

Fireman's Fund Ins. Co. v. Sims (Ga. S. C.), 42 S. E. Rep. 269; Gross v. Ins. Co. (U. S. C. C. Ga.), 22 Fed Rep. 74.

The company has the right to demand and have the insured himself appear for examination under oath, and his failure to appear for examination on demand of the company is a bar to a right of action.

Sims v. Union Assur. Soc. (U. S. C. C. Ga.), 129 Fed. Rep. 804; Fireman's Fund Ins. Co. v. Sims (Ga. S. C.), 42 S. E. Rep. 269; 31 Ins. L. J. 1049; Gross v. Ins. Co. (U. S. C. C.), 22 Fed. Rep. 74.

To constitute insured's refusal to be examined under oath a ground of defense, the insurance company must show that it named a reasonable time after notice of the fire, the place must have been a reasonably convenient one within the county where the insured resided, and it must have designated some person authorized by law to administer oaths and before whom such examination could be had.

Aetna Ins. Co. v. Simmons, 49 Neb. 811; 69 N. W. Rep. 125.

And the insured must subscribe to such examination.

Grigsby v. Ins. Co., 40 Mo. App. 276; Scottish U. & N. Ins. Co. v. Keene, 85 Md. 263; 26 Ins. L. J. 963.

Once he refuses to subscribe, he may still do so if he so wishes.

O'Brien v. Ohio Ins. Co., 52 Mich. 131.

The insured, if required, is bound to furnish duplicate bills (the originals of which have been lost), certified by the vendors, unless unable to do so.

O'Brien v. Commercial F. Ins. Co., 63 N. Y. 108.

Plaintiff is bound to show that he made a reasonable effort to comply with defendant's request to furnish duplicate bills, the originals of which were lost.

Langan v. Royal Ins. Co. (Pa. S. C.), 29 Atl. Rep. 710.

A duplicate bill is not a certified copy; the demand should be in the language of the policy to make it operative.

Ins. Cos. v. Weides, 14 Wallace U. S. 375.

Insured can not be compelled to say on what basis he settled with other companies.

Ins. Cos. v. Weides, 14 Wallace U. S. 375.

The insured is only required to answer such questions as have a material bearing on the risk.

Titus v. Glens Falls Ins. Co., 81 N. Y. 410;
Porter v. Traders Ins. Co., 164 N. Y. 504.

In the absence of any stipulation to the contrary, the proper place for examination of assured's books is the trading place of assured in the town or place where loss occurred.

Fleisch v. Ins. Co. of N. A., 58 Mo. App. 598; 23 Ins. L. J. 634;
Murphy v. North B. & M. Ins. Co., 61 Mo. App. 323.

Reasonable place means reasonable place in the locality or town where the loss occurred.

Murphy v. North B. & M. Ins. Co., 61 Mo. App. 323.
Tucker v. Colonial F. Ins. Co. (W. Va. S. C.), 34 Ins. L. J. 969.

The insurer can not require the insured to leave the State where he resides and where fire occurs to submit to examination under oath.

Amer. Central Ins. Co. v. Simpson, 43 Ill. App. 98.

And the insured may not demand that such examination shall be made at a distant place to which he has removed after the fire.

Fleisch v. Ins. Co. of N. A., 58 Mo. App. 596; 23 Ins. L. J. 634.

Where the insured endeavors to comply with the requirement to furnish duplicate bills, the jury must decide whether such efforts were reasonable under all the circumstances.

Coleman v. Ins. Co., 177 Pa. St. 239.

He is bound to comply with the request, if possible.

Langan v. Ins. Co., 162 Pa. St. 357; 23 Ins. L. J. 878;
Seibel v. Ins. Co. (Pa. S. C.), 29 Ins. L. J. 838.

The insurer's office in the adjoining county in which the loss occurs is a reasonable place for the production of books and bills.

Seibel v. Ins. Co. (Pa. S. C.), 29 Ins. L. J. 838;
Aetna Ins. Co. v. Simmons, 49 Neb. 811; 69 N. W. Rep. 125.

The time must be reasonable, and the place be reasonably conventient to where insured resides.

Aetna Ins. Co. v. Simmons, 49 Neb. 811; 69 N. W. Rep. 125;
Aurora Ins. Co. v. Johnson, 46 Ind. 315;
State Ins. Co. v. Maackens, 38 N. J. L. 564.

The failure of the insured to produce books, papers and vouchers, in the absence of a proper demand for their production, does not constitute a defense to payment under a policy of fire insurance.

[Judgment for plaintiff below. Here affirmed against company.]
Narinsky v. Fidelity Surety Co. (N. Y. S. C. App. Tr.):
92 New York Supplement (April 10,1905), 771.

The postive refusal of an insurance company to pay the loss is an absolute waiver of its right under the policy to examine the' books of the insured.

[Judgment for plaintiff below. Here affirmed against company.]
Colonial Mut. Fire Ins. Co. v. Ellinger (Ill. A. C.):
112 Ill. App. 302.

Although it might be found that it was impossible to produce duplicate bills of purchase of a certain class, that fact did not excuse the non-production of those that could have been obtained by a bona fide effort on the part of the insured.

Mispelhorn v. Ins. Co., 53 Md. 473.

Insured is not compelled to do an impossible thing, and if he can show that it was impossible to get duplicate bills, he may recover. A finding by the jury that he has done all that was possible is conclusive.

Eggleston v. Council Bluffs Ins. Co., 65 Iowa 308; 14 Ins. L. J. 365;
Miller v. Hartford F. Ins. Co., 70 Iowa 704

The insured is not obliged, when unable to do so, to furnish invoices of property destroyed.

Stepehens v. Union Assur. Soc. (Utah S. C.), 50 Pac. Rep. 626.

The insured may have his attorney present at such examination.

Thomas v. Burlington Ins. Co., 47 Mo. App. 169;
Amer. Central Ins. Co. v. Simpson, 43 Ill. App. 98.

The defense to an action on a fire policy that insured had failed to submit to an examination under oath, as required, is waived, if no notice was given to the insured, but notice was given to her husband, and as her agent he appeared and was examined.

Western Assur. Co. v. McGlathery (Ala. S. C.), 22 Southern Rep. 104.

The insurer waives the formal certification of the copy of bills and invoices furnished it, where it receives and examines the same, without objection to the absence of certificates, and makes no objection until a trial.

Johnson v. Phoenix Ins. Co., 69 Mo. App. 226.

Where the insured makes no attempt to comply with insurer's request to furnish certified copies of bills, the originals of which were destroyed, he cannot recover.

Milwaukee Mechs. Ins. Co. v. Winfield (Kan. C. A.), 51 Pac. Rep. 567.

Certified copies of bills and invoices does not mean an inventory of the stock insured owned when policy was issued.

Phoenix Ins. Co. v. Center (Texas C. C. A.), 31 S. W. Rep. 446.

The examination under oath cures defects in proofs.

Carpenter v. German-American Ins. Co., 135 N. Y. 298.

Misstatement of facts made in examination under oath will not avoid the policy unless insured knew them to be false, and made them with fraudulent intent.

Huston v. State Ins. Co. (Iowa S. C.), 69 N. W. Rep. 674.

Wilful false swearing will avoid the whole policy.

Hamberg v. St. Paul F. & M. Ins. Co. (Minn. S. C.), 26 Ins. L. J. 782.

The loss is due sixty days after proofs of loss are furnished and the duplicate bills furnished on demand of insurer are no part of the proofs of loss.

Aetna Ins. Co. v. McLeod et al. (Kan. S. C.), 25 Ins. L. J. 669.

CHAPTER VII.

FRAUD AND FALSE SWEARING.

The policy will not be avoided without proof of fraudulent intent.

Dresser v. United Firemen's Ins. Co. (N. Y.), 45 Hun. 298.

An over-valuation of the goods destroyed in the proofs of loss, unless shown to be wilful, is not even presumptive evidence of false swearing or fraud.

Unger v. People's F. Ins. Co. (N. Y.), 4 Daly 96;
Gibbs v. Continental Ins. Co. (N. Y.), 13 Hun. 611.

The misstatement as to value in proofs of loss must be false and fraudulent, but a misstatement which is but the expression of an opinion does not operate to avoid the policy.

Cheever v. Scottish U. and N. Ins. Co. (N. Y. S. C.), 86 App. Div. 328; 83 N. Y. Supp. 730.

An honest mistake, or other misstatement in proofs of loss will not forfeit claim.

Little v. Phoenix Ins. Co., 123 Mass. 380;
Parker et al. v. Amazon Ins. Co. (Wis. S. C.), 3 Ins. L. J. 567.

But if no amended statement has been furnished the insurer before suit on policy, the action can not be maintained.

Campbell v. Charter Oak Ins. Co., 92 Mass. 213;
City F. C. Sav. Bank v. Pa. F. Ins. Co., 122 Mass. 165.

To work a forfeiture the false statement must be wilfully made with respect to a material matter.

Winn v. Ins. Co., 27 Neb. 649;
Marion v. Great Rep. Ins. Co., 35 Mo. 148;
Walker v. Phoenix Ins. Co., 62 Mo. App. 209;
Hamberg v. St. Paul F. and M. Ins. Co. (Minn. S. C.), 26 Ins. L. J. 782;
Phoenix Ins. Co. v. Summerfield (Miss. S. C.), 22 Ins. L. J. 746.

And the false swearing must be either in the proofs of loss or in the examination under oath.

Schulter v. Merchants Mut. Ins. Co., 62 Mo. 236;
Ins. Cos. v. Weide (U. S. S. C.), 1 Ins. L. J. 767;
Ferris & Eaton v. North American Ins. Co. (N. Y. S. C.), 1 Hill 71; 2 Bennett 56.

Defense on ground of false swearing in proofs of loss will not avail the defendant when not pleaded.

Bear v. Atlantic Home Ins. Co. (N. Y.), 34 Misc. 613; 70 N. Y. Supp. 581.

The fact that the evidence showed that other dealers carried a much smaller line of certain articles plaintiff claimed to have had is not competent to show that plaintiff's sworn statement of loss was fraudulent.

Townsend v. Merchants Ins. Co. (N. Y.), 4 J. & S. 172; S. C. 45 How. Pr. 501.

A finding by the jury that plaintiff's loss was less than one-fourth amount claimed in his proofs of loss necessarily results in an inference of fraud and requires a verdict in favor of the defendant.

Steinfeld v. Park Ins. Co., N. Y., 50 Hun. 262; S. C. 19 St. Rep. 823; 2 N. Y. Supp. 766.

Contra:

Com'l Ins. Co. v. Friedlander, 156 Ill. 595.
Obersteller v. Com'l Assur. Co. (Cal. S. C.), 22 Ins. L. J. 392.
Moore v. Protection Ins. Co., 29 Me. 97; 2 Bennett 758.
Marchesseau v. Merchants Ins. Co., 2 Ben. 166 (La. S. C.).

The question of false swearing is one for the jury.

Dolan v. Aetna Ins. Co. (N. Y.), 22 Hun. 396.
Levy v. Brooklyn Ins. Co., 25 Wend. 687; 2 Bennett 93.

A false statement wilfully made as to the loss and value of the insured property will defeat recovery on the policy.

Lion F. Ins. Co. v. Star (Tex. S. C.), 18 Ins. L. J. 873.
Hall v. Western U. Assct., 106 Mo. App. 476.
Home Ins. Co. v. Winn (Neb. S. C.), 24 Ins. L. J. 126.

Citing:

Claflin v. Ins. Co., 110 U. S. 81.
Geib v Ins. Co., 1 Dil 443 Fed. Cas. No. 5298.
Huchberger v. Ins. Co., 4 Biss. 265 Fed. Cas. No. 6822.
Dollof v. Ins. Co., 82 Me. 266; 19 Ins. L. J. 450.
Sleeper v. Ins. Co., 56 N. H. 401.
Moore v. Ins. Co., 28 Grat. 508.
Ins. Co. v. Mannasson, 29 Mich. 316; 3 Ins. L. J. 668.

If the plaintiff knowingly and willingly inserts in his sworn statement of loss, as burned, any single article, which in fact was not in the house, or was not burned, or if he knowingly puts a false and excessive valuation on any single article, or puts such false and excessive valuation on the whole as displays a reckless and dishonest disregard of the truth in regard to the extent of the loss. Such acts are in themselves fraudulent and plaintiff cannot recover at all. Mere words are not necessarily proof, and courts are not compelled to allow justice to be perverted, because incredible evidence is not contradicted by direct and postive testimony. Such cases call for the supervisory power of the court.

> Rovinsky v. Northern Assur. Co. and another (S. J. C. Me.), 34 Ins. L. J. 800.

Practically the same doctrine is upheld in

> Schmidt v. Phil. Underwriters (La. S. C.), 32 Ins. L. J. 531.

Citing:

> Claflin v. Ins. Co., 110 U. S. 81 and Regnier v. Ins. Co., 12 La. 336; 1 Bennett 670.

And this is so where the actual loss was in excess of the amount of the policy as stated in false sworn statement.

> Dollof v. Phenix Ins. Co. and one other (S. J. C. Me.), 19 Ins. L. J. 450.

Plaintiff's affidavit that property which had been saved was destroyed worked a forfeiture of the policy

> Knop v. National F. Ins. Co. (Mich. S. C.), 25 Ins. L. J. 181.
> Mullen v. Ins. Co., 58 Vt. 113.
> West v British America Assur. Co. (U. S. C. C. Dist. Col.), 25 Ins. L. J. 689.

Plaintiff paid $3,000 for the building, but claimed it worth $6,500 in his proofs of loss. On trial of the case $3,000 was proven to be its real value. *Held*, such false statement worked a forfeiture.

> West v. British America Assur. Co. (U. S. C. C. Dist. Col.), 25 Ins. L. J. 689.

Of all the decisions one ever heard of, and one which, if upheld and generally known, will cause more attempts to defraud insurance companies than any other, the following takes the lead and is the most unreasonable and unfair:

1. A deception, in order to amount to legal fraud, must both deceive and damage. Where the company is not injured in an adjustment by the fraudulent alteration of books, the adjustment (based on and arrived at by such books)will not be defeated (disturbed).

2. The concealment of an inventory from the adjusters is not a concealment of a "material fact" within the policy, unless the company is injured thereby.

3. Evidence of the adjusters that they would not have

made the adjustment had they known of the alterations is a
mere opinion of their course under different circumstances and
is not admissible.

4. Evidence of the manager as to his reasons for the alterations is admissible.

Commercial Bank v. Firemen's Ins. Co. (Wis. S. C.), 23 Ins.
L. J. 543.

No wonder the court cites no decisions in support of its
ruling other than those of its own rendition. It was conceded
on the trial of the case that the insured's manager did, after
the fire by erasure and overwriting, reduce the manufacturing
account $13,000 and increase the lumber account $13,000. The
loss was on lumber in kilns. (Such erasurer and changes would
not throw the books out of balance.)

The inventory taken in January previous to the fire was
also concealed from the adjusters.

Would not assured's manager who had done these, things,
swear to anything? Would he ever admit that the insurance
company had been defrauded by his fraudulent acts? For what
purpose would he perpetrate a fraud? For the protection of the
insurance companies (?) of course.

How different the reasoning in this case from that of courts
of New York, Massachusetts, Maine and Louisiana, and the
U. S. S. C. and especially that of the eminent and learned Judge
Cooley in Mannasson v. Ins. Co., 29 Mich. 316; 3 Ins. L. J. 668.

Here is Wisconsin again. It was admitted that in stating
the amount of the loss in their proofs, insured included merchandise as destroyed which had been ordered before the fire,
but had not been received at the time of the fire; and that
upon their examination under oath after making of the proofs,
they testified that these goods had actually been received before
the fire. Insured claimed that these false statements were made
through innocent mistake, while the companies claimed that
they were wilfully made with intent to defraud. The proofs of
loss were made out for insured by an expert employed by them,
from information furnished by insured. The evidence showed
that the bills and invoices of insured were freely submitted to
the adjusters who in this manner ascertained the inclusion of
the goods in dispute. *Held*, That while the evidence tended to
show the inclusion of the amount of these goods in the proofs

of loss was wilful, it was a question for the jury whether they were included with fraudulent intent. [Judgment for plaintiff below. Here affirmed against company.]

Newton et al. v. Theresa Village Mut. Fire Ins. Co.;
Same v. Waterloo Mut. Fire Ins. Co.;
Same v. DeForest Mut. Fire Ins. Co. (Wis. S. C.):
104 Northwestern Reporter (July 18, 1905), 107.

CHAPTER VIII.

OPTIONS.

Option To Repair or Rebuild.

Where the insurer elects to rebuild, the contract of insurance is converted into a building contract, and the amount of damage recoverable from the breach of contract is not limited to the amount of insurance.

Heilman v. Westchester F. Ins. Co., 75 N. Y. 7, 8 Ins. L. J. 53.
Morrell v. Irving Ins. Co., 33 N. Y. 429.
Brown et al. v. Royal Ins. Co. (Queen's Bench, Eng.), 4 Bennett 371; 1 Ellis & Ellis 853.

Where two separate insurers elect to rebuild, in case of breach, the owner may recover his full damages against one of them, leaving it to seek contribution from the other on its own motion.

Morrell v. Irving Fire Ins. Co., 33 ,N. Y. 429.

The impossibility of performance by reason of action of city authorities does not relieve the insurer, it having elected to rebuild, it is liable for damages for not doing so.

Brown and others v. Royal Ins. Co. (Queen's Bench, Eng.), 4 Bennett 371; 1 Ellis & Ellis 853.
Fire Ass'n v. Rosenthal (Pa. S. C.), 15 Ins. L. J. 658.

The insurer is liable for damages including rent, resulting through delay.

Fire Ass'n v. Rosenthal supra.

But there can be no claim for rent until at least after a reasonable length of time has elapsed for making the repairs.

St. Paul F. & M. Ins. Co. v. Johnson (Ill. S. C.), 6 Ins. L. J. 434.

The assured is not bound to take any steps to restore the property to its previous condition.

Hoffman v. Aetna F. Ins. Co. (N. Y.); 1 Rob. 501.

The insurer will not be granted an injunction restraining insured from removing the goods saved, to enable the insurers to exercise their option.

N. Y. F. Ins. Co. v. Delaven, (N. Y.), 8 Paige 419.

The notice of insurer's intention to exercise the option must be given within the time named in the policy.

McAllaster v. Niagara F. Ins. Co., 156 N. Y. 80 ; 28 Ins. L. J. 769.

The insurance company having elected to rebuild is no longer under obligation to pay a money damage and it will be discharged from garnishment proceedings.

Hurst et al. v. Home Protection F. Ins. Co. (Ala. S. C.), 16 Ins. L. J. 688.
Godfrey v. Macomber and Ins. Co. (Mass. S. C.), 9 Ins. L. J. 287.

The insurer having rebuilt for sum less than the insurance, the unexhausted amount of policy remains in force on the new building in case of its destruction by fire for the unexpired term of policy.

Trull v. Roxbury Mut. Ins. Co. (Mass. S. C.), 3 Ben. 15.

The company having elected to repair, but for more than a month taking no steps to do so, is liable for damages from exposure of building to weather.

Amer. Cent'l Ins. Co. v. McLanathan (Kan. S. C.), 2 Ins. L. J. 907.

The right of option to rebuild begins to run from time proofs are served and 60 days thereafter when the loss becomes payable the option terminates and right of action accrues.

McAllaster v. Niagara F. Ins. Co. (N. Y. C. A.), 28 Ins. L. J. 769.
Clover v. Greenwich Ins. Co. 101 N. Y. 277 ; 15 Ins. L. J. 214.

And when the insurance company waives proofs of loss, it may still exercise the option within the time limited by the policy and such time begins to run from the date of such waiver.

Farmers and Merchants Ins. Co. v. Warner (Neb. S. C.), 34 Ins. L. J. 83.

There are two modes of settlement under the contract, one is payment of damages for the loss, the other the restoration of the subject of insurance to its former condition. It could not have been contemplated by the parties that both methods of performance were to be pursued. The selection by the insurance company of one of these alternatives necessarily constituted an abandonment of the other.

Wynkoop v. Niagara F. Ins. Co. (N. Y. C. A.), 12 Ins. L. J. 253.

The resort to arbitration by the insurer is an election to make payment in money.

McAllaster v. Niagara F. Ins. Co. (N. Y. C. A.), 28 Ins. L. J., 769.
Iowa Central Bldg. & L. Ass'n v. Merchants and Bankers' Fire

Ins. Co. (Ia. S. C.), 32 Ins. L. J. 852.
Alliance Co Operative Ins. Co. v. Arnold (Kan. S. C.), 31 Ins. L. J. 943.
Platt v. Aetna Ins. Co. is to same effect, but that non-waiver clause in appraisal agreement preserved company's option to rebuild, 153 Ill. 133 (Aff'g 40 Ill. App. 191), 24 Ins. L. J. 132, 38 N. E. 580.

The insurer, one of ten, and all having elected to rebuild, but afterwards all except the defendant compromised the loss. The defendant declined to settle and then demanded an appraisal, which was agreed to. The award under the appraisal exceeded the total insurance. *Held*, defendant's election to rebuild converted its policy into a building contract, and that the appraisal was without reference to any questions or matters of difference other than the loss and damage, and that plaintiff by agreeing to appraise did not, as a matter of law, waive his existing right. He was merely leaving all questions other than the loss and damage to be determined by the parties themselves, or by litigation. It was further held the liability was several and not joint, and that plaintiff had the right after the insurer had elected to rebuild to compromise and settle with any of the companies thus bound to rebuild without releasing the others from such proportionate share of the cost to rebuild.

Good v. Buckeye Mut. F. Ins. Co. (Ohio S. C.), 15 Ins. L. J., 3.

In those States having the valued-policy law, the statute forms not only part of the contract between the parties, but as was said in Reilly v. Ins. Co. (43 Wis. 456) of a statute similar in its terms, controls other provisions in the policy, so that such other provisions as far as they are inconsistent with the statute are necessarily avoided.

Ampleman v. Cit. Ins. Co., 18 Ins. L. J., 396 (Mo. App.).

Nor under such circumstances has the insurer the right to rebuild.

Marshall et al. v. Amer. Guar. F. M. I. Co., 80 Mo. App. 18.
Milwaukee Mech. I. Co. v. Russell (Ohio S. C.), 62 N. E. Rep., 338, 31 Ins. L. J., 360.

Wisconsin's standard form of policy permits the insurer, in case of total or partial loss, to rebuild or replace the property destroyed with other of like kind and quality or pay the full insurance, holding that such provision does not conflict with the valued-policy law of the State. (R. S. Wis. 1898, Sec. 1941-44.)

Temple v. Niagara Ins. Co. (Wis. S. C.), 85 N. W. Rep., 361.

Where the city ordinances will not permit the building to be repaired or rebuilt, the insurer is liable for total loss, i. e., the entire value of the building not exceeding the insurance.

O'Keefe v. L. & L. & G. Ins. Co., 140 Mo., 558 ; 41 S. W. Rep., 922.
Brady v. Ins. Co., 11 Mich., 445.
Brown v. Ins. Co., 1 Ellis & Ellis, 853.
Hamburg-Bremen F. I. Co. v. Garlington (Tex.), 15 Ins. L. J., 509.
Larkin v. Glens Falls Ins. Co. (Minn. S. C.), 83 N. W. Rep., 409.
Monteleone v. Royal I. Co. (La. S. C.), 24 Ins. L. J., 531.

And this is true where such law was enacted during the life of the policy.

Pennsylvania, etc. v. Phil, etc. (Pa. S. C.), 51 Atl. Rep., 351.

But in New York, where the standard form of policy is part of the statute law of the State, the insurer is only liable for the amount it would cost the insured to rebuild, repair or replace the building with material of like kind and quality, this regardless of laws or ordinances regulating the repair and construction of buildings.

McCready et al. v. Hartford F. Ins. Co. (N. Y. S. C., App. Div.), 70 N. Y. Supp., 778; 30 Ins. L. J., 668.

And the same is true where the policy exempts the company from loss caused by a law or ordinance regulating the repair of damaged buildings, except in those States which have a valued policy law.

Option Of Insurer To Take Over Salvage.

Option of "insurer to take all or any part of damaged property at its ascertained or appraised value * * * on giving notice within thirty days after receipt of proofs herein required, of its intention so to do."

Where assured sells the goods without giving the company the right to exercise this option, he thereby renders void his policy, and all rights thereunder.

Astrich v. German-American Ins. Co. (U. S. C. C. A., July 5, 1904), 33 Ins. L. J. 925.
Morley v. L. & L. & G. Ins. Co. (Mich. S. C.), 20 Ins. L. J. 577.

After an appraisal the company must have taken some steps to show that it wishes to avail itself of the option before it can claim breach of the condition.

Davis v. Grand Rapids F. Ins. Co., 15 Misc'l 263, S. C. 36 N. Y. Supp. 792. Affirmed, 157 N. Y. 685.

Defendants claim that assured should have kept the goods

thirty days; awaiting its option to take them was unreasonable.

Davis v. American Central Ins. Co., 7 App. Div. 488, S. C. 40 N. Y. Supp. 248. Affirmed (no opinion), 158 N. Y. 688.

Neither can the insurer with a $1,500 policy on goods valued at $16,000, insured, also, in twelve other companies, exercise this right.

Davis v. American Central Ins. Co., 7 App. Div. 488, S. C. 40 N. Y. Supp. 248. Affirmed, 158 N. Y. 688.

When two-thirds of the goods were wholly destroyed, the balance greatly damaged, and the assured had kept them eighteen days, during which time none of the thirteen companies in which assured held policies claimed the goods, the insured, after advertising the sale in two daily papers, sold the goods at public auction for $250. *Held,* That he did not thereby forfeit his claim for loss.

Davis v. American Central Ins. Co., 7 App. Div. 488, S. C. 40 N. Y. Supp. 248. Affirmed, 158 N. Y. 688.

If an insurance company fails within three days to demand an appraisal, or to exercise its option to take the goods, it waives its right to take them or to have them appraised.

Phoenix Assur. Co. v. Stenson (Tex. C. C. A.), 79 S. W. Rep. 866.

If there was no appraisement, the option to take the goods did not attach, and this regardless of whose fault caused the failure to appraise.

Swearinger v. Pacific F. Ins. Co., 66 Mo. App. 90.

The insurance company can not in one breath deny the arbitration and in the next assert and claim rights growing out of and depending on it. If it elects not to be bound by the arbitration, this is necessarily a waiver of its option to take the goods at their appraised value.

Model D. G. Co. v. N. B. and M. Ins. Co., 79 Mo. App. 550.

While nothing is said regarding the insurer's option to take the damaged property at its ascertained or appraised value in Chainless Cycle Co. v. Security Ins. Co. (N. Y. C. A.), 31 Ins. L. J. 324, yet, if not entitled to an appraisal, insurer can not exercise the option to take the stock. The opinion of the court very clearly enunciates the rights of the parties in the matter of adjustment, waiver, etc., and is well worth reading by every adjuster and lawyer. It may also be found in 169 N. Y. 304.

As regards the option in the policy to take any part of the

goods at their ascertained or appraised value, I can find no decisions affecting this option. My own opinion is that if a case is ever defended on the ground that assured has forfeited his rights by refusing to permit the insurer to exercise this option, the insured will not be held to have forfeited his claim, the reason being that if insurance companies are allowed to exercise this unfair option they thereby create a further damage to the insured's property.

If an appraisal be fairly conducted, the award thereunder is arrived at, having in view all the facts, circumstances, conditions and environments of the goods or wares appraised, so that, should the insurer feel that it has been unjustly dealt with, it may take all of the stock by paying the insured the loss and the value of the salvage as fixed by the appraisers, in which event neither party is harmed.

But suppose the property damaged be a clothing and men's furnishing stock, and the appraisers have determined the loss to be as follows: Coats, 75 per cent.; vests, 30 per cent.; pants, 60 per cent.; shirts, 20 per cent; undershirts, 66 2-3 per cent.; underdrawers, 20 per cent.; neckties, 25 per cent.; collars and cuffs, 20 per cent., and hosiery, 70 per cent. When the award is returned the adjuster says to the assured: "We have decided to take the coats, pants, undershirts and hosiery at their appraised value, leaving you the vests, shirts, drawers, neckties, collars and cuffs."

If the courts uphold the option to take any part of the goods and thus allow insurer to take the goods mentioned, it thereby permits it legally to damage the goods they force the insured to keep to the extent of at least 50 per cent. more.

In more than half of the appraisals there is a good deal of ill-feeling and bad blood engendered between the insured and the adjuster in an effort to adjust the loss; and, while some appraisals are held where there is no ill-feeling and no desire to do otherwise than to arrive at a fair estimate of the loss, yet in a great many it is a question of "do or be done," and you will see the same appraiser appraising a clothing stock, that last week appraised a household furniture loss, that the week before appraised a grocery loss, and maybe last month he appraised a shoe loss, and the month before he may have appraised a machinery loss. It is wonderful what a variegated knowledge (?) these men have as to values in different lines. Is it not true that they are selected not so much for their ability to judge values as for their skill in judging human nature?

The great objection to these men is not that they are robbers, because most of them are honest, but they would not be human if they were not biased. This bias leads them to such long delays in selecting a competent umpire, and then they further delay by assessing the damage article by article, which is unfair to the insured in more ways than one, as, for instance, what sensible merchant, if he is negotiating for the purchase of a stock of goods, will go through the stock and place a value on it article by article? He carefully examines each line of goods, and, when he gets through, makes up his mind what the entire stock is worth. That is the way the damage should be fixed in case of fire, either as a whole or by departments. The appraisers need not assess the damage article by article (Enright v. Montauk F. Ins. Co., 40 N. Y. St. Rep. 642, 5 Finch 25), nor does the policy exact such appraisal.

The assured can not select a man, except in very rare cases, who is competent to cope with these professional appraisers, for they are attending to this work nearly every day. If they make a mistake in the umpire they can easily protect their clients by running up the damage on a few lines of goods so as to enable their principals to take those articles, or force assured into a settlement different from the award by threatening to take them.

When adjusters take such advantage of a man—not all of them will do so, no matter what the provocation—it is usually because of some fancied or real wrong or meanness done them by the assured, or at the instigation of some wrecker, who promises big returns for conditioning and selling the stock at fire sale.

The adjuster is frequently justified in taking any advantage of the assured that he possibly can, were it not for that old aphorism, "two wrongs do not make a right," for sometimes the assured can act meaner than a devil and more stubborn than an ass, and in many such cases I have been compelled to admire the adjuster who could handle the adjustment without apparently losing his head or his temper. What is more, everybody else will respect and honor him, including those claimants who make fools of themselves by their mean, nasty ways.

In the case of Palatine v. Morton-Scott-Robertson Co., 106 Tenn. 558, it was held when there are several insurers, the right of each is to take only its pro-rata of the appraised salvage articles; that even if the insured sells a portion of the salvage, it is immaterial so long as enough remains unsold to enable the complaining company to exercise its option under the policy to take its pro-rata of the salvage. It would seem this is a reasonable rule.

The salvage was the property of the insured, and for its reasonable value, he must account, so that it would be unfair to require him to hold it in a deteriorating condition while the companies delayed settlement, and thus give opportunity for its further depreciation.

Where salvage is carried along with a new stock and sold as opportunity offers, it should be charged with its fair share of the expenses of the business.

North German Ins. Co. v. Morton-Scott-Robertson Co., 108 Tenn. 384; 67 S. W. Rep. 816; 31 Ins. L. J. 580.

SOME DANGERS ENCOUNTERED FROM TAKING OVER SALVAGE.

Since the advent of Salvage Companies operated by the insurance companies, many appraisals have been avoided, especially on stocks of merchandise when circumstances warrant its being taken over by the companies, in such cases where the assured is not in position to handle the damaged stock, or where the companies are in position to realize as good or better results than could the assured.

It seems to the author that in taking over these salvages not enough caution is used by the companies. For instance, it is held that where two or more companies repair a damaged building this creates a joint building contract, so that if the building is not rebuilt for any cause, the insured may sue one or all of the companies, and the company against whom he obtains judgment must look to the other company for its share of the damage recovered. This being true the same rule of law will apply when companies take over salvage—their action will be joint and not several. Therefore, should one of the companies afterwards become bankrupt, the assured could unquestionably look to the other companies for at least that portion of the proceeds of the salvage apportioned to the bankrupt company, and possibly for even more. Certainly, the insured having parted with his title or interest in the salvage, has no lien in that portion of the proceeds apportioned to such bankrupt insurance company. The fact that he once owned the stock gives him no greater right to the proceeds of the sale than has any other creditor of such bankrupt company. His only recourse is either to attach or garnish the money apportioned to the bankrupt, or let it be paid to its assignee or receiver, and sue some one or all of the other companies. Under such circumstances, the company not having paid his loss, what would be the measure of his recovery? If the value of the salvage had been agreed upon before the stock was taken over, then unquestionably he could not recover more than such bankrupt company's portion of such value. But if the value of the salvage had not been agreed to, all sorts of questions might be injected into the suit, such, for instance, as whether the salvage had been handled to the best advantage. It might be, that assured would have the right to say to the companies, "You have jointly agreed with me on the value of my stock and have taken it over for your benefit. Now I want its entire value. It was your business, not mine that you entered into this joint contract, this partnership deal, with an insolvent company. Pay me my loss."

A carefully worded agreement as to the value of the salvage, and that the companies would be looked to in a several and not joint capacity, might prevent the possibility of a come-back on the solvent companies for the default of an insolvent one.

CHAPTER IX

DUTY OF INSURED TO PROTECT PROP ERTY AT AND AFTER THE FIRE— LOSS BY THEFT, ETC.

The New York standard policy has the following provisions: "This company shall not be liable for loss caused directly or indirectly * * * by theft; or by neglect of the insured to use all reasonable means to save and protect the property at and after a fire, or when the property is endangered by fire in neighboring premises."

Lines 60 to 66 of the New York standard policy, provide that when property is removed to a place of safety to protect it from further loss the excess of its proportion for the loss and damage already done, shall cover the property so removed for five days only.

How inconsistent these clauses are. Every insurance man knows that no insurance company will insure salvage goods until after the value of same has been determined by the adjusters. Hence it is absolutely impossible to insure them in other companies and the insurers try to exempt themselves from liability after five days, when their policies compel assured to protect his property and to protect it he has been compelled to remove it and can not insure it until his loss on same is adjusted.

Here are a few decisions that may be of interest. They relate to the exemptions in the clause quoted.

Losses in removing goods from approaching fire, though not yet caught in the building where the goods are, whether by theft, loss or destruction, is to be borne by the insurance com pany when the policy does not exempt the company from them.

Agnew v. Ins. Co., 3 Phil. 193 (Pa.).
Thompson v. Montreal Ins. Co., 6 Up. Can., 2 Q. B. 319.
Case v. Hartford F. Ins. Co., 13 Ills. 676.
Lebanon Mut. F. Ins. Co. v. Hankinson, 2 Cent. Rep. 828 (Pa.).
Newmark v. L. & L. & G. Ins. Co., 30 Mo. 160.

The exemption from loss by theft is independent of the clause following it which exempts insuring company from liability from losses by means of invasions, insurrections and similar commotions. The object of the policy is to indemnify assured against any losses by fire and any loss by theft not attributable directly to the fire, would not be within the contract, (there was great noise, crowd and disturbance in the streets on the night of the fire), and when the insurer exempts itself from liability for fires which happen by reason of invasions, etc., it is superfluous to add that losses by theft occasioned by such fires would also be without the protection of the policy.

Webb. v. Protection, and Aetna Ins. Cos. 14 Mo. 3.

Unless the policy exempts the company from such losses the insurer is liable for loss by theft during and after the fire, if the theft be occasioned directly by the fire.

Newmark v. L. and L. and G. Ins.·Co., 30 Mo. 160, and following authorities there cited: 1 Phillips on Ins., Sec. 624, p. 1107; 3 Penn. 471; 13 Ill. 676; 1 Story 157.

The insurer is responsible for loss of goods stolen after a fire, in a populous city; it is a natural consequence of the peril insured against.

Tilton v. Hamilton F. Ins. Co., 1 Bos. 367 ; S. C. How. Pr. 363.

The insurer is liable for goods destroyed in blowing up a building with gun powder by civil authorities, to prevent spread of fire.

City Fire Ins. Co. v. Corlies, 21 Wend. 367.

The insurer is not liable for theft during fire.

Sklencher v. Fire Ass'n (N. J. S. C.), 60 Atlantic Rep. 232.

The assured must comply with the policy requirement, save and protect his property at and after the fire, though the policy provision does not impose any greater effort on his part than does the law, and his duty to the company, both of which requires that he do whatever is reasonable to minimize his and therefore the company's loss. The penalty for not making all reasonable efforts to save the property is not a forfeiture of the policy, but is the amount of loss caused by his failure to use such reasonable efforts.

It seems, however, he must, under penalty of forfeiture of his policy save all that remains of the property insured, and exhibit it to the company as often as required, not so much for the value of the salvage as to enable the company to form some accurate idea of what it consisted of, etc. See Thornton v.

Security Ins. Co., 117 Fed. 773, 32 Ins. L. J. 557. The company must have the right to examine the property and to have it and the loss appraised if a difference arises, Ostrich v. German-Am. Ins. Co., 65 C. C. A. 251, 131 Fed. 13, 33 Ins. L. J. 925. The company, of course, must act promptly, Chainless Co v. Security Ins. Co., 169 N. Y. 304, 31 Ins. L. J. 324, 62 N. E. 392. Flynn v. Hanover F. Ins. Co., 121 N. Y. Supp. 621. A Texas case, holds that three days' time is enough. But a reasonable time should be given, taking all circumstances into consideration.

CHAPTER X.

FALL OF BUILDING.

"If a building or any part thereof fall, except as the result of fire, all insurance by this policy on such building or its contents shall immediately cease."—New York Standard Policy.

The meaning of the clause in question, when reasonably interpreted, is that the insurer is excused from its obligation by either the fall of the building as a structure, or of such a substantial and important part thereof as impairs its usefulness as such and leaves the remaining part of the building subject to an increased risk of fire.

Nelson et al. v. Traders' Ins. Co. (N. Y. C. A.), 34 Ins. L. J. 933.

The question of fact for the jury to determine is, "was the fall caused by the fire or by some other force?" If not by fire, the insurer is not liable. A request to charge that if building was on fire before the fall, the insurer was liable, even if the fall was caused by the wind, was properly refused.

Keisel v. Sun Ins. Office (U. S. C. C. A. 8th Dist.), 28 Ins. L. J. 434.

When an explosion causes a building to fall and catch fire, it might be conceded that if the clause exempting the company from liability stood alone, the policy would be terminated immediately upon fall of the building. But that clause is governed by a specific clause, which exempts the insurer from loss by explosion of any kind unless fire ensues, and in that event for damage by fire only.

Davis v. Ins. Co. of N. A. (Mich. S. C.), 27 Ins. L. J. 184.

The clause in the policy contemplates the fall of a building caused by inherent defects, or by withdrawal of the necessary support as by digging away the underlying or adjacent soil. It might perhaps include the case of a building thrown down by storm, flood or earthquake.

Dows v. Ins. Co., 127 Mass. 346.
Leonard v. Orient Ins. Co. (U. S. C. C. A. 7th Dist.), 30 Ins. L. J. 980.
Davis v. Ins. Co. N. A. (Mich. S. C.), 27 Ins. L. J. 184.

Where there was no evidence of fire about the ruins of a building which had fallen for over an hour, and it had been, according to evidence, weakened by cutting timbers and remodeling, but six witnesses testified that a flame shot from the roof before it fell, a finding that the fall was caused by fire will not be disturbed.

Friedman v. Atlas Assur. Co., 32 Ins. L. J. 673 (Mich. S. C.).

Contents of building No. 93 were insured, one wall and half of building No. 93, and all of building 95 fell, evidence varied from 15 to 40 minutes after fall when fire occurred. Loss is within the policy.

Lewis et al. v. Springfield F. & M. Ins. Co., 76 Mass. 159.

As a direct result of fire the adjoining building fell, carrying with it the party wall and part of the insured building. *Held*, loss within the policy.

Ermentraut v. Girard F. & M. Ins. Co. (Minn. S. C.), 25 Ins. L. J. 81.

It must cease to be a building to be fallen within the meaning of the policy. So long as standing, however depreciated, it is not fallen.

Firemen's Ins. Co. v. Sholom, 80 Ill. 558.

If a building falls and afterwards burns, the insurer is not liable.

Nave v. Home Mut. Ins. Co., 37 Mo. 431.
Nichols et al. v. Sun Mut. F. Ins. Co. (Miss. S. C.), 14 S. W. Rep. 263; 23 Ins. L. J. 633.
Trans-Atlantic F. Ins. Co. v. Bamberger (Ky. C. A.), 18 Ins. L. J. 625.
Keisel v. Sun Fire Office (U. S. C. C. A. 8th Dist.), 28 Ins. L. J. 434.

Under Code Pleading, the burden of proof is on the defendant, where it admits the amount of the loss, but claims fall of building caused the fire.

Royal Ins. Co. v. Schwing (Ky. C. A.), 18 Ins. L. J. 451.
Trans-Atlantic F. Ins. Co. v. Bamberger (Ky C. A.), 18 Ins. L. J. 625.

The burden of proof is on plaintiff.

Pelican Ins. Co. v. Co-Operative Assoc. (Tex. S. C.), 19 Ins. L. J. 921.

Contra:

Friedman v. Atlas Assur. Co. (Mich. S. C.), 32 Ins. L. J. 673.
Western Assur. Co. v. Mohlman (U. S. C. C. A. 2d Dist), 27 Ins. L. J. 392.

EXPLOSIONS.

"This company shall not be liable for loss * * * unless the fire ensues, and in that event, for the damage by fire only— by explosion of any kind, or lightning; but liability for direct damage by lightning may be assumed by a specific agreement hereto."—New York Standard Policy.

So many people cannot understand why a loss to the insured's building caused by explosion, which in turn was caused by fire in an adjacent building, renders the policy void, as in such case the fire was the first or moving cause of the loss.- The insurer would be liable but for the policy contract which exempts it from liability from loss by explosions, regardless of what produced the explosion; and such exemption is wholly contractual. An insurance company insuring against loss has the right to exempt itself from any loss that may originate on the insured's property.

Sohier v. Norwich Ins. Co., 93 Mass., 336.

So where the policy against loss by fire exempted the insured from any loss occasioned by an explosion of steam boiler, it was held that a loss by fire caused by the explosion of a steam boiler in the factory insured was not within the policy.

St. John v. Mut. M. & F. Ins. Co., 11 N. Y., 516.

Nor is a loss by fire caused by an explosion where the insurer exempts itself from loss by explosion of any kind.

Hayward v. Liverpool & London F. & L. Ins, Co., 7 Bosw., 385; affd. 2 Abb. Ct. App. Dec. 349, 3 Keyes, 456 (N. Y.).

Nor where such a fire was extinguished but broke out a second and third time within two days, as it was held the existence of the fire as an effect of the explosion must be presumed to have continued as such an effect in the absence of contrary proof.

Tanneret v. Merchants' Ins. Co., 34 La. Ann., 249.

But it is, if the fire is caused by explosion of a lamp.

Heffron v. Kitanning Ins. Co., 132 Pa., 580.

Insurer is not liable for loss resulting from explosion of dynamite, gas or other substances coming in contact with lighted match or lamp.

Huer v. Westchester F. Ins. Co. (Ill. S. C.), 33 N. E. 411; 24 Ins. L. J. 471.
Phoenix Ins. Co. v. Greer (Ark. S. C.), 25 Ins. L. J. 311.
Mitchell v. Potomac Ins. Co. (U. S. S. C.), 31 Ins. L. J. 570.
Briggs v. N. B. & M. Ins. Co. (N. Y.), 53 N. Y., 446; affirming 66 Barb., 325; 2 Ins. L. J., 929.
Huer v. N. W. National Ins. Co. (Ill. S. C.), 22 Ins. L. J. 518.
German-Amer. Ins. Co. v. Hyman, 42 Col. 156, 94 Pac. 27, 37 Ins. L. J. 362.
Home Lodge v. Queen Ins. Co., 21 S. D. 165, 110 N. W. 778.
Vorse v. Jersey Plate Glass Ins. Co., 119 Ia. 556, 93 N. W. 569. (But see Contra, Furbush v. Ins. Co., 140 Ia. 240, 118 N. W. 371.)
Trans-Atlantic F. Ins. Co. v. Dorsey, 56 Md. 70, 12 Ins. L. J. 437.
United &c. Ins. Co. v. Foote, 22 Ohio St. 340, 2 Ins. L. J. 190.

Contra:

Scripture v. Lowell Ins. Co., 64 Mass. 356.
Renshaw v. Mo. State Mut. F. & M. Ins. Co., 103 Mo. 595, 20 Ins. L. J. 385.
Furbush v. Ins. Co., 140 Ia. 240, 118 N. W. 371.

Where fire in another building causes an explosion which damages plaintiff's property the loss is not within the policy.

Miller v. London & Lancashire F. Ins. Co., 41 Ill. App. 395.
Dows. v. Faneuil Hall Ins. Co., 127 Mass. 346.
Leonard v. Orient Ins. Co. (U. S. C. C. A., 7th Dist.), 30 Ins. L. J. 981.
Caballero v. Home Ins. Co., 15 La. Ann. 217, 4 Ben. 478.
Hall v. National F. Ins. Co., 35 Ins. L. J. 507, 115 Tenn. 513, 92 S. W. 402.

But if fire ensue, the insurer is liable for the loss by fire.

Miller v. London & Lancashire F. Ins. Co., 41 Ill. App. 395.
Dows v. Faneuil Hall Ins. Co., 127 Mass. 346.
Leonard v. Orient Ins. Co. (U. S. C. C. A. 7th Dist.), 30 Ins. L. J. 981.
Davis v. Ins. Co. N. A. (Mich. S. C.), 27 Ins. L. J. 184.

The same principle is involved where explosion is caused by lightning in another building 71 feet from the premises insured. And where a lightning clause is attached to policy, covering loss by lightning, subject in all other respects to the terms and conditions of the policy.

German F. Ins. Co. v. Roost (Ohio S. C.), 26 Ins. L. J. 699.

The provisions of the written form, that the policy should cover such merchandise as is usually kept for sale in retail hardware stores, was sufficient permission, the custom to keep dynamite being established by the evidence for the keeping of dynamite on the premises. [Judgment for plaintiff below. Here affirmed against company.]

Traders Ins. Co. v. Dobbins et al. (Tenn. S. C.)
        86 Southwestern Reporter (May 3, 1905), 383.

Where policy provides that it should be void if dynamite were kept on the premises, the keeping of a stick and a half of dynamite whether it caused the fire or not, worked a forfeiture.

Bastian v. British Amer. Assur. Co. (Cal. S. C.), 33 Ins. L. J. 1033

Where the explosives did not cause the fire, and were removed in time to prevent an explosion, it was held that policy was forfeited.

Kennefick-Hammond Co. v. Norwich Union F. Ins. Society (Mo. App.), 33 Ins. L. J. 664.

It is not necessary to show that the loss was due to the violation.

Norwaysz v. Thuringia Ins. Co. (Ill. S. C.), 33 Ins. L. J. 83.

Nor is the insured owner relieved by the fact that the violation was by a tenant, without his knowledge.

Norwaysz v. Thuringia Ins. Co. (Ill. S. C.), 33 Ins. L. J. 83.
La Force v. Williamsburg City F. Ins. Co., 43 Mo. App. 518.

A fire loss caused by explosion of gasoline stove on premises without consent of insured is not within the policy.

McFarland v. St. Paul F. and M. Ins. Co. (Minn. S. C.), 21 Ins. L. J. 879.

CHAPTER XII.

WAIVER—NON-WAIVER AGREEMENT.

Definition of Waiver.

A waiver is the voluntary relinquishment of some known right.

Rosen v. German Alliance Ins. Co. (Me.), 76 Atl. 688.
Scottish U. & M. Ins. Co. (Georgia), 68 S. E. 1097.
Dahrooge v. Rochester Ger. Ins. Co., 143 N. W. 608.
Gardner v. North St. M. L. Ins. Co. (N. C. S. C.), 79 S. E. 806

One's Acts, Rather Than Denial of Waiver, Looked To.

It matters not if the Insurance Company says: "We waive nothing." Its acts must be looked to to ascertain if there is a waiver. Its actual waiver cannot be affected by its statements that it is not doing that which it clearly is doing.

Summers v. Western Home Ins. Co., 45 Mo. App. 46.
Erwin v. Ins. Co., 24 Mo. App. 153.
Phillips v. Protection Ins. Co., 14 Mo. 220.

Must Know Facts Before Waiver Can Be Charged.

One cannot waive a right when ignorant of its existence, as an essential element of waiver is knowledge of the fact waived.

Security Ins. Co. v. Mette, 27 Ill. App. 324.
Rudd v. American G. F. M. F. Ins. Co., 120 Mo. App. 1.
Security Ins. Co. v. Laird, 62 So. 182 (Ala.).

An insurance adjuster knowing the policy had been forfeited by a breach of a condition, asked for and was refused a non-waiver agreement. He then stated he would not waive any of the policy conditions but required assured to make a list of destroyed property and then went away. Court held his actions a waiver of the forfeiture, comparing them to those of Julia in Byron's Don Juan—

"A little still she strove, and much repented,
And whispering, 'I will ne'er consent,' consented."
German-American Ins. Co. v. Evans (Texas C. C. A.); 61 S. W.
Rep. 536; 14 Deitch Ins. Digest, 41.

A forfeiture is waived by requiring proofs of loss or the correction of defective proofs, after knowledge of such forfeiture.

Roby. v. Ins. Co., 120 N. Y. 510.
Cobbs v. Ins. Co., 68 Mich. 463.
Cleaver v. Ins. Co., 71 Mich. 414.

Jerdee v. Ins. Co., 75 Wis. 345.
Carpenter v. Ins. Co., 61 Mich. 635.

To constitute waiver the assured must be put to some trouble or expense, or have been misled.

Roby v. Ins. Co., 120 N. Y. 510.
Weidert v. Ins. Co., 19 Ins. L. J. 740 (Oregon).
Devens v. Ins. Co., 83 N. Y. 168.
Findeisen v. Ins. Co., 15 Ins. L. J. 90 (Vermont).

There can be no waiver unless the assured relied on acts of the adjuster, or, as a prudent, careful man, had a right to do so.

Devens v. Ins. Co., 83 N. Y. 168.

NON-WAIVER AGREEMENT.

Most non-waiver agreements are entered into between the assured and adjuster sent to adjust the loss on behalf of the company. The reason for entering into such an agreement is very clearly set out by the Supreme Court of Alabama in the Draper case, first the court quotes the agreement, then shows the reason for taking a non-waiver agreement and how it may itself be waived.

"R. W. Draper insured under policy No. 5656 of the Pennsylvania Ins. Co., hereby requests W. L. Reynolds, adj., to make examination of books, papers, and other evidence of loss including assured's sworn statement if deemed necessary, which I submit to him for the purpose of ascertaining amount of loss, sustained by me by fire May 21, 1910, with the express understanding and agreement that such examination shall not be considered an acknowledgment of any liability of the said Pennsylvania Ins. Co. under said policy, nor a waiver or impairment of any rights or defenses of that company under said policy, nor a waiver or impairment of assured's obligation thereunder. It is further understood and agreed that the existing legal rights, if any, the said R. W. Draper may have under said policy are not impaired by his act in signing this request."

It thus appears that the agreement merely requests an examination of books, papers and other evidence of loss, submitted for purpose of ascertaining the amount of loss, with the understanding that such examination shall not be considered as fixing liability. * * * Giving to it a natural and reasonable construction, we think its purpose was merely to prevent a liability being fastened upon the company by virtue of the fact that the investigation would be continued after knowledge by the adjuster of the breach, recognizing that by so continuing after such knowledge it may be considered as treating the policy as valid and binding, and, therefore, that the mere continued examination might be held a waiver. (Georgia Home Ins. Co. v. Allen, 119 Ala. 436, 24 So. 399).

There is nothing in the language of the agreement to indicate the company could not be bound by positive declarations or acts evincing a clear purpose to waive any breach and treat the policy as valid.

Pennsylvania F. Ins. Co. v. Draper, 65 So. 923, will appear in 186, 187, or 188 Alabama Reports.

ONE CAN WAIVE ANY CONTRACT ONE HAS THE RIGHT TO MAKE.

If the adjuster sent by a company to adjust a loss, has the right to enter into a non-waiver agreement, he certainly has the right to waive the non-waiver agreement or any rights growing out of it, and this too when the non-waiver agreement specifically provides that he has no such rights. There is only one way an insurance company may or can prevent an adjuster from waiving its rights, that is by appointing him to do certain specified things towards adjusting or investigating the loss and then notifying the assured just what the adjuster's power and authority is. Where the assured is put on notice, he cannot be heard to complain if he has done something the adjuster had no right to require him to do. Nor can he be misled by the adjuster's unauthorized promise to pay.

Most waivers are thought of after the claim drifts into the hands of some tricky lawyer, who tells the assured his policy is void unless the adjuster said certain things. Though there are many adjusters who do not know when they commit a plain waiver. But as already stated most of these waivers originate in the fertile brain of tricky lawyers and a rascally assured. For these reasons an independent adjuster employed at so much per day should have the company's certificate of authority setting forth just what he is authorized to do, i. e., investigate the circumstances concerning the origin and circumstances of the fire and the claim growing out of it, to agree with the assured on the amount of loss if possible, failing in which he would have authority to have it appraised in accordance with the terms of the policy. But that he had no authority to admit or deny liability, nor to require the assured to do or perform any thing or act that could be construed into a waiver of the company's rights to claim a forfeiture by reason of a breach of the policy conditions, whether such breach was known to the adjuster or not. That all questions concerning the company's liability must be determined by the company itself or the courts in case it failed or refused to pay.

Of course, salaried adjusters, and salaried special agents called upon to adjust a loss, being regular employes of the company with power to give drafts in payment of the loss, could not, in the opinion of the author have their authority curtailed unless possibly the certificate of authority and the draft also, set out the fact that the draft should not be taken by the assured as an admission by the company of liability, but would be taken as the measure of the company's liability, if liable at all, and the giving by the adjuster and acceptance by the assured of the said draft was without reference to any other questions or matters of difference than the fixing of the amount of the company's liability if it should be found liable. The company could then pay the draft or not as it saw fit, if it refused payment, the draft would obviate the necessity of assured proving his claim in court, and leave the court to determine only the question of liability.

The following is a case now before the courts in Alabama, it shows the facts as given by the assured, and an opinion and brief by the author, based on assured's statement of facts.

AN ALABAMA LOSS, SHOWING EFFECTS OF IRON SAFE CLAUSE AND NON-WAIVER AGREEMENT.

Where an inventory was taken December 31, 1913, the insured has the whole of the calendar year 1914 in which to take another inventory under the form of iron-safe clause usually made a part of the policies issued in Alabama, a copy of which is shown in the McGlathery case, 115 Ala. 213, 22 So. 104. Therefore, if the next or second inventory is being taken and while in process it is destroyed by a fire which occurs before December 31, 1914, which also destroys the stock insured, such destruction of the unfinished inventory is not a violation of the iron-safe clause. The clause only provides for the production of the inventory, that is, the completed inventory, for it is no inventory at all if incomplete.

Wherever the language of the policy is susceptible of more than one construction, that construction will be placed upon it which will be most favorable to the insured. Western Assurance Co. v. McGlathery and cases there cited, 115 Ala. 213, 22 So. 104.   •

The Alabama courts only require a substantial compliance with the iron-safe clause. Queen Ins. Co. v. Vines, 174 Ala. 570, 57 So. 444.

For the sake of argument we will assume the iron-safe clause was violated in every particular in which event the company could, according to the Alabama decisions, successfully resist payment for claim under such policy. Day v. Home Ins. Co., 177 Ala. 600, 58 So. 549. But the Alabama courts hold the violation of an iron-safe clause in a fire insurance policy renders the policy voidable not void. They further hold that an adjuster may waive the iron-safe clause, Liverpool & L. & G. Ins. Co. v. Tillis, 110 Ala. 20, 17 So. 672. Georgia Home Ins. Co. v. Allen, 28 Ins. L. J. 199, 119 Ala. 436, 24 So. 399. See same (Allen) case 128 Ala. 451, 30 So. 537, 31 Ins. L. J. 60.

The insurance company may, however, take a non-waiver agreement, but such agreement is only a privilege granted the insurance company to investigate and ascertain the cause of the fire and the amount of damage done, without waiving or invalidating any of the conditions of the policy.

Pennsylvania F. Ins. Co. v. Draper, 65 So. 923, will appear in about 187 Ala.
Gish v. Ins. Co. of N. A., 16 Okla. 59, 87 Pac. 869, Annotated 13 L. R. A. (N. S.) 826.
Rudd v. American G. F. M. F. Ins. Co., 120 Mo. App. 1, 96 S. W. 237, 35 Ins. L. J. 948.
Hatcher v. Sovereign F. Assur. Co., 127 Pac. 588.

There is nothing in the language of the non-waiver agreement to indicate that the company could not be bound by positive declarations or acts evincing a clear purpose to waive any breach and treat the policy as valid.

Robert v. Sun M. Ins. Co. (Tex. C. C. A.), 35 S. W. 955.
Pennsylvania F. Ins. Co. v. Draper, 65 So. 923, Ala. Rep. about 187.
Rudd v. Amer. G. D. M. F. Ins. Co., 120 Mo. App. 1, 96 S. W. 237, 35 Ins. L. J. 948.
McMillan v. Ins. Co. of N. A., 58 S. E. 1020, 78 S. C. 433.
Gish v. Ins. Co. of N. A., 16 Okla. 59, 87 Pac. 869 annotated 13 L. R. A. (N. S.) 826.
Hatcher v. Sovereign Ins. Co., 127 Pac. 588, 42 Ins. L. J. 137 (Wash. S. C.).

A perusal of the foregoing cases will show that the company or its adjuster may treat the policy as a valid contract in several ways, that is by insisting upon the assured complying with some of the policy requirements such as the furnishing proofs of loss, the waiving of proofs of loss, the furnishing of certified copies of bills the originals of which have been lost, or requiring him to submit to examination under oath, or by taking over and conditioning the salvage or exercising its option under the contract of taking the salvage at its ascertained or appraised value, or by a promise to pay.

In other words, if the policy has been avoided by a violation of the iron-safe clause, the non-waiver agreement merely permits the company to investigate the circumstances concerning the fire and examine all the books and papers in the insured's possession pertaining to the claim for loss. But it cannot in one breath deny the contract and in the next assert' and claim rights growing out of and depending on it. If it elects not to be bound by the policy, that is necessarily a waiver of its right to insist upon the compliance with its requirements or vice versa. That is the doctrine laid down by the Missouri Appellate Court in passing on another point. See Model D. G. Co. v. North B. & M. Ins. Co., 79 Mo. App. 550.

THE ASSURED'S STATEMENT OF FACTS.

The insurance covered stock subject to the average clause in buildings A and B an alley separating them. The stock in A was almost a total loss, stock in B was not damaged. The assured had completed his inventory December 31, 1913, which had required more than a month to complete. While in process of taking the next inventory, say December 14, 1914, a fire burned the greater part of the stock and with it all the sheets of the incomplete inventory. The adjusters claimed this a violation of the iron-safe clause and would not proceed with the adjustment or investigation until a non-waiver agreement was signed.

AFTER THE NON-WAIVER AGREEMENT WAS ENTERED INTO.

The adjuster required assured to submit to examination under oath. He required assured at great expense to furnish certified copies of bills the originals of which were lost. Agreed with assured that Underwriter's Salvage Co. should condition the stock, both agreeing that this conditioning of stock did not divest assured of title and was not to be a waiver of the rights of either. Told assured that the proportion of his insurance covering in B was still in force. All of the local agents told him the same thing concerning the insurance in B. (It is well to remember that a policy covering stock only, if void in part is void altogether) though the avoidance of the insurance on stock by reason of violation of iron-safe clause does not avoid the insurance on building, both being insured under separate amounts under same policy.

Hanover Ins. Co. v. Crawford, 121 Ala. 259, 25 So. 912.

The author gave it as his opinion, the companies would be held liable if the assured's statement of facts was correct.

This loss has been settled and paid. The companies offered $160,000, assured offered to take $180,000. It was compromised for $170,000.

CHAPTER XIII.

APPRAISAL—ARBITRATION—AWARD.

First Duty Is to Try to Effect Settlement.

Where the policy provides that loss shall be ascertained or estimated by the insured and the company, or if they differ, then by appraisers as thereinafter provided, such language contemplates an actual effort to agree. When this effort fails and not until then neither party possess the right to say we differ, and our points of difference must be referred to arbitrament under the terms of the policy. Until there is some disagreement as to the amount of the loss, there is nothing to arbitrate.

Boyle v. Hamburg-Bremen F. Ins. Co., 169 Pa. 349; 32 Atl. R. 553; 24 Ins. L. J. 699.

Harrison v. Hartford F. Ins. Co., 23 Ins. L. J. 161; 59 Fed. 732.

British Am. Assur. Co. v. Darragh, 128 Fed. Rep. 890; 33 Ins. L. J. 557; 63 C. C. A. 426.

Summerfield v. N. B. & M. Ins. Co., 62 Fed. 249.

Stevens v. Norwich U. Ins. Soc., 120 Mo. App. 88; 96 S. W. R. 684.

Continental Ins. Co. v. Vallandingham, 116 Ky. 287; 76 S. W. 22.

Moyer v. Sun Ins. Off., 176 Pa. 579; 35 Atl. R. 221.

Fletcher v. German Am. Ins. Co., 79 Minn. 337; 82 N. W. R. 647; 29 Ins. L. J. 752, Harrison v. German Am. Ins. Co., 67 Fed. 577.

Kelly v. Liverpool & L. & G. Ins. Co., 94 Minn. 141; 102 N. W. 380; 34 Ins. L. J. 421.

Liverpool & L. & G. Ins. Co. v. Hall, 1 Kans. App. 18; 41 Pac. R. 65, Phoenix Fire Assur. Co. v. Murray, (U. S. C. C. A.) 187 Fed. 809.

Mutual F. Ins. Co. v. Alvord, 23 Ins. L. J. 801; 61 Fed. 752; 21 U. S. App. 228, Vangindertallen v. Phoenix Ins. Co., 82 Wis. 112, 51 N. W. 1122.

Manchester F. Assur Co. v. Simmons, 12 Tex. C. A. 607; 35 S. W. R. 722.

Farnum v. Phoenix Ins Co., 83 Cal. 246; 26 Ins. L. J. 473; 23 Pac. R. 869.

Randall v. Phoenix Ins. Co., 10 Mont. 362; 25 Pac. R. 960; 20 Ins. L. J. 613, Ohio Farmers Ins. Co. v. Titus (Ohio), 92 N. E. 82.

Wright v. Susquehana M. F. Co., 110 Pa. 29; 20 Atl. R. 716.

Hanover F. Ins. Co. v. Harper, 77 Ill. App. 453.

American F. Ins. Co. v. Stuart (Tex. C. C. A.), 38 S. W. R. 395.

Torpedo Top Co. v. Royal Ins. Co., 162 Ill. App. 338; 42 Nat'l C. Rep. 593.

Zimeriski v. Ohio Farmers Ins. Co., 91 Mich. 600; 21 Ins. L. J. 818; 52 N. W. 55.

Capital Ins. Co. v. Wallace, 50 Kans. 453; 21 Ins. L. J. 516; 31 Pac. R. 1070.

Valued Policy Law, Effect of.

In those States having a valued policy law in force, it is held that there is no consideration for an appraisal and, if had, the award will not be enforced.

Seyks v. Millers National Ins. Co. (Wis. S. C.), 41 N. W. Rep. 443.

Queen Ins. Co. v. Leslie (Ohio S. C.), 24 N. E. Rep. 1072; 19

Ins. L. J. 673.
Queen Ins. Co. v. Jefferson Ice. Co. (Tex. S. C.), 15 Ins. L. J. 109.
Home F. Ins. Co. v. Bean (Neb. S. C.), 24 Ins. L. J. 516.
German Ins. Co. v. Eddy (Neb. S. C.), 54 N. W. Rep. 856; 22
    Ins. L. J. 468.
Baker v. Phoenix Assur. Co., 57 Mo. App. 559.
Doxey v. Royal Ins. Co. (Tenn. Ch. App.), 36 S. W. Rep. 950.
Pennsylvania F. Ins. Co. v. Drackett et al. (Ohio S. C.), 57
    N. E. Rep. 962.
Aetna Ins. Co. v. Stephens (Ky. C. A.), 57 S. W. Rep. 583.
Merchants Ins. Co. v. Stephens (Ky. C. A.), 59 S. W. Rep. 511.
Ohage v. Union Ins. Co. (Minn. S. C.), 85 N. W. Rep. 212.

The delay of the insured in offering to arbitrate, which offer is a condition precedent to an action on a policy, does not bar his right of action after an offer has been made and refused, unless such delay has prejudiced the insurer.

Johnson v. Phoenix Ins. Co., 69 Mo. App. 226.
Schrepfer v. Rochford Ins. Co., 77 Minn. 291, 79 N. W. 1005.

Maine and Massachusetts Standard Policies.

The determination by arbitration of the amount of the loss having been specially made by the parties a condition precedent to suit (on the policy) it was incumbent upon the plaintiff to prove performance or a valid excuse for non-performance.

Fisher v. Merchants Ins. Co., 95 Me. 486; 50 Atl. 282.
Dunton v. Westchester F. Ins. Co. (Me.), 71 Atl. 1037.
Lamson v. Prudential Ins. Co., 171 Mass. 433, 50 N. E. 943, 28
    Ins. L. J. 70.
Weissmann v. Firemen's Ins. Co., 208 Mass. 577, 95 N. E. 411.
Paris v. Hamburg B. F. Ins. Co., 204 Mass. 90, 90 N. E. 420.

Arbitration—Appraisal—Award, Annotated Case.

1. Validity of appraisal provision of the policy.
   a In general.
   b Agreement to submit amount of loss or damage, valid.
   c Agreement to submit all matters in dispute invalid.
2. Occasion of appraisal or arbitration.
   a Preliminary requisites, presupposes a failure to agree.
   b Condition precedent to right of action.
   c Collateral and independent condition. The provision for appraisal must fix a definite method. As affected where, loss is total, or by valued policy law or statutory provision.
   d Demand of party.
   e Miscellaneous cases.
3. Requiring compliance with condition.

a Duty mutual.
b Duty of insurer.
c Duty of insured.
d When arbitration fails through no fault of· either party.

4. Effect of failure of arbitration through fault of insured is a bar to suit, as does his.
a Refusal to arbitrate.
b Or bad faith.

5. Waiver of appraisal provision.
a General cases.
b Accepting and returning proofs of loss without objection. Adjusting loss.
c Denying liability.
d Demanding or having an appraisal different from that provided by the policy.
e Acts of the parties.
1. Refusal to arbitrate.
2. Time in which appraisal may be had or demanded.
3. Other acts.
f Acts of insurance company's appraiser.

Graham v. German Am. Ins. Co., 75 Ohio St. 374, 79 N. E. 930, 36 Ins. L. J. 193, (Annotated in 15 L. R. A. (U. S.) 1055 on all points named above.)

It Is No More the Duty of the Assured Than of the Company to Demand Appraisal.

It is no more the duty of the insured than of the company to demand an appraisal in case of differences under a policy like the N. Y. Standard form. Each party is entitled to demand it, but neither can compel it, and neither has the right to insist that the other shall first demand it. If the insured refuses the company's demand for an appraisal, his right of action is suspended until he consents. If the company refuses the insured's demand for an appraisal, he may institute suit.

Western Assur. Co. v. Decker, 98 Fed. 381, 39 C. C. A. 383-9 (citing and approving Kahnweiler v. Phoenix Ins. Co., 14 C. C. A. 485, 67 Fed. 483.) Dissenting op. by Sanborn Circuit J. with valuable citations.

Common Law Agreement or Appraisal Different from that Provided by the Policy.

The agreement for submission need not be in the terms

of the policy; the parties can waive those provisions, even if they were intended to prescribe a form.

Hall v. Norwalk F. Ins. Co. (Conn. S. C.), 17 Atl. Rep. 356.
London and Lancashire F. Ins. Co. v. Storrs (U. S. C. C. A. 8th Dist.), 25 Ins. L. J. 283.
British Amer. Assur. Co. v. Darragh (U. S. C. C. A. 5th Dist.), 33 Ins. L. J. 577.
Mutual F. Ins. Co. v. Alvord (U. S. C. C. A., 1st Dist.), 23 Ins. L. J. 801.
Adams v. N. Y. Bowery F. Ins. Co. (Iowa S. C.), 51 N. W. Rep. 1149.

Where the company's adjuster appeared at the loss, examined the premises, and agreed with the insured to leave the question of amount of loss to a third person, a carpenter, the company taking no further action, this was a waiver of proofs of loss, and rendered inapplicable the arbitration clause of the policy.   `

Wholley v. Western Assur. Co., 174 Mass. 263; 54 N. E. 548; 28 Ins. L. J. 1029.

If the appraisal agreement does not follow and is not in accordance with the provisions of the policy for arbitration, it cannot be offered in evidence under the plea of failure to comply with the policy condition as to appraisal of the loss. (In this case the policy provided if differences should arise between the company and the insured as to the amount of the loss, the same should be submitted to appraisal. The appraisal agreement recited that the appraisers should ascertain the amount of the loss, and were required "to make an estimate of the actual cash cost of replacing or repairing same.")

Western Assur. Co. v. Hall, 143 Ala. 168; 38 Southern 853.

Where the policy requires appraisers to first select an umpire before proceeding with appraisal, this is generally not material and merely directory. The parties proceeding before an umpire improperly appointed by the appraisers waive all objection to his appointment. The umpire can act only after disagreement of the appraisers. Until then an umpire is not necessary. He can act as well, and with the same effect, if appointed when such a contingency occurs. The time, therefore, fixed in the contract, is not essential or material. The case of Adams v. N. Y. Bowery Ins. Co., 85 Iowa 6, 51 N. W. 1149, 21 Ins. L. J. 833, is the only case to be found in which it is held that the omission to appoint an umpire before appraisers entered upon their duties invalidated the award. The opinion is very brief (and covers other questions also invalidating the award) and as to this point cites no authority and gives no reason. We cannot follow such an authority in setting aside an award for such a merely technical omission.

The fact that the appraisers agreed in every particular is sufficient evidence that they alone were not partial or corrupt, and that their award is just and fair.

Chandos v. American F. Ins. Co., 84 Wis. 184; 22 Ins. L. J. 425; 54 N. W. 390.

To same effect except last paragraph is Doying v. Broadway Ins. Co., 25 N. J. L. 569; 23 Ins. L. J. 394, 27 Atl. 927, and Caledonian Ins. Co. v. Traub, 83 Md. 524: 25 Ins. L. J. 791; 37 Atl. 782.

An agreement between the assured and the adjuster on the amount of the loss, whether arrived at between the parties, or by leaving it to any other person or persons, in fact no matter how the amount of the loss was agreed to it is binding on both the company and the assured. It cannot be set aside except for fraud, mistake or inadequacy. (The Author.)

Assured Must Demand an Appraisal.

In case of disagreement, the insured must demand an appraisal, under a policy such as the New York standard form.

Connecticut F. Ins. Co. v. Hamilton (U. S. C. C. A. 6th Dist.), 23 Ins. L. J. 241.
Johnson v. Phoenix Ins. Co., 69 Mo. App. 226; see also 69 Mo. App. 232;
Murphy v. North B. & M. Ins. Co., 61 Mo. App. 323;
Dautel v. Pennsylvania F. Ins. Co., 65 Mo. App. 44;
McNees v. Southern Ins. Co., 69 Mo. App. 232;
Swearinger v. Pacific F. Ins. Co., 66 Mo. App. 90;
Hooker v. Phoenix Ins. Co., 69 Mo. App. 141;
Chippewa Lumber Co. v. Phoenix Ins. Co., 80 Mich. 116; 44 N. W. Rep. 1055; 19 Ins. L. J. 535;
Kahnweiler v. Phenix Ins. Co., 23 Ins. L. J. 391; 57 Fed. 562. (But in this case, Kahnweiler v. Phenix) the policy provided for appraisal on disagreement so that on appeal Kanhweiler v. Phenix Ins. Co., it was held the assured was no more obligated to demand appraisal than was the company; 67 Fed. 483; 14 C. C. A. 485.);
Western Assur. Co. v. Hall, 112 Ala. 318; 25 Ins. L. J. 874; 20 Southern 447, Earley v. Providence Wash. Ins. Co. (R. I.). 76 Atl. Rep. 753;
American Cent'l Ins. Co. v. Bass, 90 Tex. 380; 26 Ins. L. J. 718; 38 S. W. 1119;
Dee v. Key City F. Ins. Co., 104 Iowa 167; 73 N. W. 594;
Allen v. Patroup M. F. Ins. Co. (Mich.), 130 N. W. 196;
Pioneer &c. v. Phoenix Assur. Co., 106 N. C. 28; 10 S. E. 1057; 19 Ins. L. J. 408.
Veney v. Reginald, Eng., Q. B. Law R., Feby. 1888, part 2, p. 177; 1 Ins. Dig. 33;
Wolff v. L. & G. Ins. Co., 50 N. J. Law 453; 14 Atl. R. 561; 17 Ins. L. J. 714;
Gasser v. Sun Fire Off., 42 Minn. 315; 44 N. W. R. 252; 19 Ins. L. J. 243;
Blackwell v. American C. Ins. Co., 2 Mo. App. 516;

Phenix Ins. Co. et al. v. Carnahan, 63 Ohio St. 258; 58 N. E. 805;
Westenhaver v. German Am. Ins. Co., 113 Iowa 726; 84 N. W.
    717; 30 Ins. L. J. 314;
Palatine Ins. Co. v. Morton, 106 Tenn. 558; 61 S. W. 787; 30
    Ins. L. J. 481;
Mosness v. German Ins. Co., 50 Minn. 341; 52 N. W. 932; 21
    Ins. L. J. 915;
Dunton v. Westchester F. Ins. Co. (Me.), 71 Atl. Rep. 1037;
Connecticut F. Ins. Co. v. Hamilton, 59 Fed. 258; 23 Ins. L. J. 241;
Nolan v. Ocean Acc. & G. Corp., 23 Canadian Law Times 187;
Kersey v. Phoenix Ins. Co., 135 Mich. 10; 97 N. W. 57;
Exchange Bk. v. Thuringia F. Ins. Co., 109 Mo. App. 654; 83
    S. W. 534;
Law v. Commercial M. F. Co. (N. D.), 107 N. W. 59;
Graham v. German Am. Ins. Co., Royal Ins. Co. v. Silberman
    (Ohio), 79 N. E. 930; 36 Ins. L. J. 193;
Paris v. Hamburg Bremen F. Ins. Co. (Mass.), 90 N. E. 420;
Novak v. Rochester G. Ins. Co. (Ill. App.), 40 Nat. Corp. R.
    698, June, 1910;
Weismann v. Firemen's Ins. Co. (Mass. S. J. C.), 95 N. E. 411;
North B. & M. Ins. Co. v. Robinett (Va. S. C. A.), 72 S. E. 668;

Condition Precedent to Suit.

Appraisal when demanded is a condition precedent to recovery, where the policy so provides as does the New York
standard form.

Scottish U. & N. Ins. Co. v. Clancy (Tex. S. C.), 8 S. W. Rep. 630;
Wolff v. L. & L. & G. Ins. Co. (N. J. S. C.), 14 Atl. Rep. 561; 17
    Ins. L. J. 714;
Gasser v. Sun Fire Office (Minn. S. C.), 19 Ins. L. J. 247; 44 N. W.
    Rep. 252;
Chippewa Lumber Co. v. Phenix Ins. Co. (Mich. S. C.), 44 N. W.
    Rep. 1055; 80 Mich. 116;
Hamilton v. L. & L. & G. Ins. Co. (U. S. S. C.), 136 U. S. 242;
Mosnes v. German Am. Ins. Co. (Minn. S. C. July 1892), 21 Ins.
    L. J. 915;
Western Assur. Co. v. Hall (Ala. S. C.), 25 Ins. L. J. 874;
Chainless Cycle Co. v. Security Ins. Co., 169 N. Y. 304; 31 Ins.
    L. J. 324;
Phenix and other Ins. Cos. v. Carnahan et al. (Ohio S. C.),
    58 N. E. Rep. 805;
Davis v. Atlas Assur. Co. (Wash. S. C.), 47 Pac. Rep. 436;
Sun Mut. Ins. Co. v. Crist (Ky. C. A.), 39 S. W. Rep. 837; 26
    Ins. L. J. 695.

Not a Condition Precedent.

The New York standard form of policy makes an appraisal
a condition precedent to recovery only when one has been required by the insurer, it is not the duty of the insured to
initiate one.

Chainless Cycle Co. v. Security Ins. Co., 169 N. Y. 304; 31 Ins.
    L. J. 324; 62 N. E. 392;
Kahnweiler v. Phenix Ins. Co., 14 C. C. A. 485, 67 Fed. Rep. 483;
Milwaukee Mechs. Ins. Co. v. Stewart (Ind. A. C.), 42 N. E.
    Rep. 290;
Grand Rapid F. Ins. Co. v. Finn, 60 Ohio 513, 54 N. W. Rep.
    545. (Ohio now holds to the contrary.);
Davis v. Atlas Assur. Co. v. (Wash. S. C.), 47 Pac. Rep. 436;
Sun Mutual Ins. Co. v. Crist (Ky. C. A.), 39 S. W. Rep. 837;
    26 Ins. L. J. 695;
Lesure Lumber Co. v. Mut. F. Ins. Co., 101 Iowa 514; 70 N. W.
    Rep. 761;
Norris v. Equitable F. Assn. (S. C. S. D.), 102 N. W. Rep. 306;
Nerger v. Equitable F. Assn., 20 S. D. 419; 35 Ins. L. J. 556;

American Ins. Co. v. Rodenhause (Okla.), 128 Pac. 502;
Winchester v. North B. & M. Ins. Co., 160 Cal. 1; 116 Pac. 63;
Amusement &c. v. Prussian N. Ins. Co., 85 Kan. 367, 116 Pac. 620.

Where there is no disagreement as to amount of loss and the company offered to pay on same basis that other companies had settled, the policy requirement for an appraisal was thereby waived; the offer to pay being virtually an admission of the amount of insured loss.

Shook v. Retail Hardware M. F. Ins. Co. (Mo. App.), 134 S. W. 589.

To take advantage of the appraisal clause provision in a fire insurance policy such as the New York standard form, the defendant must allege in its plea that there was a disagreement between it and the plaintiff as to the amount of such loss, prior to institution of suit.

Torpedo Top Co. v. Royal Ins. Co., 162 Ill. App. 338; 42 Nat'nl Corp. Rep. 593.

Provision for Appraisal not Upheld by Pennsylvania and Nebraska Courts.

An appraisal is not a condition precedent to suit, it being revocable by either party, and the bringing of the action a revocation.

Needy v. German-Am. Ins. Co. (Pa. S. C.), 47 Atl. Rep. 739;
Yost v. McKee et al. (Pa. S. C.), 36 Atl. Rep. 317.

The Nebraska Supreme Court holds the effect of the appraisal clause is to oust the courts of their legitimate jurisdiction.

German Am. Ins. Co. v. Etherton, 41 N. W. Rep. 406.

After failure of appraisal materially different in terms from that provided in the policy, an insurance company waives right to demand new appraisal pursuant to the terms of the policy.

Davis v. Atlas Assur. Co. (Wash. S. C.), 47 Pac. Rep. 436.

A joint demand by several companies for an appraisal is not authorized by the policy; the demand must be separate.

Connecticut F. Ins. Co. v. Hamilton (U. S. C. C. A. 6th Dist.), 23 Ins. L. J. 241;
Hamilton v. Phoenix Ins. Co. (U. S. C. C. A., 6th Dist.), 23 Ins. L. J. 561.

A joint demand is not good where the policies differ.

Palatine Ins. Co. v. Morton-Scott-Robertson Co. (Tenn. S. C.), 61 S. W. Rep. 787.

Where defendant insisted on assured signing a written agreement containing provisions not in the policy, it waived its rights to appraisal.

> Walker v. German Ins. Co. (July, 1893), (Kan. S. C.), 22 Ins. L. J. 750;
> Summerfield v. North British & M. Ins. Co. (U. S. C. C. Western Dist. Va.), 24 Ins. L. J. 442.

Where the insured, after filing proofs, but before their receipt by the company, upon failure of parties to agree, advertised and sold the property against the company's protest, the latter was deprived of its rights to appraisement and was released from liability under the policy.

> Astrich v. German-Am. Ins. Co. (U. S. C. C. A. 3d Dist.), 33 Ins. L. J. 925.

The assured, after agreeing to appraisal, revoked the submission and refused to be bound. He then had the goods appraised and sold them. *Held*, A forfeiture of the policy

> Morley v. L. & L. & G. Ins. Co. (Mich S. C.), 48 N. W. Rep. 502; 20 Ins. L. J. 577;
> Providence-Washington Ins. Co. v. Wolf (Ind. A. C.), 72 N. E. Rep. 606.

The demand for appraisal iterated and reiterated is met by a denial that there was any "disagreement" or difference as to the amount of the loss, which was a distinct evasion of the demand; and it is the merest trifling with words to say that this quibbling and evasion, which was continued until an appraisal was rendered fruitless by the sale of the remnants by insured, does not amount to a refusal on the part of the insured to perform the condition as to arbitration or appraisement of the loss.

> Phoenix v. Carnahan (Ohio S. C.), 58 N. E. Rep. 805.

Citing:

> Hamilton v. Ins. Co., 136 U. S. 242; 10 Supp. Ct. 945; 34 L. Ed. 419;
> Zalesky v. Ins. Co., 102 Iowa 613; 71 N. W. Rep. 566.

All verbal demands for an appraisal and for an examination under oath touching the cause and origin of the fire are merged in a subsequent written demand therefor.

> Citizens' Ins. Co. et al. v. Herposheimer (Neb.), 109 N. W. 160.

The insured's statement that he was "ready to proceed under the provisions of the policy" is not a request for the appointment of referees (arbitration).

Vera et al. v. Mercantile F. & M. Ins. Co. and other Cos., 193 N. E. 292; 216 Mass. 154.

A local agent who issues policies is a proper person on whom to serve notice of a demand upon the company for arbitration provided for in the policy.

Phenix v. Stocks et al. (Ill. S. C.), 36 N. E. Rep. 408.

After some unsatisfactory negotiations, the insured suggested an appraisal, and afterwards wrote the insurer that unless an appraisal was agreed to within five days, he would proceed to dispose of the goods, to which no answer was made. This was held to be a waiver of the insurer's right to appraisal.

Chainless Cycle Co. v. Security Ins. Co., 169 N. Y. 304; 31 Ins. L. J. 324.

After once refusing to appraise, the insurer can not afterwards compel an appraisal.

Continental Ins. Co. v. Wilson (Kan. S. C.), 25 Pac. Rep. 629; 20 Ins. L. J. 269;
Wainer v. Milford Mut. F. Ins. Co. (Mass. S. J. C.), 23 N. E. Rep. 887;
McDowell v. Aetna Ins. Co. and other Ins. Cos. (Mass. S. J. C.), 41 N. E. Rep. 665;
Chainless Cycle Mfg. Co. v. Security Ins. Co., 169 N. Y. 304; 31 Ins. L. J. 324.

When the adjuster makes an offer in payment of the loss which assured refuses, and then withdraws his proposition, with notice that the company will insist upon every requirement of the policy, intending to terminate all negotiations for a settlement, the arbitration clause of the policy is rendered inoperative and cannot be invoked as a defense

Dautel v. Pennsylvania F. Ins. Co., 65 Mo. App. 44

Failure of the insurer after demanding appraisal at a given time and place, to appear at the time and place, is a waiver of its right to appraisal.

Northern Assur. Co. v. Samuels (Tex. C. C. A.), 33 S. W. Rep. 239.

The insurer knowing that the insured desires a prompt appraisal or adjustment, so that the property may not suffer further injury before it is sold, can not postpone its demand for an appraisal, until after the insured, misled by its act, has been placed in a position where one is impossible.

Chainless Cycle Co. v. Security Ins. Co., 169 N. Y. 304; 31 Ins. L. J. 324.

The insurer can not compel an appraisal of loss by fire

after the property has been damaged by fire a second time, since the damage by both fires constitutes but one claim, to be settled in one proceeding.

Mechanics Ins. Co. v. Hodge (Ill. S. C.), 26 Ins. L. J. 406; 37 N. E. Rep. 51.

The insured's death before award is made does not revoke the submission.

Citizens' Ins. Co. v. Coit (Ind. A. C.), 39 N. E. Rep. 766.

The company can not take advantage of the want of arbitration as provided by the policy, when its refusal defeated such arbitration, and it is immaterial that a former action was pending on the policy at the time the offer to arbitrate was made.

Johnson v. Phoenix Ins. Co., 69 Mo. App. 226.

A submission to appraisal, though made jointly by several companies, is under policies and not a common law agreement, where the policies are all alike and the submission is such as is provided for therein.

Wicking et al. v. Citizens' Mut. F. Ins. Co. (Mich. S. C.), 77 N. W. Rep. 275; 28 Ins. L. J. 230.

Appraisal is waiver of insurance company's right to rebuild.

Wynkoop v. Niagara F. Ins. Co. (N. Y. C. A.), 12 Ins. L. J. 253;
McAllaster v. Niagara F. Ins. Co. (N. Y. C. A.), 28 Ins. L. J. 769;
Iowa Cent'l B. & L. Assn. v. Merchants and Bankers F. Ins. Co. (Iowa S. C.), 32 Ins. L. J. 852;
Alliance Co-operative Ins. Co. v. Arnold (Kans. S. C.), 31 Ins. L. J. 943;
Elliott v. Merchants and Bankers F. Ins. Co. (Ia. S. C.), 28 Ins. L. J. 677.

But where appraisal agreement expressly stipulates that it is "Without reference to any other question or matter of difference within the terms and conditions of insurance than the amount of the loss," it neither waives the company's right to rebuild instead of paying, as provided for in the policy, nor excludes proof of a previous oral waiver of such right.

Platt v. Aetna Ins. Co. (Ill. S. C.), 24 Ins. L. J. 132; 38 N. E. Rep. 750.

An appraisal had by the insured and other companies is not competent evidence of the amount of the loss.

Penn. Plate Glass Co. v. Spring Garden Ins. Co. (Pa. S. C.), 28 Ins. L. J. 223;
Chenowith v. Phenix Ins. Co., 4 Finch Digest, 22 (Ky. S. C.), 12 Ky. L. Rep. 232.

If the insurers deny liability as to a portion of the loss and, in the agreement for submission to appraisal, exclude such items from the purview of the agreement, and when the award is returned the loss be paid in accordance therewith, and receipts be taken discharging the insurer from all liability by reason of the fire for which claim for loss was made, and another receipt for payment of the return premium in consideration of which the policy is canceled, still the insured may recover for the loss on items omitted from the appraisal, and which the insurer refused to pay, provided the court finds, as a matter of fact, they were covered by the policy.

Fire Ins. Assn. v. Wickham (U. S. S. C.), 21 Ins. L. J. 193.

Plaintiff dismissed his action on a fire policy and brought new suit. On receiving notice of intention to dismiss, defendant served demand for appraisal under terms of policy. *Held*, That demand was too late.

Davis v. Imperial Ins. Co. (Wash. S. C.), 47 Pac. Rep. 439.

Where the insured's action was dismissed for refusing to submit loss to appraisal and thereafter she offered to submit to appraisal, but the company refused to do so, claiming that by her previous conduct the insured had lost all rights under the policy, the insured brought this action to recover her loss. *Held*, That the doctrine between inconsistent rights or remedies is inapplicable. The plaintiff never had any election. Her refusal at first to submit to appraisal merely amounted to a waiver of her right to an appraisal, but did not extinguish her rights to recover on the policy; that the refusal of the company to submit to appraisal upon a subsequent offer of the insured to do so, was waiver of its right to an appraisal, and thereupon the insured could maintain an action on the policy without appraisal.

Schrepfer v. Rockford Ins. Co., 77 Minn. 291; 79 N. W. Rep. 1005.

Where the representative of a company that demands a separate appraisal did not join the other companies in an appraisal, but afterwards co-operated with them, and took advantage of whatever was done and was notified of all that occurred and made no objections, the company can not allege that it was not a party to the appraisal.

North German Ins. Co. v. Morton-Scott-Robertson Co. (Tenn. S. C.), 31 Ins. L. J. 580;
(See also the case of Levy v. Scottish U. & N. Ins. Co. (W. Va. S. C. A.), 52 S. E. Rep. 449).

Statute, Michigan.

The Michigan statutes prescribing the form of a standard policy to be used in that state which provides that an award of appraisers should be prima facie the amount of the loss, does not prevent the insured and insurer, after loss, from entering an arbitration of the loss and making the award of appraisers binding and conclusive as to the value of the property and the loss thereto.

Montgomery v. Amer. Cent'l Ins. Co., 108 Wis. 146; 84 N. W. 175; 30 Ins. L. J. 122.

Iowa.

A statute that the amount of the policy shall be prima facie evidence of the insurable value, at the date of the policy, doesn't prevent the company from showing depreciation, and actual value at time of fire, nor does it relieve the insured from proving the loss, nor relieve him from the operation of a clause making an appraisement a condition precedent to right of action on the policy.

Zalesky v. Home Ins. Co., 108 Iowa 341; 79 N. W. 69.

Must Produce Books for Inspection of Appraisers.

On demand of insurer, the insured directed its bookkeeper to allow appraisers to examine all its books. He, however, withheld a book containing an estimate of the cost of the destroyed articles. *Held,* Insured was bound by his acts and that his action amounted to a representation that there was no such book and that insurer was released from its agreement.

Stockton Comb. Harvester and Agricultural Works v. Glens Falls Ins. Co. (Cal. S. C.), 33 Pac. Rep. 663.

On a retrial of this case it was proven that no books were concealed from appraisers, hence judgment for plaintiff in lower court here affirmed (Cal. S. C.), 53 Pac. Rep. 565.

When appraisal fails through plaintiff's bad faith, he can not maintain an action.

Silver v. Western Assur. Co. (N. Y. C. A.), 58 N. E. Rep. 284.

Appraisal—Value of Saloon Furniture in Dry Town.

The policy limited liability to the "actual cash value, with proper deductions for the depreciation however caused." *Held*, That the value meant the price which the property would bring at a fair market; as to fixed property the value would have to be arrived at at its place of location; that as to movable property it should be ascertained at the nearest fair market for same, subject to a deduction for cost of transportation; hence on loss of saloon fixtures in a town where the sale of liquor had been prohibited, the insurer was not entitled to a valuation of the property at that place, but was obliged to pay on the basis of the value of the property at the nearest fair market for such property less cost of transportation.

Prussian National Ins. Co. v. Lawrence, (U. S. C. C. A., 4th Cir.) · 221 Federal Reporter (June 10, 1915) 931.

Insured's Right to Introduce Evidence Before Appraisers.

The authorities generally are in accord in holding that where there has been a total extinction of the property or any part of it it is not only the right of the insured to introduce evidence as to such property, but that it is the duty of the appraisers to hear evidence as to the quantity and value of such property. Where appraisers are appointed because of their knowledge and familiarity with values such as was damaged, or of the property itself, and enough of it remains from which a fair and accurate estimate may be made of its extent and value, then appraisers may refuse to hear evidence. The question is annotated in Aetna Ins. Co. v. Jester, 47 L. R. A. (N. S.) 1191.

Assured was not given an opportunity to be present with their books, or other evidence, to show the extent of their loss at any time from the beginning of the arbitration proceedings until the completion of the award in writing. This was improper. Assured should have been given this opportunity. It is true that the arbitrators were shown to be experienced men in this line of business; and, if appellants should have been permitted to be present with their evidence, it might not have changed the result. From the evidence we are not prepared to say that insurance companies or any one of the arbitrators, were guilty of fraud or an intentional wrong in arriving at the result of this arbitration; but we are convinced that mistakes, or errors, were committed to the prejudice of assured.

Harth v. Continental Ins. Co. (Ky. C. A.), 36 Ins. L. J. 603, 102 S. W. 242.

The insured has a right to be heard when he has requested

such right if the appraisers disagree, and an award of the com
pany appraiser and the umpire who have denied him that right
will be set aside.

> Chenoweth v. Phenix Ins. Co., 12 Ky. L. R. 232;
> American F. Ins. Co. v. Bell (Tex. C. C. A.), 75 S. W. 319;
> Harth v. Continental Ins. Co. et al. (Ky. C. A.), 102 S. W. 242,
> 36 Ins. L. J. 603.

The insured has the right to introduce evidence before the
appraisers as to the extent of his loss, and where he is refused
such right, the award is not binding on him. Aetna Ins. Co.
v. Jester (Okla.), 132 Pac. 130.

The rejection and exclusion of pertinent and material testimony on a hearing before appraisers is usually fatal to the
award.

> Schoenick v. American Ins. Co. (Minn.), 124 N. W. 5;
> Mosness v. German Ins. Co., 50 Minn. 341; 21 Ins. L. J. 915;
> 52 N. W. 932;
> Redner v. New York Fire Ins. Co., 92 Minn. 306; 99 N. W.
> 886; 33 Ins. L. J. 780;
> Continental Ins. Co. v. Garrett, 125 Fed. 589; 60 C. C. A. 395;
> Stout v. Phoenix Assur. Co., 69 N. J. Eq. 566; 56 Atl. 691;
> Springfield F. & M. Ins. Co. v. Payne (Kan. S. C.), 26 Ins.
> L. J. 46;
> Christianson v. Norwich U. F. Ins. Soc., 84 Minn. 526, 31 Ins.
> L. J. 218;
> Redner v. N. Y. Fire Ins. Co. (Minn. S. C.), 33 Ins. L. J. 780;
> Phoenix Ins. Co. v. Romeis (Lucas Co. Ohio C. C.), 15 C. C.
> Rep. 697.

In case of destroyed property, which an appraiser had never
seen, fairness would require that he be informed by evidence
of some sort (not necessarily under oath) as to the character
and value of the property and, unless an opportunity is afforded
to impart such information, the award will not be binding.

> Springfield F. & M. Ins. Co. v. Payne, 57 Kans. 291; 26 Ins.
> L. J. 46; 46 Pac. 315.

Where appraisers are appointed to adjust a loss to a property only partially destroyed and sufficient of it remains to
disclose the size, general character and architecture, and quality
of material used, a hearing and an opportunity to introduce
evidence of value need not be granted; but where they are un-
acquainted with the insured property, and are selected to
estimate a loss arising from total destruction of the property,
notice of the time and place of the appraisers' meeting and an
opportunity to the parties to be heard is essential to a valid
award.

> Carlston v. St. Paul F. & M. Ins. Co., 37 Mont. 118; 94 Pac. 756;
> 37 Ins. L. J. 366.

It seems that the appraisers are not obliged to give the
claimant any formal notice or to hear evidence, at least in all

cases, and yet, unless the insured waive it, he must either have notice or knowledge of the meeting of the appraisers and an opportunity to draw their attention to the items of his loss and make representations and explanations to them concerning the nature thereof.

> Kaiser v. Hamburg-Bremen F. Ins. Co., 59 (N. Y. S. C.), App. Div. 525; 69 N. Y. Supp. 344. Affirmed 172 N. Y. 663, 65 N. E. 1118.

Citing:

> Linde v. Republic F. Ins. Co., 50 N. Y. Super. Ct. 362; Remington Paper Co. v. London Assur. Corp. 12 (N. Y. S. C.), App. Div. 218.

An award of arbitrators will not be set aside on the ground that the arbitrators refused to hear pertinent testimony, when the party objecting to the award only announced his willingness to introduce testimony without actually offering any.

> Stemmer v. Scottish U. & N Ins. Co., 33 Ore. 65; 58 Pacif. R. 498; 27 Ins. L. J. 972.

The award will be set aside if appraisers refuse to consider the books in arriving at the goods assured had on hand at time of fire.

> Levine v. Lancashire Ins. Co. (Minn. S. C.), 26 Ins. L. J. 36.

Books of account are not the only evidence of the amount of the loss, and if the appraisers are satisfied that they do not show the correct amount of merchandise on hand, they may resort to other evidence, and their mere refusal to examine them in such case will not justify the setting aside of an award.

> Tyblewski v. Svea F. & L. Ins. Co., 220 Ill. 436; 35 Ins. L. J. 616; 77 N. E. 196.

Where persons are selected arbitrators by reason of special knowledge or skill possessed by them with reference to the matter in controversy, so that it is apparent that the parties intended to rely upon their personal information, investigation and judgment, they may even be justified in refusing altogether to hear evidence.

> Hall v. Norwalk F. Ins. Co., 57 Conn. 105; 18 Ins. L. J. 518; 17 Atl. 356, and cases there cited; Townsend v. Greenwich Ins. Co., 83 N. Y. Supp. 909.

There being no requirement for notice nor necessity for witnesses, an appraisement is not vitiated by the mere fact that the appraisers met without notice to the company, while officers of the insured corporation were present and pointed out the damaged property, where there is no suggestion of undue influence or bad faith, and the appraisers, made their award on their own knowledge of the subject.

American Steel Co. v. German-Am. F. Ins. Co. (U. S. C. C. A.);
187 Fed. 730;
Orient Ins. Co. v. Harmon (Tex. C. C. A.), 117 S. W. 192.

It is not necessary for either party to the submission to have notice of the meeting of the appraisers or an opportunity to present evidence. The submission did not provide for such notice or for the parties to have the opportunity to produce evidence upon the question at issue. On the contrary, the terms of submission were such as to indicate the appraisers were to proceed informally to fix the amount of plaintiff's loss, and if unable to agree, to call in the umpire to settle their differences. See Blakely v. Proctor, 134 Ga. 139, 67 S. E. 389.) Of course, the award could have been set aside for fraud, or by showing that unfair advantage had been given to one of the parties, or for palpable mistake of law, Eberhardt v. Federal Ins. Co. (ct. of App. Ga. Feby. 4, 1914), 80 S. E. 856.

An award will not be set aside for irregularity or bad faith, where one of the arbitrators privately made certain experiments as to the effect of intense heat on certain goods, the result of which he communicated to the other arbitrators at a meeting at which the respective parties and their counsel were present, without objection from them. The arbitrators also, with knowledge and consent of both parties visited the scene of the fire and made certain examinations. Two of the arbitrators talked with third persons about the fire, but both testified this had no effect on them in making up the award. Two of the arbitrators, in the absence of the third, discussed the amount of the award, but came to no conclusion until the final meeting when all three were together. Two of them privately examined the books of one of them who dealt in similar goods to those of insured, to learn the prices thereof and communicated the facts and information therefrom to the third arbitrator.

Farrell v. German-Am. Ins. Co., 175 Mass. 340; 56 N. E. 572.

The provision in the policy that "the appraisers together shall then (after choosing the umpire) estimate and appraise the loss," does not require them to view the damaged property together nor forbid them viewing it separately.

Kent v. Aetna Ins. Co. (Mo. App.), 146 S. W. 78.

Inquiries, made by one of the appraisers for his own information, in the absence of the parties or other appraisers, will not invalidate the award, unless the party is prejudiced or the award affected thereby.

Hall v. Norwalk F. Ins. Co. (Conn. S. C.), 17 Atl. Rep. 356; Farrell v. German-Am. Ins. Co. (Mass. S. C.), 29 Ins. L. J. 341.

Referees under Minnesota Standard Fire Policy have no authority to make independent investigation and base their award on the result thereof, but are required to give interested parties reasonable opportunity to present evidence bearing on case.

Schoenich v. American Ins. Co. (Minn.), 124 N. W. 5.

Where the award was rendered upon the report, information and conclusion of the loss of one of the appraisers who was the only one of the appraisers who had seen the loss, it will be declared void.

Citizens Ins Co. v. Hamilton, 48 Ill. App. 593.

Where the insured furnishes an inventory which he certifies is correct, he cannot have set aside for mistake in inventory an award based thereon.

Kentucky C. Co. v. Rochester Germ. Ins. Co., 20 Ky. L. R. 1571· 49 S. W. 780.

The company's appraiser and the umpire agreed on the amount of loss on goods totally destroyed, and accepted an expert's opinion of damage to goods saved. *Held*, no evidence could be received which showed plaintiff's loss was greater than the award.

Rogers v. Commercial U. A. Co., 15 Can. L. Times 228.

Referees under Massachusetts standard policy are not compelled to receive evidence upon the amount of the loss, but may proceed to determine that fact in any way in which they may think best.

Hanley v. Aetna Ins. Co. (Mass.), 102 N. E. 641.

Where the appraisers and umpire have before them a list of the property destroyed and the insured's statement in detail in respect to his loss, they may refuse to hear evidence.

Royal Ins. Co. v. Ries, 80 Ohio St. 272; 88 N. E. R. 638.

ARBITRATION OF ALL DIFFERENCES.

Before the New York standard form policy came into vogue, a great number of the fire policies required all differences

to be submitted to arbitration and the courts in nearly every
such case decided such clause would not be enforced, as the
effect would be to oust the courts of jurisdiction.

> National Masonic A. Ass'n v. Burr (Neb. S. C.), 62 N. W. Rep.
>   466; 24 Ins. L. J. 423;
> Prader v. Nat'l Masonic A. Ass'n (Iowa S. C.), 63 N. W. Rep. 601;
> Keefe v. Nat'l Acc. Ass'n (N. Y. S. C., App. Div.), 38 N. Y.
>   Supp. 854; 4 App. Div. 392;
> Fox v. Mason's Frat. Acc. Ass'n (Wis. S. C.), 71 N. W. Rep. 363.

Appraisal, as Used in the Policies, Means Arbitration of Only the Amount of the Loss.

But the New York standard form policy is now in general
use, except in a few of those states having a standard form of
their own, and all of the policies now provide that only the
sound value, loss and damage are to be submitted to appraisers.
The policy now in use contemplates an arbitration limited to
the amount of the loss, rather than an appraisal, and the arbitrators are termed appraisers, I presume, on account of the
courts deciding that an arbitration ousted them of jurisdiction.
But the policy is perfectly plain in defining the duties of the
appraisers and in saying that they shall be the sole arbiters
only in so far as the loss and damage is concerned, leaving all
other questions, including the liability, to be determined by the
parties, or, if they fail, then by the courts, and this is in accord
with nearly all, if not all, of the decisions.

Subject of Appraisal—Totally Destroyed Goods—Damaged Goods.

Where the amount of the loss is made payable 60 days from
date of adjusted claim and the method of adjustment provided
for in the policy in respect to the "damage to the property" is
in case the parties are unable to agree, by appraisement as
therein provided made a condition precedent to recovery, this
contemplates an appraisement of the total as well as the partial
loss.

> Gasser v. Sun Fire Office, 42 Minn. 315; 19 Ins. L. J. 243; 44
>   N. W. 252;
> Earley v. Providence Wash. Ins. Co. (R. I.), 76 Atl. Rep. 753;
> Williamson v. L. & L. & G. Ins. Co., 122 Fed. 69; 58 C. C. A. 241;
> Rutter v. Hanover F. Ins. Co., 138 Ala. 202; 35 Southern 33;
> Stout v. Phoenix Assur. Co., 65 N. J. Eq. 566; 56 Atl. 691.

Where the policy provided that in case of disagreement the
loss or damages should be submitted to appraisers to be chosen
as provided by the policy, a submission entered into by the
parties which only provided for an appraisal of the damage to
goods saved, was void as not in accord with the conditions of
the policy.

Adams v. N. Y. Bowery F. Ins. Co., 85 Iowa 6; 21 Ins. L. J. 833;
51 N. W. 1149.

When the appraisal agreement provides that "it is expressly understood that this agreement and appraisement is for the purpose of ascertaining and fixing the amount of said loss and damage only , * * * and shall not determine, waive or invalidate any other right or rights of either of the parties," the only question which can be considered as submitted to the appraisers is that of determining the value of the property totally destroyed and the injury to that not destroyed.

Germania F. Ins. Co. v. Warner, 13 Ind. App. 466; 41 N. E. 969.

A policy that provides that the amount of the loss shall be ascertained by appraisers, in case of disagreement, contemplates the articles totally obliterated as well as those which have suffered a damage only.

Palatine Ins. Co. v. Morton, 106 Tenn. 558; 61 S. W. 787; 30
Ins. L. J. 481.

A demand for appraisal of the salvage goods alone is not authorized under a policy providing that the amount of the loss shall be ascertained by appraisers in case of disagreement, and the insured is justified in declining it.

Palatine Ins. Co. v. Morton, 106 Tenn. 558; 61 S. W. 787; 30
Ins. L. J. 481.

The insured is not concluded by an award of appraisers, which, through the fault of the adjusters, is limited to the damage to such goods only as are visible at the time of the appraisal.

Hong Sling v. Scottish U. & N. Ins. Co., 7 Utah 441; 27 Pac. 170.

Where a policy insures contents of a two-story building known as the Hotel, the failure of appraisers to appraise the contents in a one-story addition will render their award invalid.

Phoenix Ins. Co. v. Moore (Texas C. C. A.), 46 S. W. Rep. 1131.

If the appraisers disregard the instructions in the agreement for submission to appraisal, the award is not binding.

Rutter v. Hanover F. Ins. Co. (Ala. S. C.), 35 Southern Rep. 33.

A provision in the policy requiring "the amount of sound value and of damage to the property" to be determined by appraisal applies only to a case of partial damage and not where the property has been totally destroyed by fire.

Rosenwald v. Phoenix Ins. Co., 50 Hun. 172; 19 St. Rep. 732; 3
N. Y. Supp. 215;

Lang v. Eagle F. Ins. Co., 12 (N. Y. S. C.), App. Div. 39; 42
    N. Y. Supp. 539.

The standard form (**N. Y.**) provides that loss on totally
destroyed goods, as well as the damage to the goods not destroyed, are to be appraised.

Stout v. Phoenix Ins. Co., 65 N. J. Eq. 566; 56 Atl. Rep. 691;
    Phenix Ins. Co. v. Carnahan (Ohio S. C.), 58 N. E. Rep. 805;
    Chippewa Lumber Co. v. Phenix Ins. Co. (Mich. S. C.), 44 N. W.
    Rep. 1055; 80 Mich. 116; 19 Ins. L. J. 535.

An appraisement omitting property claimed by the insured
to have been destroyed is void.

American F. Ins. Co. v. Bell (Tex. C. C. A.), 75 S. W. Rep. 319;
    Rutter v. Hanover F. Ins. Co. (Ala. S. C.), 35 Southern Rep. 33.

After signing the award the authority of the arbitrators
ceases, and it is not in their power to reopen it or to deal
further with the matter; the fact that one of them was misled
by the others in connection with the signing of the award, if
true, would form good ground for an application to the court
to set it aside, but did not justify him in calling in the third
arbitrator and making another award different from that to
which he was already a party.

Hall v. Queen Ins. Co., 39 Nova Scotia 295; 1 E. L. R. 295; 21
    Ins. Dig. 88.

For goods which are totally destroyed by fire no appraisement can be required, for the reason that to appraise the loss on
such goods would require appraisers to call witnesses and become arbitrators.

Pennsylvania F. Ins. Co. v. Carnahan, 19 Ohio Cir. Ct. 97,
114; 10 Ohio C. D. 186, 225; but see when these cases came before Ohio Supreme Court. Phenix Ins. Co. et al. v. Carnahan,
63 Ohio St. 258; 58 N. E. 805, it was held assured must not only
submit to appraisal; but that he must show that he has performed the condition or has a legal excuse for non-performance
thereof.

The award cannot be impeached in an action **at law** on **the**
ground that appraisers refused to consider, or to include in **the**
award, the loss on so much of the property as was totally destroyed, when such loss was clearly within the submission **and**
was covered by the terms of the award.

Georgia Home Ins. Co. v. Kline et al. (Ala. S. C.), 21 Southern
    Rep. 958.

Total Loss—Statute.

Two rules have been adopted defining total loss. The earlier one, that the loss is total whenever the building has been so injured as to lose its identity and specific character as such; and the other, that it is not totally destroyed so long as a substantial remnant remains which a prudent, uninsured person would use in rebuilding. The whole question, however, is one of fact for a jury to determine. Most of the recent cases follow the latter rule. Where the statutes provide for the amount of the insurer's liability in case of total loss, there can be no consideration for appraisal.

See case Springfield F. & M. Ins. Co. v. Homewood (annotated) for important and valuable cases bearing on the question of Constructive Total Loss, 39 L. R. A. (N. S.) 1182 (Oklahoma).

Fair—Unfair Appraisers—Conduct of Appraisers—Selection of Umpire.

The action of insurer's apraiser in nominating for umpire, names of persons unknown to assured's appraiser, and who had frequently acted as appraisers and umpires for insurance companies in other loses, was tantamount to a refusal to agree upon a disinterested umpire. This being true, the fact that an appraisal was not had is no defense to the action.

Bishop v. Agricultural Ins. Co., 130 N. Y. 488; 21 Ins. L. J. 345.

Citing:

Uhrig v. Ins. Co., 101 N. Y. 362;
Bradshaw v. Agricultural Ins. Co. (137 N. Y. 137), 22 Ins. L. J. 161.
McCullough v. Phoenix Ins. Co. (Mo. S. C.), 22 Ins. L. J. 781; 113 Mo. 606;
Brock v. Dwelling House Ins. Co., 102 Mich. 583; 24 Ins. L. J.; 464; 61 N. W. Rep. 67;
Niagara F. Ins. Co. v. Bishop (Ill. S. C.), 154 Ill. 9; 25 Ins. L. J. 24;
Hickerson v. Ins. Cos., 25 Ins. L. J. 422 (Tenn. S. C.);
Harrison v. Hartford F. Ins. Co. (Iowa S. C.), 30 Ins. L. J. 255;
Read v. Ins. Co., 103 Ia. 314;
Chapman v. Rockford Ins. Co. (Wis. S. C.), 62 N. W. Rep. 422.

Where the appraiser for the insured insisted on taking as umpire any one of a number of business men residing in the city where the loss occurred, but the appraiser for the insurance company named a number of persons not residents of said city. They were for that reason rejected by insured's appraiser, who, after trying for eleven days to agree on an umpire, resigned. *Held*, The insured was not warranted in withdrawing from the appraisal, and that neither the company nor its appraiser was at fault; that no evidence was introduced showing that either the company's appraiser or the persons nominated by him as umpire were not fair and competent.

> Kersey v. Phenix Ins. Co. (Mich. S. C.), 97 N. W. Rep. 57;
> (And see Vernon Ins. Co. v. Maitlen, 158 Ind. 393).

Where the evidence shows that the acceptance of a person as one of the appraisers of a loss by the insured is induced by the company by false statements as to his business and impartiality, such fact affords ground for setting aside an award which is grossly below the actual loss.

> Kiernan v. Dutchess Co. Mut. Ins. Co. (N. Y. C. A.), 44 N. E. Rep. 698;
> Produce Refrigerator Co. v. Norwich Union F. Ins. Society (Minn. S. C.), 97 N. W. Rep. 875.
> Bradshaw v. Agricultural Ins. Co. (N. Y. C. A., Jan., 1893), 22 Ins. L. J. 161;
> Ins. Co. of N. A. v. Hegewald (Ind. S. C.), 32 Ins. L. J. 621;
> Glover v. Rochester German Ins. Co. (Wash. S. C.), 39 Pac. Rep. 380.

The fact that one of the appraisers was an endorser of a note made by assured secured by a mortgage did not render him an interested party in the subject of arbitration.

> Bullman v. Ins. Cos. (Mass. S. C., May, 1893), 22 Ins. L. J. 668.

In selecting an umpire, the appraisers should seek an honest and competent person and one living within a reasonable distance.

> Fowble v. Phoenix Ins. Co., 106 Mo. App. 527.

Where the insurer's appraiser, being a non-resident of the place where the loss occurs, refuses to accept as umpire any of the persons resident of such place proposed by insured's appraiser, his conduct amounts to a refusal to appraise and entitles the insured to sue.

> Brock v. Dwelling House Ins. Co. (Mich. S. C.), 61 N. W. Rep. 67; 24 Ins. L. J. 464;
> Chapman v. Rockford Ins. Co. (Wis. S. C.), 62 N. W. Rep. 422;
> Hickerson v. German Am. Ins. Co. (Tenn. S. C.), 33 S. W. Rep. 1041; 25 Ins. L. J. 422.

Each appraiser presented three names; those of the insured's appraiser were objected to without cause, and those proposed by the insurer's appraiser, for the reason that they were non-residents. *Held,* Failure of appraisal was due to unreasonable conduct of the insurer's appraiser.

> Braddy v. N. Y. Bowery F. Ins. Co. (N. S. S. C.), 20 S. E. Rep. 477.

The insured's appraiser may insist that the umpire be selected from some place in the county in which the property is situated.

Niagara Ins. Co. v. Bishop, 49 Ill. App. 388.

It is no defense in an action on a policy that no appraisement was had pursuant to requirements, where the insured refused to allow the appraisers to proceed by reason of an improper proposal that was made by the company's appraiser to insured's appraiser.

Davis v. Guardian Assur. Co., 87 Hun. 414 Aff'd. on opinion below in 155 N. Y. 682.

The fact that an appraiser had before been employed as such by the company does not necessarily render him ineligible.

Stemmer v. Scottish Union and National Ins. Co. (Oregon S. C.), 27 Ins. L. J. 972.

The insured selected one G to act as appraiser on his behalf. G was an experienced builder and contractor and had made, as such, an estimate of the damage to the property by the fire, for which he had been paid prior to his selection as appraiser. *Held,* That the fact that he had made such estimate under the employment of the insured was a fact to be considered by the jury on the issue whether he was sufficiently free of bias and prejudice to be disinterested party in the appraisement. The fact that he had an intimate knowledge of the subject-matter, and on that account a preconceived opinion, did not of itself disqualify him, because it was such knowledge and such experience which made him the better qualified to ascertain the true value if he was free from bias and prejudice. In other words, this preconceived opinion as an expert, derived from personal inspection, was not a disqualification as an appraiser.

National Fire Ins. Co. v. O'Brien et al. (Ark. S. C.), 87 Southwestern Reporter (June 7, 1905) 129.

An award will not be set aside because one of the appraisers had been in the employ of the insurance company, and where the other was in the employ of the insured, and the two agreed on the loss without calling an umpire.

Remington Paper Co. v. London Assur. Corp. (N. Y. S. C., App. Div.), 43 N. Y. Supp. 431.

The question of distinterestedness of appraiser is one of fact for the jury.

Hall et al. v. Western Assur. Co. (Ala. S. C.), 32 Southern Rep. 257.

The burden of proof is on the party seeking to impeach the award, which is, in the absence of fraud, prima facie binding on both parties.

Connecticut F. Ins. Co. v. O'Fallon (Neb. S. C.), 69 N. W. Rep. 118.

A party does not assume responsibility for the consequences of irregularities and misconduct on the part of an appraiser, merely because he knew him to be a professional appraiser on behalf of interests of the other party.

Christianson v. Norwich Union F. Ins. Soc. (Minn. S. C., December, 1901), 31 Ins. L. J. 218.

But ·see

Western Assur. Co. v. Hall (Ala. S. C.), 38 S. E. Rep. 853; Bradshaw v. Agricultural Ins. Co., 137 N. Y. 137; 22 Ins. L. J. 161; Indiana Ins. Co. v. Boehm, 88 Ind. 578.

The whole question of responsibility for fairness or unfairness of appraiser is covered in the two cases of Fowble v. Phoenix Ins. Co. and Uhrig v. Ins. Co

While the appraiser is not an agent for the party who selected him, yet when it is the improper act or conduct of such appraiser which prevents the selection of an umpire, the consequence of a failure should be visited upon him who selects such appraiser.

Fowble v. Phoenix Ins. Co. (Mo. App. C.), 81 S. W. Rep. 485.

The spirit of the statute relating to arbitration of fire losses requires that the three referees shall be as free from pecuniary interest and relationship as judges and jurors are required to be, and also be as free from bias, prejudice, sympathy and partisanship as judges and jurors are presumed to be. If there is no other restriction as to the men to be nominated for the other party to choose from, or as to the third man however appointed, than that they shall not be relatives, and have no pecuniary interest, then either party may have forced upon him as referee at least one violent partisan of the other party, or at least men incompetent, opinionated, or biased. The purpose of the statute might thus be wholly defeated and made to work an injustice.

From the foregoing considerations and others we are satisfied that the insurance statute and the insurance contract require that the referees shall be "distinterested," not only in the narrow sense of being without relationship and pecuniary interest, but also in the broad, full sense of being competent, impartial, fair and opened-minded, substantially indifferent in thought and feeling between the parties, and without bias or partisanship either way. Brock v. Ins. Co., 102 Mich., 583; 61 N. W. 67; 26 L. R. A. 623; 47 Am. St. Rep. 562; Bradshaw v. Ins. Co., 137 N. Y. 137; 32 N. E. 1055; Hall v. Assurance Co., 133 Ala. 637; 32 Southern 257; Hickerson v. Ins. Co., 96 Tenn. 193; 33 S. W. 1041; 32 L. R. A. 172. Turning now to the evidence in this case, we find the following facts among others: The property insured was situated in Calais, a city on the extreme eastern frontier of the state. The referee chosen by the defendant from the three men nominated by the plaintiff was Mr. Sawyer, of Calais. The referee chosen by the plaintiff from the three men nominated by the defendant was Mr. Allen, of Portland, nearly 300 miles distant from Calais. Practically, Mr. Sawyer was the choice of the plaintiff, and Mr. Allen the choice of the defendant. When these two undertook to agree upon a man as third referee, Mr. Allen declined to agree upon any man in Calais, though freely admitting there were as good men in Calais as anywhere else in the state. He gave as a reason for his refusal that the defendant company objected to any local man.

This refusal, apart from the excuse given for it, was unreasonable. Assuming, as Mr. Allen admitted, that there were as good men in Calais as anywhere else in the state, it is not a reasonable inference from the fact of their residence in Calais and consequent probable better knowledge of local conditions affecting values there, that none of them were proper persons to act as appraising referees. His refusal to consider any of them shows that Mr. Allen was not an impartial, indifferent arbitrator, and coupled with the excuse given, it shows that he regarded himself as the representative of the defendant company. From this circumstance alone, without considering other appearing in the evidence, we think it clear that Mr. Allen was not the disinterested referee required by the statute and the policy, and hence that the award must be adjudged not binding on the plaintiff, and must be set aside. Brock v. Ins. Co., 102 Mich. 583; 61 N. W. 67; 26 L. R. A. 623; 47 Am. St. Rep. 562; McCullough v. Ins. Co., 113 Mo. 606; 21 S. W. 207; Ins. Co. v. Bishop, 154 Ill. 9; 39 N. E. 1102; 45 Am. St. Rep. 105; Hickerson v. Ins. Co., 96 Tenn. 193; 33 S. W. 1041; 32 L. R. A. 172; The defendant company refused to comply with the plaintiff's request for another arbitration of the amount of the loss, and it was stipulated in the report of the case that if the court adjudged the award invalid, judgment should be awarded for the plaintiff for the full amount of the insurance, $1,700, less $1,353.06 already paid.

Judgment for the plaintiff and interest from the date of the writ.

Young v. Aetna Ins. Co. et al., 64 Atl. 584 (Me. S. J. Ct.).

An appraiser ought not to consider himself as an agent of the party by whom he was selected, but the authorities seem to hold a party responsible when the appraiser whom he selected assumes to be his representative and improperly prevents the appraisal from being made. Under such circumstances, the act of the appraiser is regarded as the act of the party at whose instance he was named and in whose interest he assumes to act, and no direct evidence of authorization or ratification is required.

Niagara Fire Ins. Co. v. Bishop, 154 Ill. 9 ; 39 N. E. 1102 ; 45
    Am. St. Rep. 105;
Uhrig v. Ins. Co., 101 N. Y. 362 ; 4 N. E. 745 ;
Bishop v. Ins. Co., 139 N. Y. 488 ; 29 N. E. 844 ;
Harrison v. Hartford Fire Ins. Co., 112 Iowa 77 ; 83 N. W. 820 ;
McCullough v. Ins. Co., 113 Mo. 606 ; 21 S. W. 207 ;
Franklin v. Ins. Co., 70 N. H. 256 ; 47 Atl. 91 ;
Braddy v. Ins. Co., 115 N. C. 355 ; 20 S. E. 477 ;
Hickerson v. Ins. Co., 96 Tenn. 193 ; 33 S. W. 1041 ; 32 L. R. A.
    172 ;
Chapman v. Rockford Ins. Co., 89 Wis. 572 ; 62 N. W. 422 ; 28
    L. R. A. 405.

After the first attempt at arbitration had failed and was out of the way, the plaintiff requested the insurance company to appoint new referees and proceed under the provisions of the policy, and that the company refused to have anything further to do with it. This being true, the right to an appraisal was waived, and the insured was entitled to commence his action to recover upon the policy. The fact that the building had been in the meantime repaired did not justify the company in refusing to proceed with the appraisal.

O'Rourke v. German Ins. Co. (Minn. S. C.), 109 N. W. 401.

It was an unreasonable and improper requirement of the insurance companies, through their agent Young, that the umpire should not live in Bell county or vicinity, and when the appraisers broke up in February without doing anything, and it was apparent that they were not going to agree upon anything, it was incumbent upon the insurance companies, promptly within a reasonable time, to name another appraiser not a partisan, and to request of Asher to do the same, that the two new appraisers might adjust the matter or agree upon an umpire, if they were unable to agree upon the appraisement. This was not done, and, when a reasonable time had elapsed, the proposition for an appraisement must be regarded abandoued, and a subsequent demand for an appraisement could not be made. It has been well said that an habitual appraiser is not a disinterested person, within the meaning of the arbitration clause in insurance policies. The conclusions we have indicated are supported by the following authorities:

McCullough v. Phoenix Ins. Co., 113 Mo. 606; 21 S. W. 207;
Niagara Fire Ins. Co. v. Bishop, 154 Ill. 9; 39 N. E. 1102; 45 Am. St. Rep. 105;
Braddy v. Bowery Ins. Co., 115 N. C. 354; 20 S. E. 477;
Bradshaw v. Agricultural Ins. Co., 137 N. Y. 137; 32 N. E. 1055;
Glover v. Rochester German Ins. Co., 11 Wash. 143 ; 39 Pac. 380 ;
Powers v. Imperial Ins. Co., 48 Minn. 380; 51 N. W. 123; 13 Am. & Eng. Ency. of Law 362-365; 19 Cyc. 880.

A demand by two or more insurance companies for sub mission of their several liabilities in one appraisement of arbi tration is not warranted.

Wicking v. Citizens' Fire Ins. Co., 118 Mich. 640; 77 N. W. 275;
Palatine Ins. Co. v. Morton-Scott-Robertson Co., 106 Tenn. 558 ; 61 S. W. 787;
Hartford F. Ins. Co. v. Asher, (Ky.) 100 S. W. 233.

The requirement of the policies of insurance was that the appraiser and the umpire should be disinterested. Such appraisers were not in the strict sense arbitrators, and it is not probable that either party to the policies contemplated, in case of loss, that the appraisers should stand absolutely unbiased. It is more than probable that each one selected an appraiser in whom confidence was reposed as an honest man, but that, in case of any difference, his sympathies would incline toward the party by whom he was chosen. It would be expecting too much, in the present stage of progress toward the millennium, to assume that either party contemplated, when entering into the contract of insurance, that the appraisers selected should be absolutely indifferent. These tribunals are home-made, and neither their composition nor their conduct should be more closely scrutinized than is that of the tribunals selected in accordance with the statutes and long-standing judicial practice. If such appraisers are honest men, who make an honest effort to arrive at an honest award, I believe that nothing further can be demanded or expected. At the same time, all appearances of fraudulent or unfair practice should be met with the disapproval of the courts. How far the parties intended to differentiate between bias and interest is not apparent, but I think there is a distinction; and, if each party was satisfied that the opposing appraiser was free from interest, he should not have been surprised to find that he was not entirely free from bias. It would not be an extremely easy undertaking to find either an appraiser or an umpire, in a business as limited as is that of preserving fruit, who would be an entire stranger to both parties in the case.

Whalen v. Goldman, 115 N. Y. Supp. 1006.

To set aside an award of appraisers on the ground that the appraiser appointed by the company and the umpire were not "competent and disinterested," or that articles damaged were by them excluded as not insured by the policy, it must be shown that the company knew of such incompetency and interestedness, and that it was responsible for the decision excluding such articles, that a demand was made on the company that they be appraised, or it must be shown the company waived the condition of appraisement.

Early v. Providence Wash. Ins. Co. (R. I.), 76 Atl. Rep. 753.

If either of the parties to an appraisal under a clause in the policy acts in bad faith so as to defeat the object of the clause, the other is absolved from compliance therewith; when one appraisal fails by reason of default of one of the parties, the other is not bound to enter into a new appraisal agreement.

Uhrig v. Williamsburgh City F. Ins. Co., 101 N. Y. 362, affirming 31 Hun. 98.

Every presumption must be made in favor of fairness and the award should not be set aside, except upon clear and strong proof of partiality, conspiracy or fraud.

Mosness v. German-American Ins. Co. (Minn. S. C., July, 1892), 21 Ins. L. J. 915.
Citing:
Brush v. Fisher, 70 Mich. 469; Overby v. Thrasher, 47 Ga. 10; Ins. Co. v. Goehring, 99 Pa. St. 13;
Barnard v. Ins. Co. (U. S. C. C. A. 8th Dist.), 29 Ins. L. J. 631; Hartford F. Ins. Co. v. Bonner Mercantile Co., 15 U. S. App. 134.

Section 3643, Rev. St. Ohio, providing arbitrators and umpire must have been residents of the county in which loss occurred at least one year prior to said loss, is constitutional.

Germania Ins. Co. v. Cincinnati P. B. S. & P. P. Co. (Cinn. Supreme Ct. Gen. Term), 7 Ohio Decisions 571.

Where two appraisers made independent estimates, one of $5,000, the other of $115,000, and without discussing their differences, submitted them to the umpire, who took both estimates and the books to his room at a hotel, and requested both appraisers to remain within call; he had six clerks to assist him and after three days made an award of $60,624.73, in which insured's appraiser joined. *Held*, Award valid.

Hartford F. Ins. Co. v. Bonner Mercantile Co. (U. S. C. C. A. 9th Cir., May, 1893), 22 Ins. L. J. 801.

Where one appraiser in bad faith refuses to meet the other appraiser and fails or refuses to proceed with the appraisal, the other appraiser and the umpire may make a valid appraisement.

Doying v. Broadway Ins. Co. (C. of E. & A. N. J.), 23 Ins. L. J. 395; 27 Atl. Rep. 927;
American Central Ins. Co. v. Landau (N. J. Ch.), 49 Atl. Rep. 738.

Where one appraiser and the umpire refuse to deal with the other appraiser and bring in an award, it is not binding and will be set aside.

Providence-Washington Ins. Co. v. Board of Education (W. Va. S. C. A.), 30 Ins. L. J. 577;
Schmitt v. Boston Ins. Co., 81 N. Y. Supp. 767;
Christianson v. Norwich Union F. Ins. Society (Dec. 6, 1901), (Minn. S. C.), 31 Ins. L. J. 218;
Mfrs. and Builders F. Ins. Co. v. Mullen (Neb. S. C.), 67 N. W. Rep. 445;
Caledonian Ins. Co. v. Traub (Md. C. A.), 25 Ins. L. J. 791; 35 Atl. Rep. 13;
Strome v. London Assur. Corp. (N. Y. S. C. App. Div.), 47 N. Y. Supp. 481; affirmed in 162 N. Y. 627;
N. Y. Mut. S. & L. Co. v. Manchester F. Ins. Co. (N. Y. S. C. App. Div.), 87 N. Y. Supp. 1075;
Western Und. Ass'n. v. Hankins (Ill. S. C.), 35 Ins. L. J. 378.

Where one appraiser resigns, the other appraiser and the umpire can not render a valid award on items concerning which there had been no preceding conference and disagreement with the withdrawing appraiser.

Seibert v. Germania and other Co's., (Iowa S. C.), 35 Ins. L. J. 384.

Where one appraiser is called away on business engagement, and in his absence the other appraiser and umpire agreed on an award, it is a question for jury whether such award is valid or not.

Caledonian Ins. Co. v. Traub (Md. C. A.), 25 Ins. L. J. 791;
Schmitt Bros. v. Boston Ins. Co. (N. Y. S. C. App. Div.), 81 N. Y. Supp. 767.

Arbitrators are not obliged to follow strict rules of law unless it is a condition of the submission that they do so.

Hall v. Norwalk F. Ins. Co. (Conn. S. C.), 17 Atl. Rep. 356;
Levine v. Lancashire Ins. Co. (Minn. S. C.), 21 Ins. L. J. 36;

Stemmer v. Scottish U. & N. Ins. Co. (Oregon S. C.), 27 Ins. L. J. 972;
Farrell v. German American Ins. Co. (Mass. S. C.), 29 Ins. L. J. 341.

Where the arbitrators and umpire agreed that each should mark on a card his idea of damage and that the aggregate of these amounts should be divided by three and the result should be the amount of the award, it was held to be valid.

Aetna F. Ins. Co. v. Davis (Ky. C. A.), 29 Ins. L. J. 560.

Where appraisers disregard their instructions "to state separately sound value and damage" and bring in an award showing the damage, but ignoring the sound value, the award will be set aside.

Continental Ins. Co. v. Garrett (U. S. C. C. A. 6th Cir.), 125 Fed. Rep. 589.

In appraisal agreement was an unsigned direction to appraisers to affix to each article a specific damage, per yard, pound, etc. This appraisers did not do. *Held*, The award was not avoided.

Enright v. Montauk F. Ins. Co. (N. Y. S. C.), 40 N. Y. State Rep. 642.

Appraisal Must Be in Detail in Rhode Island.

An appraisal agreement is made to secure two things; First: an appraisement; and second, an award, which is the finding or judgment based upon the appraisement. Where there are numerous articles of different kinds and quality to be appraised, it is obvious that an appraisement to be of value must be founded upon an individual appraisal of the various articles. There is no provision in the agreement expressly requiring an itemized appraisal; but its implications as indicated by citations above (the only cases cited are South of v. American Central Ins. Co., 34 R. I. 324; 83 Atl. 441; Am. & Eng. Ency. Law, vol. 12, 442, 3; Cyc. 374; Continental Ins. Co. v. Garrett, 125 Fed. 589; 60 C. C. A. 395, 396) therefrom, in our judgment show that an itemized or individual appraisement was contemplated thereby. The number or articles to be appraised after different fires may be expected to vary greatly, particularly when the articles are personal property. The itemized list in such cases must also vary greatly in length. Perhaps for this reason no space for the appraisement is provided for on the form of agreement. The appraisers are apparently left to make that up themselves. In the form of the award, after the last printed word, "dollars," is a space with a dotted line upon which to write whatever may be necessary in addition. There is ample room allowed to make the itemized appraisement a part of the award by reference. * * * The evidence in this case does not warrant the presumption or inference that the form of the award, if presented by the defendant, was by it intended or calculated to deceive or mislead the appraisers or the insured as to the character of the appraisement and award desired. The court therefore held, it was the insured's duty to demand a new appraisal of his loss, the first being invalid for the reason that it failed to show that appraisers had appraised the value of each article and the loss and damage to each in detail. Riddell v. Rochester Ger. Ins. Co. (R. I. S. C.), 89 Atl. 833. '

In one of the cases cited by the Rhode Island Supreme Court (i. e. Continental Ins. Co. v. Garrett, 125 Fed. 589; 60 C. C. A. 395) as a case in point, it is true in that case the Federal Court did hold the award invalid for the reason the appraisers did not carry out the provisions of the appraisal agreement as well as those of the policy, both of which required appraisers to determine the sound value, as well as the loss thereto, whereas they omitted to find the amount of the sound value, but did find the amount of the loss. The court held the award invalid and permitted the insured to bring suit, holding that he was not required to enter into a second appraisal, the first one not being valid through no fault of his. In Enright v. Montauk Ins. Co., 40 N. Y. State Rep. 642, it was held the award was not avoided because the appraisers had not appraised the loss article by article when there was in the appraisal agreement an unsigned direction to affix to each article a specific damage. There are no other cases in line with the Rhode Island Court's decision with the single exception of one the same court decided and referred to. The Author.

By failing to furnish an arbitrator who would proceed with reasonable promptness in the discharge of his duties, any right it may have had to insist on the damages being appraised was lost. The record leaves no doubt but that the appraiser chosen by this company resorted to the familiar expedient of preventing or delaying action by demanding an umpire from afar off, and then, when something might be accomplished finding it impossible to proceed because of pressing business engagements at his home in Kansas City, Mo., there detaining him several months. That the defendant was precluded by such conduct from insisting on arbitration as a condition precedent to the maintenance of the action is well settled authority. Harrison v. Hartford F. Ins. Co., 30 Ins. L. J. 253, 112 Iowa 77 (citing Read v. Ins. Co., 103 Ia. 314; Brook v. Ins. Co., 102 Mich. 583; Bradshaw v. Ins. Co., 137 N. Y. 137; McCullough v. Ins. Co., 113 Mo. 606; Bishop v. Ins. Co., 130 N. Y. 488; Uhrig v. Ins. Co., 101 N. Y. 362).

The provision in a fire policy that the loss is payable sixty days after * * * an award of appraisers, doesn't give the insurer after it has agreed to appraisal and named its appraiser, an absolute right to sixty days in which to commence the appraisal, but it must proceed without unnecessary delay, and in a reasonable time depending on the facts in the case, so where, after the fire the parties appointed appraisers and agreed that they should commence at once to appraise the goods and insured got his appraiser and left him waiting for six days at great expense, and the insurer stated the appraiser appointed by it could not attend, and promised to procure a substitute but failed to do so, and when communicated with by telegram failed to reply, though knowing that insured was at great expense, and that the goods which were not fully insured, were being injured by delay, and that an early appraisement was necessary for insured to save anything from the stock. Such action is a refusal to appraise.

> Providence-Wash. Ins. Co. v. Wolf, 168 Ind. 690; 80 N. E. 27 overruling Ind. App., 72 N. E. 606.

Where the company fraudulently represents its appraiser as an unprejudiced one and a business man, whereas he was a professional appraiser, and it appearing the award was inadequate, it will be set aside because of a prejudiced appraiser having been fraudulently imposed on insured.

"The scheme of appraisal contemplates that the two appraisers shall estimate the amount of the loss, and in case of disagreement their differences shall be submitted to the umpire. It is not the purpose of the provision that one appraiser shall present no estimate to his co-appraiser, but confer with the umpire in the absence of and without any notice whatever to the other appraiser."

> Kaiser v. Hamburg-Bremen F. Ins. Co., 69 N. Y. Supp. 344;
> Hall v. Western Assur. Co., 133 Ala. 637; 32 Southern 257;
> Glover v. Rochester Ger. Ins. Co., 11 Wash. 143; 39 Pacif. 380.

Where the arbitration fails by reason of fraud or intermeddling of the insured, the right to sue on the policy is lost. Where the fraud or intermeddling with the appraisers is at the instance of the company, the insured may abandon the arbitration and sue on the policy. St. Paul F. & M. Ins. Co. v. Kirkpatrick (Tenn. S. C.), 164 S. W. 1186.

But this, substantially, is what was done here, and such action barely rose to the dignity of a real conference between Thomas Fleming (one of the appraisers) and David Nicholson, the umpire. Each obtained information upon "his own hook," so to express it, and then each made figures based on his private information, to a large extent, and ignoring the other appraiser proceeded to make an award. Really Fleming was ignorant of the evidence or information on which Nicholson acted, and Stultz (the other appraiser) knew little, if anything, of the real information on which either or both of the others acted. This award was not the result of information furnished to all or considered by all or by any two, or of the joint deliberation of the three or of any two. True, two signed the award, and so two agreed in the final result, but it by no means follows that the two would have agreed on that result had they consulted all the evidence and information possessed by each and deliberated thereon.

I think that an examination and consideration of the evidence of Mr. Fleming is conclusive against the fairness and justice of the award made. He testified that he gave full credit to Palmer's (a gentleman engaged by the insurance companies) report, and no credit whatever to the sworn proofs of loss and the affidavits presented by the insured.

Without going into detail, the evidence also shows that on the prior file of one of the cases against one of the companies involved in this loss Mr. Fleming made statements almost exactly opposite to the statements made on the trial of this case in important matters, * * * If it be true that he was unable to understand and comprehend the questions put to him on the trial (as he claims), a fair inference may be drawn that he was incompetent to act as an appraiser in this important matter. * * * My conclusions are that the appraisal made should be set aside, and the matter should be determined before a court and jury.

Davis v. Fireman's Fund Ins. Co., 210 Fed. 653.

It is the duty of the appraiser, undoubtedly, to bring out all the facts, favorable to the party nominating him; but he is not the agent of the party so naming him. A refusal or willful neglect of the appraiser or umpire to listen to and consider material sworn statements presented, is evidence of prejudice, bias and interest.   Davis v. Firemen's Fund Ins. Co., 210 Fed. 653 (citing Kaiser v. Hamburg-Bremen Fire Ins. Co., 59 App. Div. 525, 69 N. Y. Supp. 344, Aff'd 172 N. Y. 663, 65 N. E. 1118).

While an award of appraisers will be presumed to be just and proper, yet where the evidence shows that the company's appraiser was an expert in adjusting losses, and that, in entering upon the appraisement of the destroyed property he practically ignored the insured's appraiser, and refused to take any account of the estimated depreciation made by an appraisal company who had personally examined the property about a year before the fire, but arbitrarily depreciated the property 50 per cent., it was no such effort at a fair and impartial appraisement as the standard policy contemplates.   Davis v. Stuyvesant Ins. Co., 145 N. Y. Supp. 192.

Mere inadequacy alone is not sufficient to set aside an award; but, if the inadequacy be so gross and palpable as to shock the moral sense, it is sufficient evidence to be submitted to the jury on the issues relating to fraud and corruption or partially and bias.   The arbitrators awarded insured damages in the amount of $73.50.   The jury found that insured's loss amounted to $750.   *Held*, That the award in such case ought not to be permitted to stand.

Perry v. Greenwich Ins. Co. (N. C. S. C.) 49 Southeastern Reporter (March 11, 1905), 889.

Where an award was signed by one appraiser with the un derstanding that certain items not considered were improperly omitted, it should not be final, and afterwards such omission was found improper, such award can not be claimed as final.

Herndon v. Imperial F. Ins. Co. (N. C. S. C. March, 1892), 21 Ins. L. J. 193.

Where the award was based on an inventory furnished by the insured and certified by him to be correct, he can not have the award set aside for a mistake in the inventory.

Kentucky Chair Co. v. Rochester German Ins. Co. (Ky. C. A.), 28 Ins. L. J. 361.

Neither party can avoid the award on the ground that appraisers erred in judgment as to the law or facts.

Hall v. Norwalk F. Ins. Co. (Conn. S. C.), 17 Atl. Rep. 356; Stemmer v. Scottish U. & N. Ins. Co. (Oregon S. C.), 27 Ins. L. J. 973.

An appraiser or umpire may inform himself by calling in

the aid of a third person skilled in a special branch embraced in the appraisal and give to such estimate of such third person such weight and evidence as he sees fit, even to adopting it as his own judgment.

> Bangor Savings Bank v. Niagara F. Ins. Co. (Me. S. C.), 23 Ins. L. J. 292;
> Rogers v. Com'l Union Assur. Co. (Manitoba O. B.), 15 Canadian L. Times 228.

The award of appraisers was not binding where they did not appraise the damage to all the articles embraced in the schedule, but held that some of them were not covered by the policy. A policy of insurance covering "tools used in the manufacture of boots and shoes" covers patterns for making boots and shoes.

> Adams v. N. Y. Bowery F. Ins. Co. (Iowa S. C.), 51 N. W. Rep. 1149.

In this state courts of equity will set aside awards not only for fraud and for corrupt practices on the part of arbitrators or parties, but for mistake, or willful misconduct of the arbitrators. Commercial Assur. Co. v. Parker, 119 Ill. App. 126, citing Citizens Ins. Co. v. Hamilton, 48 Ill. App. 593; Catlett v. Dougherty, 114 Ill. 568.

The policy requires the parties to choose appraisers only once and if that fail through no fault of assured, he may bring suit.

> Braddy v. N. Y. Bowery F. Ins. Co., 115 N. C. 354, 20 S. E. 477;
> Harrison v. German Am. Ins. Co., 67 Fed. 577;
> Hickerson v. Royal Ins. Co., 96 Tenn. 193, 33 S. W. 1041;
> Niagara F. Ins. Co. v. Bishop, 154 Ill. 9, 39 N. E. 1102, 25 Ins. L. J. 24;
> Connecticut F. Ins. Co. v. Cohen, 97 Md. 294, 55 Atl. 675;
> Western Assur. Co. v. Decker, 39 C. C. A. 383, 98 Fed. 381;
> Brock v. Dwelling Ho. Ins. Co., 102 Mich. 583, 61 N. W. 67;
> Davis v. Atlas Assur. Co., 16 Wash. 232, 47 Pacif. 436, 885;
> Capitol Ins. Co. v. Wallace, 50 Kans. 454, 31 Pacif. 1070;
> McCullough v. Phoenix Ins. Co., 113 Mo. 606, 21 S. W. 207;
> Chapman v. Rockford Ins. Co., 89 Wis. 572, 62 N. W. 422;
> Uhrig v. Williamsburgh City F. Ins. Co., 101 N. Y. 362, 4 N. E. 745;
> Davenport v. Long Island Ins. Co., 10 Daly 538;
> Bishop v. Agricultural Ins. Co., 130 N. Y. 488, 29 N. E. 844;
> Randall v. Phoenix Ins. Co., 10 Mont. 362, 25 Pacif. 960;
> Fire Assn. v. Appel, 76 Ohio St. 1, 80 N. E. 952, 36 Ins. L. J. 769;
> O'Rourke v. German Ins. Co., 99 Minn. 293, 104 N. W. 900;
> Bernhard v. Rochester G. Ins. Co., 79 Conn. 388, 65 Atl. 134;
> Pretzfelder v. Merchants Ins. Co., 116 N. C. 491, 21 S. E. 302, 28 Ins. L. J. 169;
> Shawnee F. Ins. Co. v. Pontfield, 110 Md. 356, 72 Atl. 835;
> Sharp v. Niagara F. Ins. Co. (Mo. App.), 147 S. W. 154;
> Continental Ins. Co. v. Wilson, 45 Kans. 250, 25 Pacif. 629, 20 Ins. L. J. 269;
> St. Paul F. & M. Ins. Co. v. Kirkpatrick (Tenn. S. C.), 164 S. W. 1186;
> German Am. Ins. Co. v. Jerrills, 82 Kans. 320, 108 Pac. 114, annotated in 28 L. R. A. (N. S.) 104;
> Aetna Ins. Co. v. Jester, 37 Okla. 413, 132 Pac. 130, annotated in 39 L. R. A. (N. S.) 1191.

Where the policy makes appraisal a condition precedent, and the appraisers after making an honest effort to agree on an umpire and fail to do so, the assured is not justified in refusing to proceed with the appraisal by selection of a new appraiser, and in suing for the amount of his loss.

> Westenhaver v. German Am. Ins. Co., 113 Iowa 726; 84 N. W. 717;
> Vernon Ins. Co. & T. Co. v. Maitlen, 158 Ind. App. 393; 62 N. E. 755;
> Baumgarth v. Fireman's Fund Ins. Co. (Mich.), 116 N. W. 449, 37 Ins. L. J. 577 (citing Davenport v. Ins. Co., 10 Daly (N. Y.) 535);
> Grady v. Home F. & M. Ins. Co., 27 R. I. 435;
> Kersey v. Phoenix Ins. Co., 135 Mich. 10, 97 N. W. 57.

It is not unreasonable for the insured to refuse to submit to a second appraisal (the first having failed) unless the insurer waives the provision in the policy that loss should not become due until sixty days after award of appraisers.

> Michel v. American Cent'l Ins. Co. (N. Y. S. C. App. Div.), 44 N. Y. Supp. 832.

If an appraisal fails, through no fault of insurer, assured has no standing in court until a new appraisement is had.

> Levine v. Lancashire Ins. Co. (Minn. S. C.), 26 Ins. L. J. 36;
> Carp v. Queen Ins. Co. (Mo. C. of A.), 79 S. W. Rep. 757.

But, if it fail through no fault of either party, this does not justify insured from refusing further arbitration and bringing suit; other appraisers should be selected.

> Westenhaver et al. v. German-Am. Ins. Co. (Ia. S. C.), 30 Ins. L. J. 314;
> Fisher v. Merchants Ins. Co. (Me. S. J. C.), 31 Ins. L. J. 45;
> Vernon Ins. and Trust Co. v. Maitlen (Ind. S. C.), 31 Ins. L. J. 672;
> Carp v. Queen Ins. Co., 104 Mo. App. 502.

The Mass. Rev. Law as c 118 S. 60 provides that where the referees are unable to agree on a third referee within ten days, the insurance commissioner will on request of either party appoint the third referee. The Mass. standard policy makes arbitration as to the amount of the loss a condition precedent to suit. Upon a disagreement the insured and the company each selected referees who failed to agree on a third within ten days, whereupon the insured notified one of the referees that he wished the third appointed by the insurance commissioner but no written application was made by plaintiff to the commissioner as is required by statue, but he asked for the appointment of new referees. About twenty days after their appointment the two referees agreed on a third. The plaintiff refused to abide by the selection because it was not made in ten days of the appointment of the referees. The company declined to waive its right to have the loss determined by the referees. It was held that the selection of the third referee after ten days was legal, and that the arbitration as condition precedent was not waived.

Paris v. Hamburg-Bremen F. Ins. Co. (Mass.), 90 N. E. 420.

Waiver.

Where the insurer knew the policy was avoided by breach of a condition and then entered into an appraisal, it is estopped from setting up such a defense.

McFarland v. Kittanning Ins. Co. (Pa. S. C.), 21 Ins. L. J. 555;
Hickerson v. Ins. Cos. (Tenn. S. C.), 25 Ins. L. J. 422.

Insurer's demand for appraisal waives proofs.

Walker v. German Ins. Co. (July, 1893), (Kan. S. C.), 22 Ins.
L. J. 750;
Home F. Ins. Co. v. Bean (Neb. S. C.), 24 Ins. L. J. 516;
Smith v. Herd et al. (K. C. A.), 30 Ins. L. J. 393;
Branigan v. Jefferson Mut. Ins. Co., 102 Mo. App. 70; 76 S. W.
Rep. 643.

An appraisal which provides that no questions are to be determined other than the loss is no waiver of forfeiture.

Queen Ins. Co. v. Young (Ala. S. C.), 5 Southern Rep. 102;
Holbrook v. Baloise F. Ins. Co. (Cal. S. C.), 49 Pac. Rep. 555.

Even though such forfeiture be known to the insurer before agreeing to appraisal where agreement specified, it should not decide liability under the policy.

Johnson v. American F. Ins. Co. (Minn. S. C.), 41 Minn. 396, 43
N. W. Rep. 59.

Nor where the insurer learned of such forfeiture after entering into appraisal and did not withdraw from the appraisal and the award was not rendered for a month afterwards.

Gibson Electric Co. v. Liverpool & London & Globe Ins. Co. (N. Y.
C. A.), 28 Ins. L. J. 629.

The insurer may deny liability and still insist on the appraisement as conclusive of the amount of the loss under Texas standard policy.

American Cent'l Ins. Co. v. Bass et al. (Tex. S. C.), 38 S. W.
Rep. 1119.

Nor does it waive proofs of loss.

Wicking et al. v. Citizens' Mut. F. Ins. Co. (Mich. S. C.), 28 Ins.
L. J. 230;
Fournier v. German Am. Ins. Co. (R. I. S. C.), 30 Ins. L. J. 715;
Cook v. North B. & M. Ins. Co. (Mass. S. C.), 31 Ins. L. J. 385.

Where a policy of insurance contains one provision requiring proofs of loss and another requiring an appraisal, both can not be in operation at the same time, so that where the com pany offers to pay what it believes to be the loss, it implies that it is satisfied with the integrity of the loss, but if the insured declines the offer it brings into operation the appraisal clause, and insured must allege an award of appraisers, or that he has endeavored to secure one.

Murphy v. North B. & M. Ins. Co., 70 Mo. App. 78.

So where an answer pleads failure to arbitrate, it impliedly admits the necessary proofs of loss.

Exchange Bank v. Thuringia F. Ins. Co., 109 Mo. App. 654; 83 S. W. 534.

As the award, both by the terms of the submission to ap praisers and by the terms of the policy, merely limited the deter mination of the amount of loss without reference to other ques tions or matters of differences, it had only the effect of fixing the amount of the liability in the event the company should be found liable.

Smith v. British Am. Assur. Co., 110 Ky. 56, 60 S. W. 841.

Where the appraisal agreement provided that the appraiser should ascertain, pursuant to the terms and conditions of the policy, the actual cash value, etc., and further that the appraise ment "does not in any respect waive any of the provisions or conditions of said policies of insurance or of any forfeiture thereof, or the proof of such loss and damages required by the policies of insurance thereon." The company may refuse to accept proofs not made out in conformity with the award of appraisers, but if the proofs were not served within the sixty days after the fire as provided for in the policy, the company's construction of the policy contract was sound when it informed the insured, "if it shall be alleged or claimed by you that award. of appraisers for any reason is not binding upon you, then this company objects to the papers purporting to be proofs of loss, and declines to accept them for the reason that they were not served upon this company within sixty days after the fire as required by the terms and conditions of said policy. The papers are returned herewith."

Commercial Union Assur. Co. v. Dalzell, 210 Fed. Rep. 605 (C. C. A. 3d Circuit Jany. 29, 1914, Nos. 1792, 1793.).

Having once waived the appraisal by its conduct (in selecting a professional appraiser), the insurer can not require another appraisal.

Continental Ins. Co. v. Vallandingham (Ky. C. A.), 32 Ins. L. J. 1032.

The refusal of an insurance company to join in an appraisal of the loss with the insured and the other companies does not estop it from disputing the loss as estimated by the appraisers so appointed and such an appraisement is never conclusive, and is not even evidence at all, unless made so by the parties uniting in it. It gets its entire force from the joint act of the parties through their agents, and where it is exparte, and though averred by plaintiff in his statement, is denied by defendant, it goes for naught, and is not evidence at all, either on motion for judgment or at the trial.

Penn. P. G. Co. v. Spring G. Ins. Co. 189 Pa. 255; 42 Atl. 138; 28 Ins. L. J. 223.

It merely waives Co.'s right to afterwards insist upon an appraisal.

McDowell v. Aetna Ins. Co. et al., 164 Mass. 444; 41 N. E. 665; 25 Ins. L. J. 156.

An offer to submit a loss to appraisement made by the company in ignorance' of facts rendering the policy void, and promptly withdrawn upon learning the facts, is no waiver of its right to deny liability for the loss.

Greenwood v. Georgia R. Ins. Co., 72 Miss. 46; 17 Southern 83.

Neither the company nor the insured is bound by an award under appraisal between the insured and another company.

Chenoweth v. Phenix Ins. Co., 12 Ky. L. R. 232;
Penn Plate G. Co. v. Spring G. Ins. Co., 189 Pa. 255; 42 Atl. 138; 28 Ins. L. J. 223.

Where the insurance company's adjuster did not take part in the early negotiations for a joint appraisal, but was kept informed on the steps taken, and was co-operating with the other insurers and taking advantage of whatever was done that could benefit him and later was present with the other adjusters and co-operated with them, and after leaving the conference was notified of what was being done, his company is bound by and participated in the joint appraisal, notwithstanding the fact he had demanded a separate appraisal.

North German Ins. Co. v. Morton, 108 Tenn. 384; 68 S. W. 816; 31 Ins. L. J. 580.

The failure of the insured to object to the appraiser selected by the company for bias, prejudice or incompetency before the award is made, will not estop him from afterwards setting up the existence of such incompetency in avoidance of the award. Whether appraisers were competent and disinterested is a question for the jury.

Royal Ins. Co. et al. v. Parlin & Orendorff Co., 12 Tex. C. A. 572; 34 S. W. 401, 3 and 4.

But where in such case appraisal being a condition precedent the adjuster and the insured negotiated as to the amount of the loss without agreeing, and the company demanded further proofs of loss, refusing to pay anything until they were furnished, but never offered to submit the loss to appraisal, it cannot claim that a suit brought on the policy four months thereafter was a violation of its terms as to arbitration.

Milwaukee Mchs. Ins. Co. v. Stewart, 13 Ind. App. 640; 42 N. E. 290.

Where the policy provides that an appraisement by arbitrators shall not determine the validity of the policy, the company's liability nor any question but the amount of the loss, an agreement for submission to appraisal under such policy by the company's adjuster appointing appraisers, but stipulating that no other question shall thereby be affected is no waiver of a forfeiture of the policy.

Queen Ins. Co. v. Young, 86 Ala. 424; 5 Southern R. 116; Johnson v. American F. Ins. Co., 41 Minn., 396; 43 N. W. R. 59.

When after disagreement with the insured the company demands an appraisal to which both parties agree, this waives the provision of the policy requiring proofs of loss.

Ross v. Phenix Ins. Co. (Kans. S. C.), 114 Pac. R. 1054.

An award of appraisers appointed under a provision of the policy, nullifies the twelve months limitation clause of the policy in which the insured must institute suit.

Fellman v. Royal Ins. Co. (U. S. C. C. A.), 184 Fed. 577.

Waiver of Assured's Sale of Salvage.

The insured's breach of policy in selling salvage was waived by a subsequent demand of the company for arbitration and appraisal of the loss.

St. Paul F. & M. Ins. Co. v. Kirkpatrick (Tenn. S. C.), 164 S. W. 1186.

A demand for appraisal 65 days after receipt of proofs of loss, and 72 days after the fire under N. Y. standard policy is too late. The company has only a reasonable period depending on the facts in the case in which to demand an appraisal.

Langsner v. German Alliance Ins. Co., 123 N. Y. Supp. 144.

The loss being due sixty days after proofs are furnished the company, its demand for any appraisal made fifty-nine days thereafter is too late, the demand must be made early enough to permit arbitration to be had before the expiration of the time.

Firemen's Fund Ins. Co. v. Caye (Ky. S. C.), 14 Ky. L. R. 810.

The policy stipulating that insured shall have sixty days after fire in which to deliver proofs, and that the loss shall not be payable until sixty days after such delivery of proofs, including an award by appraisers, where an appraisal has been required, the company has the right at any time within sixty days after proofs are delivered to demand an appraisal.

North B. & M. Ins. Co. v. Robinett (Va. S. C. A.), 72 S. E. 668.

Competent and Disinterested Appraiser.

As a "competent and disinterested appraiser," the fact that the appraiser (a public insurance adjuster) one who had acted in that capacity for other persons on similar occasions does not, as a matter of law, render him incompetent or interested; but that question is one of fact for the jury.

Meyerson v. Hartford F. Ins. Co., 39 N. Y. Supp. 329; 17 Misc'l 121.

Law Requiring Appraiser to Be Resident of State Is Valid.

The Minnesota laws which provide that referees appointed to adjust fire losses under the Minnesota standard policy must be residents of that state is mandatory, and a failure to comply therewith renders the award void.

Schoenich v. American Ins. Co. (Minn.); 124 N. W. 5.

Mortgagor—Mortgagee.

Where policy is payable to mortgagee as his interest may appear, notice to or consent of such mortgagee of the appraisement is not necessary to its validity.

Chandos v. Amer. Fire Ins. Co. (Wis. S. C., January, 1893), 22 Ins. L. J. 425;
Collinsville Savings Bank v. Boston Ins. Co. (S. C. of E. Conn.), 34 Ins. L. J. 1031; 60 Atl. Rep. 647.

Mortgagee, to whom a policy is payable, it not concluded by an appraisal between the owner and insurance company.

Bergman v. Com'l Ins. Co. et al. (Ky. C. A.), 13 Ky. Law Rep. 720; 21 Ins. L. J. 271;
Georgia Home Ins. Co. v. Stein et al. (Miss. S. C.), 18 Southern Rep. 414;
Morris v. German Am. Ins. Co. (Ky. Sup. C.), 14 Ky. L. R. 859.

Where a mortgage clause is attached to the policy and provides that the insurance as to the interest of the mortgagee or trustee, should not be invalidated by any act or neglect of the owner, the trustee is not bound by an agreement between the owner and the company as to the amount of the loss. The effect of attaching the mortgage clause to the policy was to effect a new and separate contract with the mortgagee, and to effect a separate insurance of the interest of the mortgagee dependent for its validity solely upon the course of action of the company and the mortgagee, unaffected by any act or neglect of the mortgagor of which the mortgagee is ignorant.

Scottish U. & N. Ins. Co. v. Field, 18 Colo. App. 68; 70 Pacif. 149.

Under a policy which was made payable to a mortgagee "as their mortgage interest may appear," where the policy provided "if with the consent of the company an interest under this policy shall exist in favor of a mortgagee or of any person or corporation having an interest in the subject of insurance other than the interest of the insured as described herein, the conditions hereinbefore contained shall apply in the manner expressed in such provisions and conditions of insurance relating to such interest as shall be written upon, attached or appended hereto." The mortgagee is not entitled to participate in the adjustment nor to question the validity of an award of appraisers to whom the insured and the company have submitted the amount of the loss.

Collinsville S. S. v. Boston Ins. Co., 77 Conn. 676; 60 Atl. 647.

The fact that the mortgagee does not comply with the requirements of the policy after the fire, such as the furnishing of proofs of loss, or his failure or refusal to submit the loss to appraisal will not avoid the policy in so far as the mortgage or trustee is concerned, if the standard mortgage clause be attached to the policy.

Gillespie v. Scottish Union & N. Ins. Co. 61 W. Va. 169; 56 S. E. 213, 36 Ins. L. J. 300 (annotated in 11 L. R. A. [N. S.] 143);
Bacot v. Phoenix Ins. Co., 96 Miss. 223; 50 So. 729, 39 Ins. L. J. 214, (annotated in 25 L. R. A. [N. S.] 1226);
Franklin F. Ins. Co. v. Martin, 40 N. J. L. 575;
Kupferschmidt v. Agricultural Ins. Co., 80 N. J. L. 441, 78 Atl. 225, (annotated in 34 L. R. A. [N. S.] 503);
Stanley v. Royal Exch. Assur. Co. (Kans. S. C.), 145 Pac. 563.

Nor can the assured bind the mortgagee or trustee under a mortgage clause, by a settlement with the company or by an award of appraisers.

Hartford F. Ins. Co. v. Alcott, 97 Ill. 439 (citing and approving Hastings v. Westchester F. Ins. Co.), 73 N. Y. 141, 7 Ins. L. J. 430.

Massachusetts and Ohio hold that such mortgagee is bound to furnish notice, and proofs and submit loss to arbitration if the assured fails to do so.

Union Inst. Co. v. Phoenix Ins. Co., 196 Mass. 230, 81 N. E. 994 (annotated in 14 L. R. A. [N. S.] 459) ;
Erie Brewing Co. v. Ohio F. Ins. Co., 81 Ohio St. 1; 89 N. E. 1065, 39 Ins. L. J. 200 (annotated in 25 L. R. A. [N. S.] 740, and in 18 Am. & Eng. Anno. Cas. 265).

The safest and surest way is to have the submission to appraisal agreed to by both the owner or mortgagor and the mortgagee.

The ordinary clause, "Loss if any payable to mortgagee, as his interest may appear" seems to have no such contingencies, as under such circumstances the party to whom the loss is payable has only the right to have whatever may be found to be due the assured payable to him as his interest may appear. But even in such cases it is better to have both parties agree to the adjustment, or submission to appraisal.

While it is held in New Jersey that the mortgagee or trustee to whom the loss is payable under a mortgage clause is not bound to furnish proofs, nor required to submit to appraisal of the loss, the Illinois case does not go so far, it merely holds no act of the owner or mortgagee may diminish his claim, such as effecting other insurance, or adjusting the loss by agreement or by appraisal. (The Author.)

CHAPTER XIV.

WHAT IS NOT OTHER CONTRIBUTING INSURANCE.

"This company shall not be liable under this policy for a greater proportion of any loss on the described property * * * than the amount hereby insured shall bear to the whole insurance, whether valid or not, or by solvent or insolvent insurers."—(N. Y. Standard Policy.)

As to the term valid or not, see Deitch, Standard Fire Policy, p. 92, in which he cites Parks v. Ins. Co., 100 Mo. 373 and Phenix Ins. Co. v. Lamar, 106 Ind. 513, to show that absolutely void insurance can not be made to contribute, thereby reducing the assured's claim.

If a company fails and is placed in the hands of a receiver, that very act cancels all outstanding policies, and the holders of such policies only have a claim for the unearned premium, but not for any loss that may occur subsequent to the appointment of such receiver.

Doane v. Milville Mut. M. and F. Ins. Co. (N. J. Ch. C.), 11 Atl. Rep. 739; 1 Ins. Digest 27;
Taylor v. Ins. Co. et al. (Minn. S. C.), 48 N. W. Rep. 772; 20 Ins. L. J. 562;
Reliance Lumber Co. v. Brown (Ind. S. C.), 30 N. E. Rep. 625;
In re. Commercial Ins. Co. (R. I. S. C.), 36 Atl. Rep. 930; 10 Ins. Digest 368;
a is v. She e et al. (Wis. S. C.), 62 N. W. Rep. 1050; 8 Ins. D vDigest 92ar r
Boston and Albany R. R. Co. et al. v. Merc. Trust Co. et al. (Md. C. A.), 34 Atl. Rep. 778; 9 Ins. Digest 305;
See also Joyce on Ins., Sec. 1454;
Michel, Secty. of State v. Southern Ins. Co., 128 La. 562, 54 So. 1010 annotated in 24 Am. & Eng. Anno. Cas. 810;
Gleason v. Prudential F. Ins. Co. (Tenn.), 151 S. W. 1030.
Contra:
Fink v. National M. F. Ins. Co., 90 S. C. 544, 74 S. E. 33.

As a natural consequence, therefore, if the policy is canceled, it ceases to be other insurance, and the assured is not liable legally to have such canceled insurance brought in for contribution, thereby reducing his claim against the solvent insurance held by him, and this is so whether such cancellation is by agreement between the parties or by operation of law.

To require contribution from another policy it must have been on the same interest, in the same property, or some part thereof.

Lowell Mfg. Co. v. Safeguard F. Ins. Co., 88 N. Y. 591;
Sunderlin v. Aetna Ins. Co. (N. Y.), 18 Hun. 522;
Cannon v. Home Ins. Co. (La. S. C.), 26 Ins. L. J. 737.

If an equitable owner insure the property, his policy is not affected by a subsequent insurance by an adverse claimant of the title.

Acer v. Merchants Ins. Co. (N. Y.), 57 Barb. 68.

Where two policies cover separate and distinct interests, that of the mortgagee and that of the owner, it is not other insurance within the meaning of the clause.

Hastings v. Westchester F. Ins. Co., 73 N. Y. 141;
Cannon v. Home Ins. Co. (La. S. C.), 26 Ins. L. J. 737;
Connecticut F. Ins. Co. v. Merchants and Mech's Ins. Co. (Va. S. C. A.), 15 Ins. L. J. 615.

CHAPTER XV.

APPORTIONMENT OF NON-CONCURRENT INSURANCE—VARIOUS RULES AND EXAMPLES—CONTRIBUTION.

READING RULE IN FORCE IN MASSACHUSETTS AND VERMONT.

Specific insurance for $2,250 covered as follows: $825 on Item A; $987.50 on Item B; $437.50 on Item C. In addition, there was insurance for $12,700 covering blanket on all the items. The loss on the respective items was total as follows: Item A, $3,491.48; Item B, $6,230.37; Item C, $2,014.70. *Held*, That the blanket policies should be made to cover specifically on each item in the proportion that the value of each bears to the aggregate value of all the items; that Item A was 29,748 per cent. of the whole value; Item B 53.085 per cent. and Item C 17.166 per cent; it necessarily followed that these percentages of the blanket insurance attached respectively to the several items, hence, the following apportionment:

	Item A		Item B		Item C	
	Insures	Pays	Insures	Pays	Insures	Pays
Specific Insurance	$ 825.00	6 625.77	$ 987.50	$ 796.00	$ 437.50	$ 336.73
Blanket Insurance	3,778.09	2,865.71	6,741.82	5,434.37	2,180.09	1,677.97
	$4,603.09	$3,491.48	$7,729.32	$6,230.37	$2,617.59	$2,014.70

Chandler v. Ins. Co. of N. A. (Vt. S. C.), 28 Ins. L. J. 1028;
Blake v. Exchange M. Ins. Co., 12 Gray (Mass.) 265, 4 Bennett 306;
Taber V. Continental Ins. Co., 213 Mass. 487, 100 N. E. 636.

CROMIE RULE.

The blanket policy must first pay the loss on items not covered by the specific policy and the unexhausted amount will contribute with the specific policy in paying the loss on the items covered by both policies.

Anglerodt v. Delaware M. Ins. Co., 31 Mo. 593, 4 Bennett 589;
Meigs v. London Assur. Corp. 126 Fed. 781, 33 Ins. L. J. 251;
Cromie v. Ky. L. M. Ins. Co., 15 B. Monroe (Ky.) 432, 3 Bennett 785.

CONNECTICUT AND NEW JERSEY RULE.

One set of policies covered blanket on building, machinery and stock; one set covered a specific amount on each item.

It is conceded assured must be paid his loss. Any method

of apportionment which in a given case fails to afford him the full measure of his just indemnity, must give place to another that will.

The court rejected the rule making the blanket policies cover specifically on each item in the proportion as the value of each bore to the aggregate value of all, also making them specific on each in proportion as the loss on each bears to the loss on all. It also rejected the rule proposed by the specific insurance, that the blanket insurance be made to contribute for the full amount of the blanket policy on each item with the specific insurance, and held that the blanket insurance should pro rate with the specific insurance on the item of greatest loss, the unexhausted amount with the specific insurance on the item of next greatest loss and so on with each item, where this produces substantial equity to all parties. But no rule of unvarying application can be made.

Schmaelze v. London and Lancashire F. Ins. Co., 75 Conn. 397, 53 Atl. 853, 33 Ins. L. J. 632;
Grollimund v. Germania F. Ins. Co., 82 N. J. L. 618, 83 Atl. 1108.

PAGE RULE.

Company A insures $10,000 specific on lumber on Block No. 1. Company B insures $40,000 blanket on lumber on Blocks Nos. 1 and 2. If fire destroys lumber on Block 1, doing no damage to lumber on Block 2, Company A will pay one-fifth the loss and Company B four-fifths.

Page v. Sun Ins. Office (U. S. C. C. A., 8th Dist.), 20 C. C. A. 397; 25 Ins. L. J. 865;
Liverpool & L. & G. Ins. Co. v. Delta, etc. (Tex. C. C. A.), 121 S. W. 599;
Scottish Union & N. Ins. Co. v. Moore (Okla.), 43 Pac. 12.

MEIGS OR CROMIE RULE.

Class A companies insured $130,000 on main buildings and $50,000 on contents, permission granted to make additions, alterations and repairs, and this insurance to cover on and in same, and for other insurance. Class B companies insured $60,000 on wing addition built subsequent to date of Class A policies, and $7,500 on contents thereof, and permitted other insurance.

Both the plaintiff and agent for Class B companies treated the insurance on the wing or addition as specific insurance and supposed the Class A companies did not cover the wing. The agent of Class A companies informed plaintiff no endorsement was necessary, as his policies granted privilege to make additions and to take out other insurance.

After the completion of the wing or addition a fire occurred which damaged the property as follows: East wing (addition), $26,668.50; contents thereof (including $4,500 on students' clothing), $13,250; main building, $1,815.65; contents of main building, $2,332.30.

Held, Loss should be apportioned as follows: Class A companies first pay $1,815.65 on main building, leaving a balance of $218,184.35; and $2,332.30 on contents of main building, leaving a balance on contents of $47,667.70. Class B companies must pay the loss of $4,500 on students' clothing, as those articles are not covered under Class A, hence following apportionment of balance of loss:

	Addition		Contents of Addition.	
	Insures	Pays	Insures	Pays
Class A	$128,184.35	$19,527.94	$47,667.70	$8,231.93
Class B	60,000.00	9,140.56	3,000.00	518.07

Double insurance is, or ought to be, wherever there are two separate insurers, liable for the same loss. The fact that one policy covers more property than the other does not prevent the insurance being double on the subjects covered by both.

Meigs v. London Assur. Co. (U. S. C. C. Eastern Dist. Pa.), 32 Ins. L. J. 251.

The doctrine laid down by U. S. C. C., Eastern Dist. Pa., in the case of Meigs v. London Assur., 32 Ins. L. J., 251, i. e., that Class A Companies covered the addition is borne out by N. Y. C. A. in Arlington v. Colonial Assur. Co., 180 N. Y. 337; 73 N. E. Rep. 34.

PENNSYLVANIA NOT IN ACCORD WITH FEDERAL COURT ON MEIGS RULE.

Pennsylvania S. C. held that Class A policies did not cover the property covered by Class B policies.

Meigs v. Ins. Co., 205 Pa. 378.

MARYLAND.

Where a warehouseman takes out insurance on goods his own, held in trust, or in which he has an interest, the words held in trust will also cover those goods with which he is entrusted in the ordinary sense of the word and not those goods only that are held in trust in a strict technical sense. And where the owner of a part of these goods stored with the warehouseman from whom he has borrowed money on them, takes out insurance on those specific goods, the policies being made payable to the warehouseman in case of loss, such insurance will inure to the benefit of the warehouseman. They will be considered as in favor of the same assured, on the same interest, in the same subject, and against the same risks as the insurance issued directly to the warehouseman; and with the latter policies constitute a double or other insurance; and both sets of policies will contribute their respective proportions of the loss.

Hough v. Peoples F. Ins. Co., 36 Md. 398, 2 Ins. L. J. 353; Home Ins. Co. v. Baltimore W. Ho. Co., 93 U. S. 527, 6 Ins. L. J. 39.

NEW YORK.

The Reading rule is adopted in modified form. That is, where the insurance exceeds the value, it is held the Reading rule works entire equity between the insurers. That rule is where several parcels of property are insured together (blanket) under one policy for one entire sum, and one or each one of these parcels is specifically or separately insured by one or more policies, the sum insured by the more general or blanket policy is to be distributed among the several parcels in the proportion that the value of each parcel of property bears to the aggregate value of all the parcels of property. But where there is no over insurance and where the loss exceeds the aggregate insurance, there is no occasion for any apportionment.

Ogden v. East River Ins. Co., 50 N. Y. 388, 5 Bennett 439, 2 Ins. L. J. 134;

The New York Supreme Court (which is not a court of last resort), citing the Ogden v. East River Ins. Co. as its authority, applied the Finn rule of apportionment, which was applied by the arbitration committee of the New York Board of Fire Underwriters in the instant case (which merely shows how lawyers and courts become confused in applying these intricate rules, and there is no wonder when so few insurance men, who are supposed to understand them, cannot agree on a method, and not all of them even understand the application of a rule when it is explained to them).

Meyer v. American Ins. Co., 4 N. Y. Supp. 617a; appeal dismissed, 23 N. Y. Supp. 71, 18 Ins. L. J. 156.

When There Is No Occasion for Apportionment.

To make this question perfectly clear, we will say there are five parcels of property, which we will designate A, B, C, D, and E. One set of policies is divided into two items. Item No. 1 covers a specific amount on parcel A. Item No. 2 covers a specific amount on parcel B. Another set of policies cover a specific amount under item No. 1 on parcel C, a specific amount under item No. 2 on parcel D. Another set of policies is divided into three items, covering a specific amount each on parcels D and E. Another set of policies cover blanket on parcels A, B and C, another set of policies cover blanket on all of the parcels A, B, C, D and E.

Under such conditions if the loss on all the parcels exceeds the aggregate specific insurance on each and all, and in addition the blanket insurance, there is in the absence of any co-insurance or average clause, no occasion for an apportionment, the loss will be total under all of the policies, whether blanket or specific, according to most of the decisions.

Ogden v. East R. Ins. Co., 50 N. Y. 388; 6 Bennett 439; 2 Ins. L. J. 134;
Niagara F. Ins. Co. v. Heenan, 81 Ill. App. 678;
American C. Ins. Co. v. Heath, 29 Tex. C. A. 445; 69 S. W. 235;
Royal Ins. Co. v. Roedel, 78 Penn. 19; 4 Ins. L. J. 840;
Baltimore F. Ins. Co. v. Loney, 20 Md. 20; 4 Bennett 646;
Hough v. Peoples F. Ins. Co., 36 Md. 398; 2 Ins. L. J. 353;
LeSuer, etc. v. Mutual F. Ins. Co., 101 Iowa 514; 70 N. W. 761;
Anglerodt v. Delaware Ins. Co., 31 Mo. 593; 4 Bennett 589;
Cromie v. Ky. & L. M. Ins. Co., 15 B. Monroe (Ky.) 432; 3 Bennett 785;
Page v. Sun Ins. Office, 20 C. C. A. 397; 36 U. S. Ap. 672; 25 Ins. L. J. 865; 74 Fed. 203;
Liverpool & L. & G. Ins. Co. v. Delta, etc. (Tex. C. C. A.), 121 S W. 599;
Scottish U. & N. Ins. Co. v. Moore (Okla.), 43 Pac. 12;
Meigs v. London Assur. Corp., 126 Fed. 781; 33 Ins. L. J. 251.

Apportionment Under Co-Insurance Clause.

Where the policy is subject to the co-insurance clause (or same thing, the reduced rate agreement), which provides a different method of apportionment if the insurance be less than the amount required under such agreement (the full, or 100 per cent. clause, requires the assured to carry insurance equal to or exceeding the full value of the property. The 90 per cent. clause requiring the insurance to equal or exceed 90 per cent. of the value of the property, the 80 per cent. clause requiring the insurance to equal or exceed 80 per cent. of the value of the property, and so on, down to the 50 per cent. clause), then such policy will pay the loss in accordance with the provision of such co-insurance without regard to the amount apportioned to the other policies. And if the other policies are not subject to the co-insurance clause or reduced rate agreement, they will pay the loss in the proportion that the amount of insurance thereunder bears to the aggregate amount of all the insurance without reference to the co-insurance clause. The amount of loss which the assured bears under one policy by reason of the operation of the co-insurance clause or reduced rate agreement, cannot be added to the liability of the company which has no such clause or agreement in its policy.

Farmers, etc. v. Scottish U. & N. Ins. Co., 173 N. Y. 241; 65 N. E. 1105;
Kansas City, etc. v. American F. Ins. Co., 100 Mo. App. 691; 75 S. W. 186;.
Barnes v. Hartford F. Ins. Co., 3 McCray 22; 9 Fed. 813; 11 Ins. L. J. 110.

Co-Insurance Clause or Reduced Rate Agreement.

Is in conflict with §7023, R. S. Mo. 1909, and therefore void
Alsop v. Continental Ins. Co. (Mo. App.), 162 S. W. 313.

It is void for the same reason in Kentucky and Mississippi.
Sachs v. London & L. Ins. Co., 113 Ky. 88; 67 S. W. 23;
Hartford F. Ins. Co. v. Schlencker, 80 Miss. 667; 32 So. 155.

It is held not to conflict with the Georgia statute, which provides that the full amount of the fire loss, not exceeding the amount of the policy, must be paid by the insurance company, any policy provision to the contrary notwithstanding.
Fireman's Fund Ins. Co. v. Pekor, 106 Ga. 1; 31 S. E. 779.

The co-insurance clause or reduced rate agreement is valid unless in conflict with the statutes.
Peoria F. & M. Ins. Co. v. Wilson, 5 Minn. 3; 4 Bennett 497;
Pennsylvania F. Ins. Co. v. Moore, 21 Tex. C. A. 528; 51 S. W. 878;
Armour v. Reading F. Ins. Co., 67 Mo. App. 215;
Chesebrough v. Home Ins. Co., 61 Mich. 333; 28 N. W. 110; 15 Ins. L. J. 515;
Quinn v. Fire Assct., 180 Mass. 560; 62 N. E. 980;
Barnes v. Hartford F. Ins. Co., 9 Fed. 813; 11 Ins. L. J. 110.

The Average or Distribution Clause.

The following clause was held to apply at the time the policy was issued, but not at the time of the loss, which occurred some time after the issuance of the policy. But, the court added, the insurance company could have made it to apply at the time of the fire had it chosen so to write it. The form on which the decision was based is as follows:

"It is hereby agreed that in case of loss this policy shall attach in or on each building or division in such proportion as the value in or on each building or division bears to the aggregate of the subjects insured."

Scottish U. & N. Ins. Co. v. Moore (Okla.), 143 Pac. 12.

It was held otherwise as to almost identically the same clause in Missouri and Iowa, where it seems it does not conflict with the statute law prohibiting the use of the co-insurance or other clause providing for the payment of a sum less than the loss.

U. S. Cooperage Co. v. Fireman's Fund Ins. Co. (Mo. App.), 174 S. W. 193;
Dahms v. German F. Ins. Co. (Iowa S. C.), 132 N. W. 870.

Three-Quarter Clause.

The three-fourths clause is valid.
Coffey v. East Tex. Ins. Co., 61 Tex. 287.

But it is not valid when in conflict with the statutes.
Queen v. Jefferson Ice Co., 64 Tex. 578, 15 Ins. L. J. 109;
Darden v. L. & L. & G. Ins. Co. (Miss. S. C.), 68 So. 485.

FORMS SUGGESTED AS COMPLYING WITH THE OKLAHOMA COURT'S SUGGESTIONS.

Average Clause. It is understood and agreed that this insurance shall at the happening of any loss cover and attach in or on each building or location in the proportion that the value in or on each building or location shall at that time bear to the aggregate value of the property insured in or on all of within described buildings or locations. If this policy be divided into two or more items, the foregoing average clause shall apply to each item separately.

Full or 100% Co-Insurance Clause. It is understood and agreed that in case of loss or damage by fire, this company shall not be liable for any greater proportion thereof than the amount hereby insured shall then bear to 50, 75, 80, 90 or any other per cent. of (as the case may be if you want a 50, 75, 80 or 90 per cent. clause) the whole cash value of the property hereby insured, and in no event shall this company be liable for a greater proportion of any loss on the described property than the amount hereby insured shall bear to the whole insurance, whether valid or not, or by solvent or insolvent insurers, covering such property. If this policy be divided into two or more items the foregoing co-insurance clause shall apply to each item separately.

Reduced Rate Agreement. In consideration of the rate of premium at which this policy is written it is expressly stipulated and made a condition of this contract that this company shall not be liable for a greater proportion of any loss than the amount hereby insured shall then bear to (50, 75, 80 or 90 per cent. of as the case may be) the whole cash value of the property hereby insured, and in no event shall this company be liable for a greater proportion of any loss on the described property, than the amount hereby insured shall bear to the whole insurance, whether valid or not, or by solvent or insolvent insurers, covering such property. If this policy be divided into two or more items the foregoing reduced rate agreement shall apply to each item separately.

While there is a slight difference in the phraseology there is none in the result of the application of the co-insurance and the reduced rate agreement. The assured collects the same amount under each. The object of both is the same, to force the assured to carry a reasonable amount of insurance. A clause not worded like our full value co-insurance clause, but having the same effect, is used in Germany, France and England.

CO INSURANCE AND AVERAGE CLAUSES

The following report made by the Committee on Fire Insurance to the National Association of Credit Men, and a reply thereto by the author, gives two views upon the subject of co-insurance and the workings of co-insurance and average clauses:

"Average Clause in Blanket Insurance Not Recommended."

"One of the members of a California Association has written to this committee, and submitted what is known as an Average Clause, which is a rider attached to a Blanket Insurance Policy, whereby stocks and merchandise in two separate buildings are supposed to be insured jointly. He has requested that a detailed explanation be furnished as to the settlement which would be effected in the event of loss on either or both properties.

"The principal clause in this Average Clause rider, reads as follows:

" 'It is hereby understood and agreed that in case of loss this policy shall attach in each of the two buildings in such proportion as the value in each building bears to the aggregate value of the property hereby insured.'

"This clause alone, in the event of a fire or total loss would mean the loss of considerable money to the party insured, and we would explain the matter in the following manner:

"The clause referred to in this form is what is known as the Average Clause. Its chief effect is to eliminate the blanket feature from what might otherwise be a blanket form, and really transforms a blanket form into a specific one.

"The practical workings of this Clause are as follows: Suppose the insured had two buildings, A and B, with a total value therein of $10,000 and total insurance of $10,000. If the values in building A and building B are equal, namely, $5,000 each, the recovery under this set of facts would be full, namely, in a loss on building B the insured would recover under the terms of the clause 5-10 or ½ of the amount of insurance, or $5,000, which really amounts to two specific items of $5,000 each on the contents of each building.

"If the values were $6,000 in building A and $4,000 in building B and the amount of insurance equal to the aggregate value, the recovery would still be in full, and not be affected by this clause.

"Suppose, however, that the aggregate value were $15,000, distributed as follows: Building A, $10,000 and building B, $5,000, with total insurance of $10,000. In this case, in a total loss on building B the insured would recover one-third of the amount of insurance, or $3,333.33, and in the same proportion on building A. Without this clause the insured would recover the full amount of $5,000 in a loss on building B, and could in any case recover the full amount of his insurance and would only lose the difference between the amount of insurance and the aggregate value. Many persons carry a blanket form with this clause inserted, and labor under the impression that they have all the advantages of a blanket form, whereas in reality it is a specific form. It can be also seen that it differs radically from flat insurance.

"We, therefore, feel justified in stating that in the event of a total loss, the insured would be able to recover a far greater proportion of his loss if he would carry either co-insurance or straight insurance than he would be able to recover under the present conditions with this Average Clause attached, and we hope that our members will investigate their insurance, and be satisfied that this clause would operate against them in the event of a loss.   Yours very truly,

"FIRE INSURANCE COMMITEE,

·"Geo. W. Ryan,

"Chairman."

Chicago, Ill., March 20, 1907

Editor "Bulletin National Association of Credit Men," 41 Park Row, New York:

Dear Sir—I notice an article in the March "Bulletin," under title, "Average Clause in Blanket Insurance Not Recommended," and the statement is signed, "Fire Insurance Commitee, Geo. W. Ryan, Chairman."

Answering the statement in seventh paragraph, will say Mr. pany will insure a stock contained in two separate and distinct buildings, without either the average clause, or at least a 90 per cent. co-insurance clause, and in most instances they would insist on writing the policy with either the average or full value co-insurance clause. Otherwise, by issuing a $5,000 policy they would be carrying double liability for one premium.

Answering the statement in seventh paragraph, will say Mr. Ryan is right in his statement, that with value in building A $10,000. Value in building B $5,000. Insurance $10,000, blanket policy covering both buildings with the average clause, the policy would pay $3,333.33 in case building B's contents were totally destroyed.

If any company were foolish enough to write a blanket policy without an average clause, but containing an 80 per cent. co-insurance clause, the assured would recover the loss in proportion as his insurance of $10,000 would bear to 80 per cent. of the value, or $12,000, or 10/12, equalling $4,166.66.

Under the 90 per cent. co-insurance clause he would recover in proportion as his insurance would bear to 90 per cent. of the value or 100/135, equalling $3,703.70.

Under the 100 per cent. or full co-insurance clause, he would recover in proportion as his insurance would bear to the full value, or 10/15, equalling $3,333.33.

But suppose with the same insurance and same values the loss in building B was only $3,333.33, and the value of the salvage was $1,666.67, then we find that under the average clause the assured would collect $3,333.33.

Under the 80 per cent. co-insurance clause he would collect $2,777.77.

Under the 90 per cent. co-insurance clause he would collect $2,466.67.

Under the full co-insurance clause he would collect $2,222.22.

Here is an example of the workings of the 90 per cent. co-insurance clause:

Insurance Co. insures	$10,000	Pays	$2,466.67
Assured co-insures	3,500	Pays	866.66
Insurance required under 90 per cent. clause	$13,500	Pays	$3,333.33

Suppose that with what Mr. Ryan calls "flat insurance" (the term is new to me, but I presume he means specific insurance), of say $5,000 in each building, a fire should entirely destroy the contents of both, the assured's books would show the aggregate value of the stock in both buildings, but there would be no way of telling how much was in each. Hence, how much does the Chicago Insurance Company owe and how much does the New York Insurance Company owe? With the average clause, both companies' interests are identical and both know they must pay a total loss. Truly yours,

THRASHER HALL.

WISCONSIN RULE.

The insured is entitled to full indemnity under his contract, and a rule of apportionment which fails to furnish this is error.

The Insurance.

Company A insured on live stock $1,500, no limitation. Company B insured on live stock $1,667, being not to exceed $500 on any one animal. Company C insured on live stock $1,667, no one animal to be valued at more than $500.

The Loss.

One bull, $2,000; three steers, $336; total loss $2,336.
The companies first pay the loss on the three steers.

	Insures	Pays
Company A	$1,500	$104.00
Company B	1,667	116.00
Company C	1,667	116.00
	$4,834	$336.00

Company A pays $1,345 on bull, Company B pays $482, and Company C $173 (in round numbers).

Sherman v. Madison M. Ins. Co., 39 Wis. 104; 5 Ins. L. J. 285.

CANADIAN (OR ALBANY RULE).

The defendant insured $2,000 on building and $2,000 on furniture, the British America insured $2,000 in one amount covering blanket on building and furniture. There was a partial loss to both building and furniture. The defendant was held for two-thirds the loss.

Trustees First Unitarian Church v. Western Assur. Co., 26 Upper Can. 2 B. 175; 5 Bennett 94.

FLOATING POLICY.

Floating or excess insurance will not contribute in the payment of any loss on property until such property is brought within its protection.

Peabody v. Liverpool & L. & G. Ins. Co., 171 Mass. 114; 50 N. E. 526.

When a Specific Policy is Exhausted.

A specific policy is exhausted when neither the loss nor the policy is paid in full by reason of a co-insurance or other clause which may have the effect of limiting the amount to be paid under such policy.

Cutting, Ins. Comr. v. Atlas M. Ins. Co. In re. Downs, 199 Mass. 380; 85 N. E. 174; 37 Ins. L. J. 924.

READING RULE.
Value to Value.

The compound or blanket policy will be made to cover as many parcels, groups or items of property as are fixed by specific insurance, in the proportion that the value of each parcel, item or group of property. For instance, if stock be insured specifically under policy of Company A, which also insures a specific amount on furniture and fixtures, and a third specific amount on machinery, this makes three items, parcels or groups. Therefore, Company B's policy, which insures all of these items, parcels or groups under a single sum, is called a blanket or compound policy. The Reading rule makes this blanket policy cover on each item in proportion as the value of each bears to the aggregate value of all three items, and the amounts thus found will contribute with the specific insurance on each item in the payment of the loss thereon.

In the opinion of the author there is very little reason in this apportionment and it is an arbitrary, unfair rule. Nothing in the policy contract provides for any such rule of apportionment, and it is liable to cause the assured to lose heavily. Why blanket insurance should be made to cover the several items in a different method from what they would ordinarily, merely because there was other insurance which separated these blanket items by covering them specifically, is beyond the writer's knowledge. The Federal Courts and those of Missouri, Maryland and Connecticut have adopted the most equitable rule, and the only one which seems to the writer to be in accordance with the idea that assured must not bear any part of his loss so long as there is enough insurance to pay it. However, it has the approval of the courts of Massachusetts and Vermont.

FINN RULE.

Substitute the word loss wherever the word value appears in the Reading rule and you have this rule, i. e., the blanket policy covers each item, parcel or group of property, in proportion as the loss on each group, item or parcel of property bears to the aggregate loss on all of the groups, items or parcels of property, and the amounts thus found will pro rate with the specific insurance on each group, item or parcel. There will be as many groups, items or parcels as there are specific items in the specific policy on which there is a loss, and sometimes one more, as where one policy insures a specific amount on' stock, and a specific amount on store furniture, and the blanket or compound policy insures both of these items, groups or parcels as well as another group consisting of machinery.

This rule seems more in line with the Page rule, but differs from the Cromie and Missouri rule in that it does not first pay the loss on the items covered only by the blanket policy and the remainder or unexhausted amount is not then made to pro rate with the specific policy in paying the loss on the other items. This rule is the first rule of apportionment of the Kinne rule, which has been approved and agreed to by all of the insurance companies operating west of the Rocky Mountains. It seems the Finn rule is used in the New York Board of Fire Underwriters. See Meyer v. American Ins. Co., 23 N. Y. Supp. 71; 18 Ins. L. J. 156.

If the loss is on but one item, group or parcel of property, the Finn rule makes the entire blanket or compound policy contribute with the specific policy, and therein it conforms to the Page rule.

ALBANY RULE.

This rule means, that in so far as the assured is concerned,

that in dealing with each company all other insurance, to its
full amount, must be treated as other contributing insurance.
To illustrate: If Company A's policy covered $1,000 on house-
hold furniture, Company B's policy covered $1,000 on house-
hold furniture and wearing apparel, and Company C's policy
covered $1,000 on household furniture, wearing apparel and
jewelry. The loss being $1,000 on furniture, $500 on wearing
apparel, $500 on jewelry. Under the Albany rule there would be
three apportionments. First, Company A would apportion the
loss as follows:

	Insures on Furniture	Pays on Furniture
Company A	$1,000	$333.33
Company B	1,000	333.33
Company C	1,000	333.34
Totals	$3,000	$1,000.00

Company B would apportion the loss as follows:

	Insures on Furniture & Wearing Apparel	Pays on Furniture & Wearing Apparel
Company A	$1,000	$500.00
Company B	1,000	500.00
Company C	1,000	500.00
Totals	$3,000	$1,500.00

Company C would apportion the loss as follows:

	Insures on Jewelry Furniture & Wearing Apparel	Pays on Jewelry Furniture & Wearing Apparel
Company A	$1,000	$666.66 2/3
Company B	1,000	666.66 2/3
Company C	1,000	666.66 2/3
Totals	$3,000	$2,000.00

Under this apportionment the insured would receive from
Company A, as per its apportionment, $333.33. From Company
B, as per its apportionment, $500. From Company C, as per its
apportionment, $666.67, or a total of $1,500 for his loss of
$2,000.

This apportionment may seem very unfair, but it is in accord with the New York standard policy provision, which reads: "This company shall not be liable under this policy for a greater proportion of any loss on the described property than the amount hereby insured shall bear to the whole insurance whether valid or not, or by solvent or insolvent insurers." The standard policies of other states are not materially different. The only construction that can be placed on the language of the policy is that given it in the Albany rule. Where two separate companies are liable for the same loss, the fact that one of them covers more property and in more locations than the other does not give it the right to have less than its policy pro rate with the more specific policy in paying the loss.

Liverpool & L. & G. Ins. Co. v. Delta, etc. (Tex. C. C. A.), 121 S. W. 599;
Scottish U. & N. Ins. Co. v. Moore (Okla.), 143 Pac. 12;
Page v. Sun . Office, 20 C. C. A. 397; 36 U. S. App. 672; 25 Ins. L. J. 865Ins

Giving a correct construction to the language of the contribution provision of the policy quoted above, and applying the reasoning of the courts in the foregoing cases, how can a result be reached differing with the Albany rule?

FINN RULE.

Applying the Finn rule to the loss stated in the preceding case illustrating the Albany rule, we get the following result.

	Insures on Furniture	Pays on Furniture	Insures on Wear. Ap.	Pays on Wear. Ap.
Company A	$1,000.00	$ 461.53		
Company B	666.67	307.70	$333.33	$285.71
Company C	500.00	230.77	250.00	214.29
Totals	$2,166.67	$1,000.00	$583.33	$500.00

	Insures Jewelry	Pays on Jewelry
Company C insures jewelry alone for.......	$250.00	$250.00

KINNE RULE.

Applying the Kinne rule, we get the following result:

As the loss to loss method of the Finn rule does not pay but half the loss on jewelry, we must take enough of Company C's policy to pay the $500 loss on that group, parcel or item (i. e., jewelry). Company B's policy and the $500 unexhausted insurance under Company C's policy is then made to apply on furniture proportionately as the loss on that group of property, $1,000, bears to aggregate loss on that group, and the group consisting of wearing apparel (on which the loss is $500), or a total on both groups of $1,500. The loss on furniture being two-thirds of the whole loss on furniture and wearing apparel, and the loss on wearing apparel being one-third of this whole loss, two-thirds of Company B's policy, or $666.67, and of the remaining $500 under Company C's policy, or $333.33, covers furniture; one-third of Company B's policy, or $333.33, and one-third of the remainder under Company C's policy, or $166.67, covers wearing apparel, the loss is, therefore, re-apportioned as follows:

Company A insures furniture......$1,000.00	Pays...$	500.00
Company B insures furniture...... 666.67	Pays...	333.33
Company C insures furniture...... 333.33	Pays...	166.67
Company B insures wearing apparel 333.33	Pays...	333.33
Company C insures wearing apparel 166.67	Pays...	166.67
Company C insures jewelry....... 500.00	Pays...	500.00

Assured therefore collects........................$2,000.00

CROMIE RULE.

Applying the Cromie (Kentucky and Missouri) rule, i. e., "the more general policies first pay the loss not covered by the other policies, leaving the remainder or unexhausted amount to pro rate with the other insurance in paying the balance of the loss," we obtain the following result:

Company C-first pays the $500 loss on jewelry, which is not insured by either Company A or B. The unexhausted amount of Company C's policy, i. e., $500, pro rates with Company B's $1,000 policy in paying the loss of $1,000 on wearing apparel, Company B paying two-thirds of the loss, or $333.33, and Company C paying one-third, or $166.66. This leaves Company B with $666.66 unexhausted insurance and Company C with $166.66 to pro rate with Company A's $1,000 to pay the $1,000 loss on furniture, Company A, therefore, pays $545.46, Company B pays on furniture $363.63, Company C pays on furniture $90.91.

CONNECTICUT AND NEW JERSEY RULE.

Under the New Jersey and Connecticut rule, "the blanket

policy pays the largest loss first, the second largest loss next and so on until the entire loss is paid, but states there can be no fixed rule to govern all cases." Hence the following apportionment: The largest loss being on furniture, each policy is made to pay that loss first, and each policy being for $1,000 and the loss being $1,000, each pays on that item, $333.33. The next step is for Company C, with its $666.67 unexhausted insurance, to pay the $500 loss on jewelry, which neither of the other companies insure, thus leaving it with $166.67 unexhausted insurance to pro rate with Company B's $666.67 unexhausted insurance to pay $500 loss on wearing apparel, not insured by Company A, but which is insured by Companies B and C, hence Company B pays on wearing apparel $400 and Company C $100.

WISCONSIN RULE.

Under the Wisconsin rule, the smallest loss is first paid by the more general or blanket policy; applying that rule we get the following result: The smallest loss to the companies in the instant case would be wearing apparel, as there are two companies to pay it, whereas there is but one to pay the jewelry loss, the loss on both items being the same, i. e., $500. Both Companies B and C have $1,000 insurance each, so that each pays $250 on wearing apparel. The next smallest loss being on jewelry, Company C pays the whole $500, that item not being insured by either of the other policies.

This leaves $750 unexhausted insurance under Company B's policy, and $250 unexhausted insurance under Company C's policy to pro rate with Company A's $1,000 policy in paying the $1,000 loss on furniture. So that company having half the insurance, pays $500. Company B having 37½ per cent., pays $375, and Company C having 12½ per cent., pays $125 on the furniture.

READING RULE.

In order to apply the Reading rule, we must assume values; we will therefore assume the whole value was $4,000, the value of the furniture being $3,000, with a loss of $1,000, the value and loss being $500 each on jewelry and wearing apparel. Company B's liability being fixed on furniture and wearing apparel proportionate to value, and Company C's on those two items and jewelry in the same manner.

	Furniture		Wearing Apparel		Jewelry	
	Insures	Pays	Insures	Pays	Insures	Pays
Co. A...	$1,000.00	$ 383.57				
Co. B...	857.14	328.76	$142.86	$142.86		
Co. C...	750.00	287.67	125.00	125.00	$125.00	$125.00
	$2,627.14	$1,000.00	$267.86	$267.86	$125.00	$125.00

RECAPITULATION OF NET RESULTS OF THE VARIOUS RULES, APPLIED TO THE SAME LOSS.

The Value and Loss.

	Value	Loss
Household furniture ...	$3,000	$1,000
Wearing Apparel	500	500
Jewelry	500	500
Totals	$4,000	$2,000

The Insurance

	Furniture	Wearing Apparel	Jewelry
Company A	$1,000	Nil	Nil
Specific on furniture			
Company B	$1,000		Nil
Blanket on furniture and wearing apparel.			
Company C		$1,000	
Blanket on furniture, wearing apparel and jewelry.			

Reading Rule.

Company A pays....................................	$ 383.57
Company B pays....................................	471.62
Company C pays....................................	537.67
Total	$1,392.86

Assured loses $607.14.

Albany Rule.

Company A pays....................................	$ 333.33
Company B pays....................................	500.00
Company C pays....................................	666.67
Total	$1,500.00

Assured loses $500.

Finn Rule.

Company A pays......................................$ 461.53
Company B pays......................................   593.41
Company C pays......................................   464.21

Total $1,519.15
Assured loses $480.77.

Kinne Rule.

Company A pays......................................$ 500.00
Company B pays......................................   666.67
Company C pays......................................   833.33

Total $2,000.00
Assured loses nothing.

Wisconsin Rule.

Company A pays................................ ..$ 500.00
Company B pays................................   625.00
Company C pays................................   ..   875.00

Total $2,000.00
Assured loses nothing.

New Jersey and Connecticut Rule.

Company A pays......................................$ 333.33
Company B pays.......................... ....   733.34
Company C pays......................................   933.33

Total $2,000.00
Assured loses nothing.

Cromie, or Kentucky and Missouri United States Rule.

Company A pays......................................$ 545.46
Company B pays......................................   696.96
Company C pays......................................   757.58

Total $2,000.00
Assured loses nothing.

The author, as already stated, is of the opinion that if the provisions of the contract are to be followed, the Albany rule should govern. Of course, this works a hardship on the assured, but the contract in each policy provides that it shall pay in proportion as its policy bears to the total insurance. The fact that some other policy covers other property does not give the assured the right to have that part lopped off from contribution.

If the contract is not to be followed, pay your money and take your choice of any of the foregoing rules. It would seem to the author if the courts and insurance men depart from the contract, then the thing to do is take that rule which is the simplest and the easiest to apply, or the complicated Kinne rule. The assured will collect his full loss under either as long as there is any insurance unexhausted which will cover his loss. It will require a very competent expert to apply the Kinne rule in some cases, but not in a simple case like that in the foregoing example, but in the preceding example the Cromie rule comes nearer equalizing the amounts paid by the several companies than does any of the others.

The Kinne rule and some examples of its workings by its author follow:

THE KINNE RULE.
The Principle.

The principle governing all apportionments of non-concurrent policies is that general and specific insurances must be regarded as co-insurances; and general insurance must float over and contribute to loss on all subjects under its protection, in the proportions of the respective losses thereon, until the insured is indemnified, or the policy exhausted.

Steps to be Taken.

The correct method of applying the principle has been formulated in the following:

First—Ascertain the non-concurrence of the various policies and classify the various items covered, into as many groups as the non-concurrence demands, whether of property, location or ownership.

Second—Ascertain the loss on each group of items separately.

Third—If but a single group is found with a loss upon it, the amount of all policies covering the group contribute pro rata.

Fourth—If more than one group has sustained a loss, and such loss on one or more groups be equal to or greater than the totals of general and specific insurance thereon, then let the whole amount of such insurances apply to the payment of loss on such groups.

Apportionment.

Fifth—If more than one group has sustained a loss, and such loss be more than the totals of unexhausted general and specific insurances thereon, then apportion the amount of each policy covering on such groups generally, to cover specifically on each group, in the same proportion that the sum of the losses on such groups bears to the loss on each individual group.

Note.—When a group is covered by one or more general policies it would be well to see at once if an apportionment as above on that group would equal the loss, as in case it will not, it will show, without further calculation, that the whole amount of loss on such group must be met by such policies pro rata, and the remainder only apportioned. In such cases, carrying out step 6 simply accomplishes by a longer process what is indicated above.

Reapportionment

Sixth—If the loss on any group or groups is then found to be greater than the sum of the now specific insurance is apportioned, add sufficient to such specific insurances to make up the loss on the group, taking the amount of the deficiency from the now specific insurances of the heretofore general amounts previously covering the now deficient groups, which cover on groups having an excess of insurance, in the proportion that their sums bear to their individual amounts.

Note.—Very rarely are new deficiencies created by the reapportionment, but if so, repeat step 6.

Seventh—Cause the amounts of all the now specific insuranecs to severally contribute pro rata to pay the partial losses, and it will be found that the whole scheme has resulted in the claimant being fully indemnified in accordance with the various contracts and on a basis which preserves the equity between the companies throughout.

The Argument.

Mr. Griswold says that "it is only a question of how to properly apply a proportional rule to cause it to become entirely general," and in this connection I beg attention to the following, in which the theory of evolution is plainly evident.

Rules.

Reading...........Value to Value.

Finn..............Loss to Loss—no reapportionment.

Albany............Insurance to Insurance.

Rule IV...........Insurance to Value.

National Board.....Value to Value—Value to Insurance.

Griswold..........Loss to Ins.—Loss to Loss—Ins. to Ins.

Kinne.............Loss to Loss—Loss to Loss—Loss to Loss.

Compound policies give rise to three general classes of problems, viz.: When their non-concurrency is Partial, General or Mixed.

SOME PRACTICAL WORKINGS OF THE KINNE RULE.

The following examples, if thoroughly analyzed, will enable the adjuster more fully to understand the propriety and unchanging equity of the rule:

Example 1.

Example, Page 732, Text Book (Griswold).

Groups	A	B	C	D	Ins. to Pay.
School Books......				5,000	8,000
Other Books......			5,000		2,000
Stationery.........	10,000	5,000			3,500
Pictures...........					500
Fancy Goods......					2,000
	10,000	5,000	5,000	5,000 25,000	16,000

2-16 of $10,000 is less than $2,000, required to pay loss on fancy goods, we have $2,000 of A to pay loss on fancy goods. Dividing the remaining $8,000 of A and the $5,000 each of B and C as stated in step 5, we have the following:

Apportionment.

Groups	A	B	C	D	Ins.	To pay	Def.
School Books	4,571.41	2,857.16	2,962.96	5,000	15,391.53	8,000	
Other Books	1,142.87	714.28	740.74		2,597.89	2,000	
Stationery	2,000.00	1,250.00	1,296.30		4,546.30	3,500	
Pictures	285.72	178.56			464.28	500	35.72
Fancy Goods	2,000.00				2,000.00	2,000	
Totals	10,000.00	5,000.00	5,000.00	5,000	25,000.00	16,000	35.72

The deficiency of $35.72 on pictures is made up under step 6, by taking pro rata sums from the now specific amounts of A and B, which have an excess of insurance, which is quickly done, and we have the following:

Reapportionment.

Groups	A	B	C	D	Ins.	To pay
School Books	4,558.38	2,849.02	2,962.96	5,000.00	15,370.36	8,000
Other Books	1,139.62	712.24	740.74		2,592.60	2,000
Stationery	1,994.30	1,246.44	1,296.30		4,537.04	3,500
Pictures	307.70	192.30			500.00	500
Fancy Goods	2,000.00				2,000.00	2,000
Totals	10,000.00	5,000.00	5,000.00	5,000.00	25,000.00	16,000
Paying	7,098.45	3,686.60	3,112.31	2,602.64	16,500.00	16,000
Saving	2,901.55	1,813.40	1,887.69	2,397.36	9,000.00	

Example 2.

An actual case of recent date.

Apportionment.

Item 1. Hotel	1,000	1,000	1,000.00	666.67	1,666.67	400
Item 2. Hall			270.27	333.33	603.60	200
Item 3. Addition	500	100	108.11	66.67	174.78	80
Item 4. Coops			54.06	33.33	87.39	40
Item 5. Barn			67.56		67.56	50
	1,500	1,100	1,500.00	1,100.00	2,600.00	770

A covers $1,000 on Item No. 1, and $500 on Items Nos. 2, 3, 4 and 5; B covers $1,000 on Items Nos. 1 and 2, and $100 on Items Nos. 3 and 4.

CHAPTER XVI.

COURT DEFINITIONS OF INSURANCE TERMS.

"This entire policy, unless otherwise provided by agreement hereon, or added hereto, shall be void * * * if (any usage or custom of trade or manufacture to the contrary notwithstanding) there be kept, used or allowed, on the above described premises, benzine, benzole, dynamite, ether, fireworks, gasoline, greek fire, gun powder, exceeding twenty-five pounds in quantity, naphtha, nitroglycerine or other explosives, phosporus, * * *"

"Premises" means the building insured or containing the property insured and not the yard or other buildings adjacent thereto.

Allemannia Fire Ins. Co. v. Pittsburg Expo. Co. (Pa. S. C.), 11 Atl. Rep. 572;
Sperry v. Ins. Co. of N. A. (U. S. C. C.), 14 Ins. L. J. 141; 22 Fed. Rep. 516;
Rau v. Westchester F. Ins. Co. (N. Y. S. C.), 36 N. Y. S. C. App. Div. 516; 28 Ins. L. J. 182;
Fireman's Fund Ins. Co. v. Shearman, 20 Tex. C. C. A. 243, 50 S. W. Rep. 598;
Thomas v. Hartford F. Ins. Co. (Ky. C. A.), 53 S. W. Rep. 297;
Northwestern Mut. Life. Ins. Co. v. Germania F. Ins. Co., 40 Wis. 446.

When the use of any such prohibited articles is usual and necessary in the conduct of the insured's business, or, if they be usually kept in similar establishments, it will not avoid the policy. On the doctrine that when a repugnancy exists between the written portion of the policy or rider attached thereto, and the printed conditions of the policy, the provisions of the rider or written portion will prevail. It would be an absurdity to say that a policy is void because of the keeping of such prohibited articles, when the policy itself insured them, as for instance, "on stock of paints, oil, varnishes and other articles usually kept in a paint shop," and by insuring them it is "otherwise provided by agreement, indorsed on the policy," that such articles may be kept on the premises.

Plinsky v. Germania Ins. Co. (U. S. C. C.), 32 Fed. Rep. 47;
Faust v. American F. Ins. Co. (Wis. S. C.), 64 N. W. Rep. 883;
Maril v. Connecticut F. Ins. Co. (Ga. S. C.), 23 S. E. Rep. 463;
Fink v. Lancashire F. Ins. Co., 60 Mo. App. 673;

Tubb v. L. & L. & G. Ins. Co. (Ala. S. C.), 17 Southern Rep. 615;
Yoch v. Home Mut. Ins. Co. (Cal. S. C.), 44 Pacif. Rep. 189;
Fraim v. National F. Ins. Co. (Pa. S. C.), 32 Atl. Rep. 613;
Mascot v. Granite State F. Ins. Co. (Vt. S. C.), 35 Atl. Rep. 75;
Barnard v. National F. Ins. Co., 27 Mo. App. 26;
Phoenix Ins. Co. v. Fleming et al. (Ark. S. C.), 27 Ins. L. J. 584;
    44 S. W. Rep. 464;
Amer. Cent'l Ins. Co. v. Green et al. (Tex. C. C. A.), 41 S. W
    Rep. 74;
Davis v. Pioneer Furn. Co. (Wis. S. C.), 28 Ins. L. J. 474; 78
    N. W. Rep. 596;
Ackley v. Phenix Ins. Co. (Mont. S. C.), 64 Pacif. Rep. 665;
Traders Ins. Co. v. Dobbins (Tenn. S. C.), 86 S. W. Rep. 383;
Haley v. Dorchester M. Ins. Co., 12 Gray 545;
Collins v. Farmville Ins. & Bkg. Co., 79 N. C. 279;
Baumgartner v. Ins. Co., 1 W. N. C. (Penn.), 119.

It is not admissible to show custom among merchants to keep such prohibited articles in limited quantities as part of the stock.

Beer v. Ins. Co., 39 Ohio St. 109;
Birmingham F. Ins. Co. v. Kroegher, 83 Pa. St. 64;
Lancaster F. Ins. Co. v. Lenheim, 89 Pa. St. 497;
Mason v. Hartford F. Ins. Co., 29 Up. Can. Q. B. 585;
Western Assur. Co. v. Rector, 9 Ky. Law Rep. 3.

It is for the jury to determine whether such prohibited articles were included in the description of the property insured.

Carrington v. Lycoming F. Ins. Co., 53 Vt. 418;
Niagara F. Ins. Co. v. De Groff, 12 Mich. 124.

It is not sufficient to show that the prohibited article was one usual to the trade; it must be shown that it is included in the specific words used to describe the property insured.

Liverpool & L. & G. Ins. Co. v. Van Os., 63 Miss. 431.

"Mechanics" as used in a policy does not mean common painters, and a condition rendering policy void if "gasoline be kept, used or allowed in the building" does not prevent the keeping in the building of gasoline to be used in the filling of gasoline torches for use by painters in removing paint from the building. (The fire originated in cornice about fifteen feet from where painter had last used the torch.) The use of such torch does not, as a matter of law, increase the hazard.

Smith, County Treasurer, v. German Ins. Co. (Mich. S. C.), 25
    Ins. L. J. 192; 65 N. W. Rep. 236.

As to definition of total loss and rights of insured in party wall, see N. W. Mut. Life Ins. Co. v. Ins. Cos., 88 N. W. Rep. 265 and 272.

"Fire-proof safe" means a safe of the kind generally known as fire-proof.

Knoxville F. Ins. Co. v. Hird (Tex. C. C. A.), 23 S. W. Rep. 393;
23 Ins. L. J. 16.

"Plate" does not mean articles of common or ordinary use such as silver forks or spoons, but only the more pretentious articles which are displayed on the tables of the wealthy or ostentations, and which are to be considered rather as articles of luxury than as household furniture.

Hanover F. Ins. Co. v. Manassen (Mich. S. C.), 3 Ins. L. J. 668.

"Store" means shop and includes a bakery or restaurant.

Richards v. Washington Ins. Co., 60 Mich. 420.

"£250· Insurance against any one accident." (One of the plaintiff's cars overturned, injuring forty persons) means that £250 is the limit of liability for accident to any one person, and that, if more than one is hurt, plaintiff may recover for its liability not exceeding £250 to each person.

South Staffordshire Tramways Co., Ltd. v. Sickness & Accident Ass'n, Ltd. (Eng. C. A. Q. B. Div.), 1 Queen's Bench Div. Law Reports (March 2, 1891), 402.

"Any and all risks and perils of fire, and inland navigation, and transportation, while on vessels, steam-boats, railroads, or in hotels, stores, or depots in the United States, and while in custody of the assured or traveling salesman. The printed conditions of the policy providing that the insurer would be liable for loss to the property insured laden on board the good vessel or vessels, boat or boats, railroad or carriages, lost or not lost, at and from port or places, to ports and places on a regular and lawful route, named herein," covers a loss to the property from water wetting the goods where the salesman with the goods in a carriage, crossed a stream at the usual place of crossing.

Kratzenstein v. Western Assur. Co. (N. Y. C. A.), 22 N. E. Rep. 221.

"Subject to three-fourths value clause" is meaningless, there being nothing in the policy to explain the meaning thereof, furnishes no intelligent agreement for the court to construe.

Parks et/al. v. Hartford F. Ins. Co. (Mo. S. C.), 12 S. W. Rep. 1058.

"Concurrent insurance" is that which to any extent insures the same interest, against the same casualty, at the same time, and that would bear the loss proportionately with the primary insurance.

New Jersey Rubber Co. v. Commercial U. Assur. Co. (N. J. C. E. and A.), 46 Atl. Rep. 777.

"Their own, held in trust or on commission," plaintiff must show that he adopted warehouseman's act in procuring such insurance, and so notified him, before he can claim any benefit under a policy issued to defendant.

Pittman v. Harris (Tex. C. C. A.), 59 S. W. Rep. 1121.

"Plate glass in windows and doors, the dimensions whereof are nine square feet or more," does not mean a plate glass front which was immovable and stationary, though the glass therein was of greater dimensions than nine square feet.

Hale v. Springfield F. & M. Ins. Co., 46 Mo. App. 508.

"Sporting House," has an innocent as well as a guilty meaning. Without proof of the sense in which it was used, it does not show conclusively that premises were occupied for unlawful purposes.

White v. Western Assur. Co. (Minn. S. C.), 54 N. W. Rep. 195; 22 Ins. L. J. 305.

"Gasoline clause in policy," the word "allowed" is to be construed as meaning "allowed to be kept or used," and the condition is not violated by merely permitting gasoline to be carried through the building on the premises.

London & Lanc. F. Ins. Co. v. Fischer (U. S. C. C. A. 6th Cir.), 92 Fed. Rep. 500.

"$750 on building on lot 6; $250 on boiler contained therein; $1,000 on machinery, patterns and other tools," will include patterns not in the building.

Aetna Ins. Co. v. Strout, 16 Ind. App. 160; 44 N. E. Rep. 934.

"Adjacent" means "near," "close," "in proximity."

Hanover F. Ins. Co. et al. v. Stoddard et al. (Neb. S. C.), 27 Ins. L. J. 120 ; 73 N. W. Rep. 291.

"$3,300 on horses being not over $110 per head," does not limit the risk to 30 head of horses.

Springfield F. & M. Ins. Co. v. Crozier (Ky. Super. Ct.), 12 Ky. L. J. 143.

"$2,500 total concurrent insurance permitted" in a policy for $2,500 held to mean assured could take out $5,000 total insurance.

L'Engle v. Scottish U. & N. F. Ins. Co. (Fla. S. C.), 37 S. W. Rep. 462.

"Twelve o'clock noon" means the common or solar time.

Grabbs v. Farmers Mut. F. Ins. Assn. (N. C. S. C.), 34 S. E. Rep. 503.

Parol evidence is admissible to show that standard time had been adopted by established custom.

Rochester German Ins. Co. v. Peaslee-Gaulbert Co. (Ky. C. A.), and Pacific Ins. Co. v. Louisville Lead and Color Co. (Ky. C. A.), 87 S. W. Rep. 1115.

WHAT IS NOT INSURED.

"Fixtures" does not include casks, bottles and packing cases in a brewery.

Fitzgerald v. Atlanta Home Ins. Co. (N. Y. S. C., App. Div.), 70 N. Y. Supp. 552.

"All other implements of trade" does not include stationery and glove boxes of a glove manufacturer.

Stemmer v. Scottish U. & N. Ins. Co. (Ore. S. C.), 53 Pacif. Rep. 498.

"Saloon fixtures" does not include chairs.

Manchester F. Assur. Co. v. Feibelman (Ala. S. C.), 23 Southern Rep. 759.

"Carriages and all such goods usually kept in a livery barn and sales stable" does not include goods held in trust or on commission, and $3,000 additional concurrent insurance" the assured having taken out that much additional insurance which covered not only those goods belonging to the assured, but goods held in trust or on commission did not render them non-concurrent with first policy.

Corkery v. Security F. Ins. Co. (Iowa S. C.), 68 N. W. Rep. 792.

"Harvester while in use" does not mean while it is stored in a shed.

Slinkard v. Manchester F. Assur. Co. (Cal. S. C.), 55 Pacif. Rep. 417.

"Harvesting machine operating in grain fields and in transit from place to place in connection with harvesting," does not cover a loss to the machine after it had been taken from place of storage and sent to shop for repair, and there burned about the day the harvesting season opened.

Mawhinney v. Southern Ins. Co. (Cal. S. C.), 32 Pacif. Rep. 945; 22 Ins. L. J. 596.

"Household furniture" does not include furniture purchased after policy was issued.

Phoenix Ins. Co. v. Dunn. (Tex. C. C. A.), 41 S. W. Rep. 109.

"Machinery, shafting, belting, iron working lathes, planers, upright drills, milling machinery and fixtures and other machinery and implements used in his business as a machinist" does not include articles carried in stock for sale.

Michel v. American Central Ins. Co., 17 Hun. 87.

"Builders' risk" on a house plaintiff contracted to remove does not cover his loss on tools in the house at time of fire.

Planters & Merchants Ins. Co. v. Thurston (Ala. S. C.), 9 Southern Rep. 268; 20 Ins. L. J. 746.

"Stock of vinegar in store and in tank, mash and low wines" does not cover mixtures in process of manufacture.

Purves v. Germania Ins. Co. (La. S. C.), 10 Southern Rep. 495; 21 Ins. L. J. 306.

"Decorations to walls and ceilings" does not include painting of the outside walls of the building.

Sherlock v. German Amer. Ins. Co. (N. Y. S. C.), 47 N. Y. Supp. 315.

"Frame barn, and contents therein," does not cover, against loss on a horse usually kept in the barn, when the loss to such horse was sustained when it was 50 feet distant from the barn.

Farmers Mut. F. Ins. Ass'n. v. Kryder (Ind. App. C.), 31 N. E. Rep. 851.

"Materials" do not include benzine, unless it is commonly used in the business.

McFarland v. Peabody Ins. Co., 6 W. Va. 425.

"On property belonging to the insured, or on any property for which they may be liable," does not include those articles from which the policy exempts the insurer from liability, unless specifically insured.

The Commonwealth v. Hide & Leather Ins. Co. (S. J. C. Mass.), 3 Ins. L. J. 671.

But it does include merchandise in transit over their road whether in their own cars or on the cars of other common carriers.

The Commonwealth v. Hide and Leather Ins. Co. (S. J. C. Mass.), 3 Ins. L. J. 671.

"Three-story brick building occupied as a pottery, and known as 'Pottery Building'" does not include a boiler house adjoining, used on one floor as a boiler house and one floor for storage of pottery, power being furnished from said boiler house to the pottery, and to box and yarn factories in adjoining buildings.

Forbes v. American Ins. Co. (S. J. C. Mass.), 41 N. E. Rep. 656.

"Blankets purchased with insurer's consent, to protect insured's property from fire burning in adjacent building," is not a loss within the policy.

Welles v. Boston Ins. Co., 6 Pick. 182.

"Unfinished house" does not include timbers lying in adjoining building to be used in its construction.

Ellmaker v. Franklin F. Ins. Co., 5 Penn. St. 183; 6 W. S. 439.

"Jewelry and clothing, being stock in trade," limits liability to jewelry and clothing only.

Rafel v. Nashville M. & F. Ins. Co., 7 La. An. 244.

"English, American and West India goods" does not include tea or nutmegs unless they are English, American and West Indian goods.

Huckins v. People's M. F. Ins. Co., 31 N, H. 238.

"Merchandise" means all those things which assured, as a merchant, sells, and not articles of personal property not intended for sale.

Kent v. Liverpool & L. & G. Ins. Co., 26 Ind. 294.

"Stock of wearing apparel and household furniture" does not include linen sheets and shirts smuggled and kept for clandestine sale.

Clary v. Protection Ins. Co., 1 Wright 228;
Watchorn v. Langford, 3 Camp. 422.

"Stock and Materials" do not include retorts in a smelting plant.

American Smelter Co. v. Providence-Wash. Ins. Co., 64 Mo. App. 438.

"Lumber, Lath and Pickets" do not include shingles, though if the word lumber alone is used it might.

West Branch Lumberman's Exch. v. American Ins. Co., 183 Pa. St. 136; 27 Ins. L. J. 305; 38 Atl. Rep. 1081.

"Stock of hair manufactured or in process" does not include goods of other material, even though usually kept in such stocks.

Medina v. Builders Ins. Co., 120 Mass. 225.

"Household Furniture" does not include a watch.

Clary v. Protection Ins. Co., 1 Wright Ohio 228.

"Oil in tank cars in transit" * * * "insurance to continue and endure until said goods and merchandise are safely landed at.........., as aforesaid," means that the latter clause, when properly filled out, applied only to sea carriage, and was no part of contract made by this policy, which insured "oil in tank cars in transit," and when a tank car of oil covered by the policy had been delivered by the railroad which transported to the insured, by being placed by its direction upon its private switch alongside its warehouse, the oil was no longer "in transit."

Crew v. British and Foreign M. Ins. Co. (U. S. C. C. A., 3rd Dist.), 103 Fed. Rep. 48.

"Occupied as a dwelling" is a warranty that the building is so occupied at the time.

Hamburg-Bremen F. Ins. Co. v. Lewis (D. C. C. A.), 4 App. D. C. 66.

"Occupied as a dwelling" does not permit building to be used in part as a grocery store.

Greenwich Ins. Co. v. Dougherty (N. J. S. C.), 42 Atl. Rep. 485.

Permission to use the building for "any mercantile purpose" does not authorize its use as a restaurant.

Garretson v. Mcts. & Bkrs. Co. (Iowa S. C.), 45 N. W. Rep. 1047.

WHAT IS INSURED.

"On lines owned, leased or operated by," means owned, leased or operated at the time the policy was issued, though not so owned, leased or operated at time of fire; to hold otherwise would make insurer liable for loss it never had in contemplation.

Northern Pacif. Exp. Co. v. Traders Ins. Co. (Ill. S. C.), 55 N. E. Rep. 702.

"Baled cotton held for compression or compressed, but not loaded on cars, and for which a compress shipper's receipt has been issued for certain railroads, while contained on open platforms, and under sheds of insured, loss, if any, payable to said railroads as their several interests may appear at the time of the fire," covers all cotton held by plaintiff for any owner, situate as described for which compress receipt had been issued for shipment over any of the railroads, that the word "for" in connection "for which," etc., is not used to indicate ownership of the cotton, but simply the lines over which it is to be routed.

Hope Oil Mill Comp. & Mfg. Co. v. Phoenix Assur. Co. (Miss. S. C.), 21 Southern Rep. 132.

"On cotton in bales for which bills of lading have been issued by its duly authorized agents, and for which it may be liable." (Policy containing this clause was issued to H. & T. C. R. R. Co. The bills of lading provided the carriers were not to be liable for any loss or damage by fire. The R. R. Co., according to custom placed the cotton in the yards of a compress to be compressed. While there it was accidentally damaged by fire). It was held that insurer was liable.

Germania Ins. Co. v. Anderson (Tex. C. C. A.), 40 S. W. Rep. 200.

"Rolling stock on line of assured's road, its branches, spurs, side tracks and yards, owned or operated by assured, but not on line of any road leased by assured unless such road is specified as being insured in part under this policy," covers rolling stock which is destroyed in a yard operated by the insured in connection with its own line of road, but not owned by it, though the owner of the yard is not specified.

L. & L. & G. Ins. Co. v. McNeill (U. S. C. C. A. 9th Cir.), 89 Fed. Rep. 131.

"Cars leased and for which assured is liable" must be construed with reference to the known business of the insured and covers foreign cars coming into its possession in such business. The assured owned only a few cars, and was engaged in the handling of cars for other railroad companies.

Phenix Ins. Co. v. Belt Ry. Co., 82 Ill. App. 265.

"Freight cars owned or used by assured" will cover cars owned by others while in transit on assured's tracks.

The Commonwealth v. Hide & Leather Ins. Co. (S. J. C. Mass.), 3 Ins. L. J. 671.

"Insurance by warehouseman to secure property held in trust for others" are floating policies, and broad enough to cover property of others stored with him, subsequently to their issue.

Smith v. Carmack et al. (Tenn. Ch. App.), 64 S. W. Rep. 372.

"Held in trust" embraces goods held by the insured as bailee.

Beideman v. Powell, 10 Mo. App. 280.

"Their own, held in trust, on commission, or on' joint account with others, or sold but not delivered, contained in their warehouse," covers goods stored with assured.

> Pelzer Mfg. Co. v. St. Paul F. & M. Ins. Co. and other Ins. Cos. (U. S. C. C. Dist. S. C.), 19 Ins. L. J. 372.

"Held in trust, or sold and not delivered," covers lumber sold, piled by itself and marked for purchaser ready for shipment.

> Michigan Pipe Co. v. Michigan F. & M. Ins. Co. (Mich. S. C.), 52 N. W. Rep. 1070;
> Waring et al. v. Indemnity F. Ins. Co. (N. Y. C. A.), 1 Ins. L. J. 672.

"Its own, held in trust, on commissions, or in storage or for repairs, or sold, but not removed," will cover full value of goods left for repair or sale, and not merely the insured's insurable interest therein.

> Johnson v. Arbresch (Wis. S. C.), 101 N. W. Rep. 395, 34 Ins. L. J. 203.

"Held in trust" will cover goods held by an agent employed to manage a store, carrying on business in his own name, who is required to keep an account of all transactions to his principal and turn over all the property at the end of his employment.

> Roberts v. Firemen's Ins. Co. et al. (Pa. S. C.), 30 Atl. Rep. 450.

"Their own, or held by them in trust, or on which they have an interest or liability, and have agreed to insure under this policy, and not removed, stored or hereafter stored during the continuance of this policy," insures to the extent of insured's storage liens on merchandise stored with them as warehousemen, and for which they have issued warehouse receipts, expressly stipulating they would not be liable for loss by fire.

> Pittsburgh Storage Co. v. Scottish U. & N. Ins. Co. (Pa. S. C.), 32 Atl. Rep. 58.

"Assured, a warehouseman, insured his goods and those of others." One of the depositors who had paid the warehouseman for insurance was only entitled to share with the warehouseman and other depositors in the amount paid on the loss, less the amount paid for the insurance.

> Boyd v. McKee et al. (Va. S. C. A.), 37 S. E. Rep. 810.

"For account of whom it may concern, or equivalent terms," clearly indicates a purpose to keep insured the entire title to the property, and one who purchases an interest therein and adopts the insurance may recover, though printed stipulation of the policy is inconsistent with such right.

Hagan v. Scottish U. & N. Ins. Co. (U. S. D. C., Eastern Dist. Pa.), 98 Fed. Rep. 129.

"Held in trust" will include goods stored with assured, a warehouseman.

Southern Cold Storage W. Ho. v. Dechman (Tex. C. C. A.), 73 S. W. 545.

"Held in store" will embrace the property of others kept in assured's warehouse at time of fire.

Strohn v. Hartford F. Ins. Co., 3 Ins. L. J. 288.

"Held in trust" means goods with which the insured is intrusted in the ordinary sense of the word and not in the strict technical sense.

Hough et al. v. Peoples Ins. Co. (Md. C. A.), 2 Ins. L. J. 353.

This is one of the well known Baltimore Warehouse cases, citing:

Waters v. Assur. Co., 85 Eng. C. L. Rep. 879.

"Contained in their factory" will include all buildings constituting the factory, as factory does not necessarily mean one building or edifice.

Liebenstein v. Baltic F. Ins. Co., 45 Ill. 301.

"Articles used in packing hogs, cattle, etc.," includes coal or fuel used to generate steam for purpose of packing.

Home Ins. Co. v. Favorite, 46 Ill. 263;
Phoenix Ins. Co. v. Favorite, 49 Ill. 259.

Clause in policy reading, "$800 on household and kitchen furniture" * * * and "$......on family wearing apparel" covers wearing apparel.

German F. Ins. Co. v. Seibert (Ind. A. C.), 56 N. E. Rep. 686.

"Three-story building occupied as a store at No. 72 E. street" includes a one-story addition in rear and opened into it by a window and a door, and for a long time occupied as part of the store.

Boyer v. Grand Rapids F. Ins. Co. (Mich. S. C.), 83 N. W. Rep. 124.

And the keeping of gasoline in such addition will render the policy void.

Boyer v. Grand Rapids F. Ins. Co. (Mich. S. C.), 83 N. W. Rep. 124.

"Church Building" includes altars therein.

Caraker v. Royal Ins. Co., 63 Hun. 82; 17 N. Y. Supp. 858; aff'd
  • no op. 136 N. Y. 645.

"Brick building and additions, including gas, steam and water pipes, yard fixtures, railings, stoops and sidewalks in front of and all fixtures contained in or attached thereto at 160 M Street, occupied for stores and dwellings" covers either or both of two buildings owned by assured at that number, one at front and other at rear of the lot and connected externally by an intervening structure.

Rickerson v. Hartford F. Ins. Co., 149 N. Y. 307.

"Brick building and additions thereto occupied as a dwelling" includes a building occupied by his servants, and as a laundry, even though it is not annexed to the brick dwelling provided there is no other building in assured's yard which can possibly be claimed as an addition to the main building and not built in it as part of the house originally.

Phenix Ins. Co. v. Martin (Miss. S. C.), 16 Southern Rep. 417;
  24 Ins. L. J. 319.

"Steam Saw Mill" includes not only building but machinery.

Bigler v. N. Y. Central Ins. Co., 20 Barb. 635; aff'd 22 N. Y. 402.

"Starch factory, including machinery and fixtures," includes all fixtures used in the manufacture of starch.

Peoria M. & F. Ins. Co. v. Lewis, 18 Ill. 553.

"Frame dwelling house," covers frame wing sodded up on three sides.

McNamara v. Dakota F. & M. Ins. Co. (S. Dak. S. C.), 47 N. W.
  Rep. 288.

"Planing mill building and addition, and machinery therein" covers engine room and machinery therein, 22 feet distant, the only connection between them being a shaft for motive power and a spout or shavings conveyor.

Home Mut. Ins. Co. v. Roe (Wis. S. C.), 36 N. W. Rep. 594.

"Two-story brick dwelling house and its additions, adjoining and communicating," includes a frame addition, adjoining and communicating.

Carpenter v. Allemannia F. Ins. Co. (Pa. S. C.), 26 Atl. Rep. 781.

"Main building and all additions thereto, adjoining and com-

municating," includes dryhouse, twelve feet away, and the engine house, four feet from dryhouse.

> Marsh v. New Hampshire F. Ins. Co. (N. H. S. C.), 49 Atl.
> Rep. 88.

"Two-story frame building and additions thereto with shingle roof occupied by insured as a dwelling" covers a room called
his carriage house in which he kept his carriages and horses,
and which was under the same shingle roof as the rest of the
building, and was separated from the woodshed which connected
with the kitchen by a single partition of plain boards. This partition did not extend to the second story. Insured's hired man
slept in room over carriage house, which was furnished same as
any bed room in the house.

> Hannan v. Williamsburgh City Fire Ins. Co. (Mich. S. C.), 45
> N. W. Rep. 1120.

"Three-story brick building, basement, additions, foundations and area walls" includes gas piping and fixtures, heating
apparatus, elevator and plumbing, and this, too, when those articles are specifically insured under another item of the policy,
when the insurance under that item is not sufficient to cover the
value of such articles.

> Niagara v. Heenan (Ill. S. C.), 54 N. E. Rep. 1052.

"One-story brick building, and attached additions occupied
as saloon, No. 129½ L street," is question for the jury to determine, whether or not a one-story frame building occupied as a
restaurant, No. 131 L street, attached to and communicating
with the brick building, was insured.

> Connecticut F. Ins. Co. v. Hilbrant (Tex. C. C. A.), 73 S. W.
> Rep. 558.

"Eggs in pickle," where agent who wrote policy testifies he
understood the insurance was to cover the stock "while being
pickled and disposed of," covers the entire stock whether in
pickling vats or not.

> Hall v. Concordia F. Ins. Co. (Mich. S. C.), 51 N. W. Rep. 524.

"Wholesale stock of drugs, paints, oils, dye stuffs, and other
goods on hand for sale" covers not only the wholesale stock but
all other goods contained in the building, and this, too, notwithstanding assured's wholesale and retail stores were separated by
a partition.

> Wilson Drug Co. v. Phoenix Assur. Co. (N. C. S. C.), 14 S. E.
> Rep. 790.

"Tools used in the manufacture of boots and shoes" covers patterns for making boots and shoes.

> Adams v. N. Y. Bowery F. Ins. Co. (Iowa S. C.), 51 N. W. Rep. 1149.

Contra:

> Johnston v. Niagara F. Ins. Co. (N. C. S. C.), 25 Ins. L. J. 558; 24 S. E. Rep. 424.

"Grain" in barn includes corn and millet hay.

> Norris v. Farmers Mut. F. Ins. Co., 65 Mo. App. 632.

"Stock in two-story brick building," includes stock in a one-story rear addition.

> Carr v. Hibernia Ins. Co., 2 Mo. App. 466.

"Grain" includes broom corn in bale, but not the baled panicles from which the seed has been threshed.

> Reavis v. Farmers M. F. Ins. Co., 78 Mo. App. 14.

"Grain and seed" includes flax seed which was afterwards converted into oil çake, especially so, as the agent who took the risk knew that the oil cake was the only subject to be included in the description.

> Marsh Oil Co. v. Aetna Ins. Co., 79 Mo. App. 21.

Policy issued to painter, "on his paints, oils, brushes, varnish and such other merchandise," covers such other articles of convenience or necessity as are used in his business, whether intended for sale or not.

> Hartwell v. California Ins. Co. (Me. S. J. C.), 24 Atl. Rep. 954.

"Merchandise" includes butter and eggs.

> Lake Sup. P. & Cold Storage Co. v. Concordia F. Ins. Co. (Minn. S. C.), 104 N. W. Rep. 560.

"Blacksmith and carriage maker's stock, manufactured and in process of manufacture," will include unmanufactured or raw stock.

> Spratley v. Hartford F. Ins. Co., 1 Dil. C. C. 392.

"Stock in trade as a baker" includes tools and implements necessary for carrying on the business of a baker.

> Moadinger v. Mechanics F. Ins. Co., 2 Hall 490.

"Stock of watches, watch trimmings, etc.," was not limited to watches and watch trimmings, but included general stock.

> Crosby v. Franklin Ins. Co., 5 Gray 504.

"Engine and machinery for the manufacture of tinware" includes dies.

Seavy v. Central Mut. F. Ins. Co., 111 Mass. 540.

"Stock of merchandise consisting of family groceries, lamps, scales and other such merchandise" includes lamps and scales used by assured as store furniture and not kept for sale.

Georgia Home Ins. Co. v. Allen (Ala. S. C.), 24 Southern Rep. 399.

Lumber piled in mill building, on cars under mill sheds, and in sheds adjoining to said mill sheds." Held, To cover five sheds where lumber was piled, and not merely to lumber piled in mill under ten or twelve feet of projecting roofs at either side of mill, built to protect men and lumber when loading and unloading cars in stormy weather.

Wolverine Lumber Co. v. Palatine Ins. Co. (Mich. S. C.), 102 N. W. Rep. 991.

"Stock in brick building and additions attached" will include stock in a frame building on next lot, extending over and against the rear of the brick building two inches and used in connection therewith as a store room, it being the only building attached or connected with the brick.

Maisel v. Fire Ass'n (N. Y. S. C., App. Div.), 69 N. Y. Supp. 181.

"Farming utensils" includes hay press used on assured's farm.

Phenix Ins. Co. v. Stewart, 53 Ill. App. 273.

"Engine and machinery used for the manufacture of tinware, sheet iron, japaned and fancy painted ware," includes "dies" and all essential parts of the machinery used in manufacturing such articles as the insured manufactured.

Seavy et al. v. Central Mut. F. Ins. Co. (S. J. C. Mass.), 3 Ins. L. J. 576.

"Butter and cheese manufactured and in process of manufacture, and all materials and supplies used in the manufacture of same, including packages," includes milk cans.

Cronin v. Fire Ass'n (Mich. S. C.), 70 N. W. Rep. 448.

"Implements including binders and such goods kept for sale in a general implement store" includes binding twine.

Davis v. Anchor Mut. F. Ins. Co. (Iowa S. C.), 64 N. W. Rep. 687.

"Ship tackle, ordnance, ammunition, artillery and furniture of ship" includes provisions for use of crew.

Brough v. Whitmore, 4 Term. 206.

"On grain, while contained in frame iron-clad building occupied by storage and handling grain, known as 'St. Anthony Elevator'" covers in either "Main Building" or "Annex A," 300 feet distant connected by an iron-clad gallery. Both buildings were of same construction and the entire plant was known as St. Anthony Elevator.

Pettit et al. v. State Ins. Co. (Minn. S. C.), 19 Ins. L. J. 138;
43 N. W. Rep. 378;
Cargill et al. v. Millers & Mfrs. Mut. Ins. Co. (Minn. S. C.), 19
Ins. L. J. 876.

"Fixtures" include anything that is a fixture as between the insured and his landlord.

Clark v. Svea Ins. Co. (Cal. S. C.), 36 Pacif. Rep. 587.

"Threshing outfit" includes self-feeder.

Minneapolis Threshing Mch. Co. v. Darnall (S. Dak. S. C.), 83
N. W. Rep. 266.

"Household furniture, useful and ornamental" includes Japanese vase.

Bowne v. Hartford F. Ins. Co., 46 Mo. App. 473.

"Household furniture, useful and ornamental, and family stores" includes books, games, writing materials, child's swing, and child's walker.

Huston v. State Ins. Co. (Iowa S. C.), 69 N. W. Rep. 674.

Household furniture includes carpets and bedding.

Patrons Mut. Aid Society v. Hall (Ind. A. C.), 49 N. E. Rep. 279.

"Household furniture" includes all articles necessary and convenient for housekeeping such as sausage mill, churn, cookstove, dishes, kettles, etc., not particularly specified.

Reynolds et al. v. Iowa & Neb. Ins. Co. et al. (Iowa S. C.), 46
N. W. Rep. 659.

"Loss of rents * * * during such period as may be necessary to restore the premises to same condition as before the fire" includes the period necessary to make the contract as well as the time actually necessary in making the repairs.

Hartford F. Ins. Co. v. Pires (Tex. C. A. A.), 165 S. W. 565.

"Merchandise of .every description incidental to assured's business consisting chiefly of grain and grain products," will include malt.

Johnson v. Stewart, 243 Pa. 485, 90 Atl. 349.

"Held in trust" as used in a warehouseman's policy will cover goods stored with him, such a policy cannot be subject to the construction that it was only intended to cover goods of shippers who had made arrangements with assured to that effect.

Johnson v. Stewart, 243 Pa. 485, 90 Atl. 349.

"In cars on side tracks within 100 feet" covers only in such cars as are within 100 feet, and not in cars on side track within 100 feet. The policy refers to the cars rather than to the tracks.

Smith v. Phoenix Ins. Co. (Mo. App.) 168 S. W. 831.

"Premises" as used in an insurance policy means merely the space leased by the insured and does not include other parts of the building over which he has no control.

Central & Co. v. North B. & M. Ins. Co., 245 Pa. St. 272; 91 Atl. 662.

"Renewal of lease" does not constitute a change of lessees interest.

Home Ins. Co. v. Coker, 43 Okla. 331, 142 Pac. 1195.

Coinsurance—Concurrent Insurance; coinsurance is where the assured bears a portion of the loss; concurrent insurance is other insurance covering the same property against same risks.

Oppenheim v. Fireman's F. Ins. Co. (Minn. S. C.), 138 N. W. 777.

"Lien for rent" is not a chattel mortgage within the meaning of a fire insurance policy.

Phoenix Ins. Co. v. Fleenor, 104 Ark. 119, 148 S. W. 650;
Raulet v. Northwestern N. Ins. Co., 157 Cal. 213, 107 Pac. 292.

"Open for business." A store is not open for business within the meaning of a fire insurance policy, where the assured closes his store to go to lunch, only intending to be gone a half hour.

Joffee v. Niagara F. Ins. Co., 116 Md. 155; 81 Atl. 281.

"Within 60 days after the fire," means after the fire has terminated. Slocum v. Saratoga & W. F. Ins. Co., 134 N. Y. Supp. 78, National W. P. Co. v. Associated Mfrs. M. F. Ins. Co., 175 N. Y. 226. The time begins to run after destruction of the prop-

erty. Johnson v. Humboldt Ins. Co., 91 Ill. 92. It begins to run
from the time the fire started. Western, etc., v. Traders Ins.
Co., 122 Ill. App. 138. The Illinois Court of Appeals is not as
high as the Illinois Supreme Court. (The Author.)

"Ready to proceed under the provisions of the policy," a
statement to that effect is not a compliance with the policy provisions requiring the loss to be submitted to referees.

Vera v. Mercantile F. & M. Ins. Co., 216 Mass. 154, 103 N. E. 292.

"Void" as used in a fire insurance policy means null and
of no effect.

Tolliver v. Granite St. F. Ins. Co., 111 Me. 275, 89 Atl. 8.

"Insurance proceeds exempt" when collected for destruction of a homestead.

Johnson v. Hall (Tex. C. C. A.), 163 S. W. 399.

"While occupied as" constitutes a warranty that the property would be used as warranted. Occupied implies an actual
use for the purpose designated.

Washington F. Ins. Co. v. Cobb (Tex. C. C. A.), 163 S. W. 608.

"Toilet articles, labels, bottles and powder" will also include
corn starch.

Aachen & Munich F. Ins. Co. v. Arabian T. G. Co., 64 So. 635,
(10 Ala. App. 395).

"Red Top Seed," whether it is grain or not is for the jury.

Coen v. Denver T. M. F. Ins. Co., 155 Ill. App. 332.

"Stock—Merchandise," in mercantile law "stock" is the
goods which a tradesman holds for sale or traffic, "merchan
dise" is the object of commerce.

Spring Garden Ins. Co. v. Brown (Tex. C. C. A.), 143 S. W. 292.

"Inventory." An inventory is not an invoice, an inventory
means a list of goods in the store, an invoice is also a list of
goods but is made out by the seller or consignor and does not
show that the goods so listed were ever received in the assured's store. Hartford F. Ins. Co. v. Adams (Tex. C. C. A.),
158 S. W. 231; Day v. Home Ins. Co., 177 Ala. 600, 58 So. 549,
and the same doctrine applies where the assured himself shipped
the goods from a branch store. Phoenix Ins. Co. v. Dorsey
(Miss. S. C.), 58 So. 778.

"Furniture" will include an iron safe not attached in any way to the building.

Mecca. Ins. Co. v. First State Bank (Tex. C. C. A.), 135 S. W. 1083.

"Stock of grain" will include bran, a product thereof.

German F. Ins. Co. v. Walker (Tex. C. C. A.), 146 S. W. 606.

"Inventory." The bunching of articles without itemizing i. e. giving the total value of each group is not an inventory as

Shawnee F. Ins. Co. v. Thompson, 30 Okla. 466, 119 Pac. 985.
Houff v. German Am. Ins. Co., 3 Va. App. 986, 66 S. E. 831.

"Inventory." But while the grouping of articles is not a compliance with the policy provisions requiring an inventory, this does not affect that part of the inventory which is itemized and therefore does not avoid the policy.

Arnold v. Indemnity F. Ins. Co., 152 N. C. 232, 67 S. E. 574.

"Vacant and unoccupied." Vacancy can only occur when the building is empty, contains substantially nothing; while occupancy, when speaking of residences, refers more particularly to human habitation, or actually living in the house.

Norman v. Missouri T. M. Ins. Co., 74 Mo. App. 456.

"Vacant or unoccupied" when applied to a dwelling house means that no ones lives in it, a mere supervision of it does not constitute occupancy.

Cook v. Continental Ins. Co., 70 Mo. App. 610;
Hoover v. Mercantile T. M. Ins. Co., 93 Mo. App. 111; 69 S. W. 42;
Craig v. Springfield F. & M. Ins. Co., 34 Mo. App. 481;
Wheeler v. Phoenix Ins. Co., 53 Mo. App. 446;
Waddle v. Commonwealth Ins. Co., 170 S. W. 682, 184 Mo. App. 571.

"Dental books" are not covered under the description, "furniture, chairs, gas apparatus, pictures, paintings, instruments, appliances, and material incidental to a dental office."

American F. Ins. Co. v. Bell (Tex. C. C. A.), 75 S. W. 319.

"Grain," includes millet hay.

Norris v. Farmers M. F. Ins. Co., 65 Mo. App. 639.

"Valued policy law of Texas," means that neither notice nor proofs of loss is necessary, the claim being due on demand, interest begins to run from the date of the fire or from the date of the demand.

Camden F Ins. Ass'n. v. Bomar (Tex. C. C. A.), 176 S. W. 156.

5

"Machinery" is realty when owned by the same owner who owns the building and is within the purview of the valued policy law, when the policy insures the building and machinery of a mill. A special agreement between the insured and the insurer attempting to fix the legal status of machinery in a building as personality is void under the valued policy law.

Havens v. Germania F. Ins. Co., 135 Mo. 649, 37 S. W. 497; 24 Ins. L. J. 321;
Murphy v. N. Y. Bowery Ins. Co., 62 Mo. App. 495.
Darden v. L. & L. & G. Ins. Co. (Miss. S. C.), 68 So. 485.

"A building" is personal property when it stands on leased ground. (The Author.) See also Fixtures, Bouvier's Law Directory and Sharp v. Niagara F. Ins. Co., 147 S. W. 154, 164 Mo. App. 475. But it is held otherwise by Tex. Civil Appeals Court in Orient Ins. Co. v. Parlin, 38 S. W. 60, and Fidelity-Phenix Ins. Co. v. O'Bannon, 178 S. W. 731, although the Texas valued policy specifically excludes from its protection personal property.

"Mortgage clause" relates to the owners subsequent acts or neglect and does not apply to his application for insurance or his statements of omission therein. The policy may be void from its inception. Liverpool L. & G. Ins. Co. v. Agricultural S. & L. Co., 33 Can. S. C. 94. When after the loss the mortgage is foreclosed, the mortgagee can only recover the balance due on the mortgage. Hadley v. New Hampshire Ins. Co., 55 N. H. 110. The mortgage clause creates a separate and distinct contract for the benefit of the mortgagee, Bacot v. Phoenix Ins. Co., 96 Miss. 223, 50 So. 729; 39 Ins. L. J. 214; Reed v. Ins. Co., 76 N. J. L. 11, 69 Atl. 724; Smith v. Union Ins. Co., 25 R. I. 260, 55 Atl. 718; Franklin F. Ins. Co. v. Martin, 40 N. J. L. 575; Kupferschmidt v. Agricultural Ins. Co., 80 N. J. L. 441, 78 Atl. 225; Burnham v. Royal Ins. Co., 57 Mo. App. 394. If the owner or mortgagor takes out other insurance it cannot pro rate in paying the loss, as he can not do anything by which the mortgagee's insurance will be diminished. Laurenzi v. Atlas Ins. Co. (Tenn. S. C.), 176 S. W. 1022; Hastings v. Westchester F. Ins. Co., 73 N. Y. 141, 7 Ins. L. J. 430; Union Inst., etc., v. Phoenix Ins. Co., 196 Mass. 230, 81 N. E. 994; Hartford F. Ins. Co. v. Olcott, 97 Ill. 439. Neither can he make an adjustment, nor enter into an appraisal agreement which will bind the mortgagee or trustee. Laurenzi v. Atlas Ins. Co. (Tenn. S. C.), 176 S. W. 1022; Hartford F. Ins. Co. v. Olcott, 97 Ill. 439; Hastings v. Westchester, 73 N. Y. 141, 7 Ins. L. J. 430. But it is held otherwise in Massachusetts and Ohio, not only this, but that the mortgagee has no standing in court until the amount of the loss has been arbitrated or arbitration waived. Union Inst. Co. v. Phoenix Ins. Co., 196 Mass. 230, 81 N. E. 994; Erie Brewing Co. v. Ohio F. Ins. Co., 81 Ohio St. 1, 89 N. E. 1065, 39 Ins. L. J. 200. New Jersey holds to the contrary and that the mortgage clause relieves the mortgagee from every compliance with conditions to be performed after the fire. Reed v. Firemen's Ins. Co., 81 N. J. L. 523, 80 Atl. 462.

"**Loss if any payable to—as interest may appear.**" This merely gives the payee the right to have paid over to him any money that may be found due under the contract and takes from the assured none of his rights. He is not the assured, but only his appointee. Brecht v. Law M. & C. Ins. Co., 160 Fed. 399, 87 C. C. A. 351 (annotated in 18 L. R. A. ([N. S.] 197); Woods v. Ins. Co. St. of Pa., 87 Wash. 563, 144 Pac. 650. Such a loss payable clause is not even notice to the insurance company that the payee holds a chattel mortgage on the property. Woods v. Ins. Co. St. of Pa., 82 Wash. 563, 144 Pac. 650. But it is held in Mississippi by reason of a statute, and in Kentucky that a mortgagee to whom a policy is made payable is not bound by an adjustment or appraisal made by the owner or mortgagor. In entering into an appraisal it is always best to be on the safe side and have the mortgagee to whom the policy is payable a party to the appraisal agreement, so that he cannot be heard to complain. (The Author.).

"**Merchandise and materials for making same**" as used in a policy of fire insurance means all articles which are necessarily or conveniently used in insured's business, embracing tools, apparatus, and implements used by him in his business. Oklahoma F. Ins. Co. v. McKey (Tex. C. C. A.), 152 S. W. 440.

Proximate cause of loss is the one which puts the other cause into motion.
Hocking v. British Am. Assur. Co., 62 Wash. 73, 113 Pac. 259.

"**Life estate and reversioner,**" both are entitled to have the funds from a fire insurance policy applied to the repair of the damaged building.
Brough v. Higgins, 2 Gratt. (Va.) 408; 2 Bennett 443.

"**Insurance on** boat," does not cover materials and lumber in the shipyard where it was being built and intended for use in its construction.

Mason v. Franklin F. Ins. Co., 12 Gill & J. (Md.) 468; 2 Bennett 214.

Same principle of law:

Ellmaker's Exec. v. Franklin F. Ins. Co. (Pa. S. C.), 5 Barr. 183; 2 Bennett 519.

"Loss by mob." A destruction of a building by fire caused by mob is not a loss by "any usurped power whatsoever."

Drinkwater v. London Assur. Corporation (Eng.), 2 Wilson 363; 1 Bennett 12.

"Civil commotion." A clause in a policy exempting the insurers in case of a loss by "civil commotion," applies to a destruction by a riot.

Landsdale v. Mason et al. (Eng.), 1 Marshall on Ins. 688; 1 Bennett 16.

"Linen," as used in a fire insurance policy covering household furniture, will not protect linen drapery goods subsequently purchased on speculation.

Watchorn v. Langford (Eng.), 3 Campbell 422; 1 Bennett 91.

"Held in trust." A policy taken out by the consignee in his own name insuring goods held "in trust" will only cover his interest in such goods, and not any loss which the consignor alone sustains.

Parks v. General Interest Assur. Co., 5 Pick. (Mass.) 34; 1 Bennett 184. Contra.
De Forest v. Fulton F. Ins. Co. (S. C., N. Y.), 1 Hall 84, and many other cases; in fact, the author knows of but one other in harmony with the Massachusetts case, i. e. a Louisiana case.

"Blowing up, drowning, etc." A shipment of negroes insured against the dangers of navigation, such as blowing up, drowning, etc., will cover the loss of a negro by drowning without any disaster happening to the boat.

Moore v. Perpetual Ins. Co., 16 Mo. 98.

"Property on premises owned or occupied by assured" will include a dredge fastened to a wharf owned by them.

Farmers' Loan & Tr. Co. v. Harmony F. & M. Ins. Co. (S. C., N. Y.), 51 Barbour 33; 5 Bennett 174.

"Prosecuted," as used in a fire insurance policy, is synonymous with the word suit.

Merchants M. Ins. Co. v. Lacroix, 35 Tex. 249; 5 Bennett 455.

"Assured's working interest" in leased property, which he agreed to restore at end of lease in good condition, and to replace with other of equal if destroyed, will include the entire value of the property.

Imperial Ins. Co. v. Murray, 73 Pa. St. 13; 5 Bennett 526.

"Merchandise, his own, in trust, or on commission, for which he is responsible," does not include merchandise sold and paid for where warehouse receipts were endorsed over to the purchaser.

North B. & M. Ins. Co. v. Moffat, (Eng.) Law Reports 7; Common Pleas 25; 5 Bennett 381.

"Stock of watches, watch trimmings, etc.," will include assured's entire stock of jewelry.

Crosby v. Franklin Ins. Co., 5 Gray (Mass.) 504; 4 Bennett 35.

"Manufacturer of brass clocks," as describing the insured's business in a fire insurance policy, covers and permits the use of all articles ordinarily employed in that manufacture.

Bryant v. Poughkeepsie M. F. Ins. Co. (S. C., N. Y.), 21 Barb. 154; 4 Bennett 37.

"Tax title," where the tax collector was not shown to have made his return of the sale within the time prescribed by law, must be regarded as fatally defective. See Shimmin v. Inman, 26 Me. 228; Andrews v. Senter, 32 Me. 394.

Pinkham v. Morang & Monmouth M. F. Ins. Co., 40 Me. 587; 4 Bennett 43.

"Clerk sleeps in store" in an application for fire insurance is merely descriptive of present occupancy and not a warranty for the future.

Frisbie v. Fayette M. Ins. Co., 27 Pa. St. 325; 5 Bennett 159.

"Insurance against fire by lightning" does not contemplate a loss by lightning unless fire ensued.

Babcock v. Montgomery Co. M. Ins. Co., 4 Comstock (N. Y.) 326; 3 Bennett 154.

"Policy to co-partners" does not cover the interest of one who purchases his partner's interest, where the policy provides it shall be void if the property be alienated by sale or otherwise.

Tillou v. Kingston M. Ins. Co., 5 N. Y. 405; 3 Bennett 238.

"For account of whom it may concern," as used in a fire in

surance policy, only protects such interests as were intended to be insured at the time the insurance was effected.

Steele v. Franklin F. Ins. Co., 17 Pa. St. 290; 3 Bennett 278.

"Held in trust" includes goods held by pawnbroker, and are not covered by a policy which provides goods held in trust or on commission are not covered unless mentioned in the policy as being insured, nor does the term, "Jewelry and Clothing, Being Stock in Trade," include such articles as musical instruments, surgical instruments, guns, pistols and books.

Rafel v. Nashville M. & F. Ins. Co., 7 La. An. 244; 3 Bennett 336.

"Dissolution of partnership" and division of the property is such a change of title as will avoid the policy provisions, rendering it void if there be any transfer or change of title in property insured.

Dreher v. Aetna Ins. Co., 18 Mo. 128; 3 Bennett 514.

"Insured and or assured" is the person who owns the property, applies for the insurance, pays the premiums and signs the deposit note, and not another to whom the money may be made payable in case of loss, though he may have a lease on the premises.

Sanford v. Mechanics Mutual F. Ins. Co., 12 Cush. (Mass.) 541; 3 Bennett 619.

"Crude petroleum—Camphene." The keeping of a little crude petroleum for medical purposes is not a storing within the meaning of a policy, and it seems that using camphene for a light in a sleeping apartment will not avoid a policy prohibiting its use.

Williams v. Fireman's F. Ins. Co., 54 N. Y. 569; 5 Bennett 537.

"Foreclosure." Filing a mechanic's lien is not a commencement of foreclosure proceedings, nor is a levy obtained under an execution to enforce the lien on real estate within the meaning of a policy referring to levy on personal property.

Colt v. Phoenix F. Ins. Co., 54 N. Y. 595; 5 Bennett 537.

"Until a certain date" includes that date.

Isaacs v. Royal Ins. Co., Law Reports; 5 Exchequer 296.

"Warranty—Representation." A representation is part of the preliminary proceedings to a contract, a misrepresentation of an immaterial matter not fraudulently made will not avoid·the policy, but a warranty must be literally performed.

Dewees v. Manhattan Ins. Co., 34 N. J. Law 244; 5 Bennett 244;
American Ins. Co. v. Barnett, 73 Mo. 364;
Hamilton v. Home Ins. Co., 92 Mo. 353.

"Gunpowder." The policy insuring "general stock of hardware" does not include gunpowder nor permit the keeping of same in stock, where the policy provisions rendered the policy void if it were kept in stock.

Mason v. Hartford F. Ins. Co., 29 Up. Can. O. B. 585; 5 Bennett 294.

Same principle of law:

Pindar v. Continental Ins. Co. et al., 47 N. Y. 114; 5 Bennett 185;
Dewees v. Manhattan Ins. Co., 35 N. J. Law 366; 5 Bennett 314;
Appleby v. Astor F. Ins. Co., 54 N. Y. 253; 45 Barbour 454; 5 Bennett 490;
McFarland v. Peabody Ins. Co. et al., 6 West Va. 425, 437; 5 Bennett 490.

"Immediate notice," as used in a fire insurance policy, means reasonable time under the circumstances.

Cashau v. Northwestern N. Ins. Co., 5 Bissell (U. S. C. C.) 476; 5 Bennett 501.

"In quantities exceeding one barrel." In view of the punctuation, the permit was applicable to all the prohibited materials specified.

Ins. Co. v. Slaughter (U. S. S. C.), 12 Wallace 404; 5 Bennett 340.

"Laws relating to fire insurance" do not apply to tornado insurance.

Nally v. Home Ins. Co., 250 Mo. 452; 157 S. W. 769.

"Keeping or storing." Keeping a wooden barrel of benzine on the premises only for the time required to fill the receptacle permitted by the policy was not a keeping or storing within the meaning of the policy.

Maryland F. Ins. Co. v. Whiteford, 31 Md. 219; 5 Bennett 240.

"Refined coal or earth oils," as used in a fire insurance policy, refers only to articles as dangerous, as naphtha, benzine or benzole.

Morse v. Buffalo F. & M. Ins. Co., 30 Wis. 534; 5 Bennett 424.

"Leasehold or other interest not absolute" in the property insured by a fire insurance policy. A mortgagor under such policy holds an equitable fee simple, which need not be represented to the company or expressed in the policy.

Washington F. Ins. Co. et al. v. Kelly, 32 Md. 421; 5 Bennett 303.

"Machine and repair shop" has no technical insurance meaning. It is for the jury to determine whether assured's business was or was not included in the term.

Chaplin v. Provincial Ins. Co., 23 Up. Can. C. P. 218; 5 Bennett 503.

"Particular and detailed account of the loss." A policy requiring such is complied with where the assured's account showed value of stock at a given date; the amount of stock received since that date; the amount of stock saved, and the amount of the loss claimed.

Stickney v. Niagara F. M. Ins. Co., 23 Up. Can. C. P. 372; 5 Bennett 503.

"Mortgagee." His indorsement of mortgage note to his assignee of the mortgage gives him an insurable interest in the mortgaged property.

Williams v. Roger Williams Ins. Co., 107 Mass. 377; 5 Bennett 373.

"Owner" has no definite meaning, and is a question for the jury, where the assured represented himself as the owner of a building that stood on leased ground.

Hopkins v. Provincial Ins. Co., 18 Up. Can. C. P. 74; 5 Bennett 159.

"Plate," as used in a policy which excludes it as not insured, does mean silver forks, tea and tablespoons.

Hanover F. Ins. Co. v. Mannasson, 29 Mich. 316; 5 Bennett 541.

"Change within the control of assured" material to the risk, as used in a fire policy, refers to police regulations to prevent fires, and not to the erection of buildings, or the use of neighboring premises.

Commercial Ins. Co. v. Mehlman, 48 Ill. 313; 5 Bennett 190.

"Contained in," as used in a fire insurance policy, contemplates a limitation of the risk taken, so that the insurer will not be liable for a loss occurring while the engine and car are out of the house in which they were described as contained in.

Annapolis, Etc., R. R. Co. v. Baltimore F. Ins. Co., 32 Md. 37; 5 Bennett 258.

"Deliver in," as used in a fire insurance policy, means deliver in writing.

Davis v. Scotland Provincial Ins. Co., 16 Up. Can. C. P. 176; 5 Bennett 61.

"Dwelling." The fact that the owner of the store and his

clerk slept in a back room of the store does not constitute the store a dwelling.

Cerf v. Home Ins. Co., 44 Cal. 320; 5 Bennett 426.

"Factory," as used in a fire insurance policy, may mean a single building, or several when all are used for a common purpose and together constitute the factory.

Liebenstein v. Baltic Fire Ins. Co., also v. Metropolitan Ins. Co., 45 Ill. 301, 305; 5 Bennett 115.

"Fireworks." Where a policy prohibited the keeping of fireworks, evidence showing that such articles constitute the business of a "German jobber and importer" is inadmissible where the policy covered that kind of stock and permitted assured to keep firecrackers for sale.

Steinbach v. Ins. Co., 13 Wallace (U. S. S. C.) 183; 5 Bennett 394.

"Fire insurance on a certain quantity of coal" will cover not only the coal deposited at the time, but that deposited since, and covers also the risk arising from spontaneous combustion of such coal.

British Am. Ins. Co. v. Joseph, 9 Lower Can. R. 448; 4 Bennett 161.

"Consisting of" excludes everything not enumerated, so that while "Stock in Trade" would include the articles sued for, but where this term is limited in its meaning by the words "consisting of" and the articles sued on are not named and do not come under the meaning of those articles enumerated, the insurer is not liable.

Joel v. Harvey (England), 5 Weekly Rep. 488; 4 Bennett 185.

"Privileged for a printing office" will permit the use of a prohibited article by the policy, where such article is in common use among printers, and this too where the case of such article accidentally caused the fire.

Harper v. Albany M. Ins. Co., 17 N. Y. 194; 4 Bennett 247;
Harper v. N. Y. City Ins. Co., 22 N. Y. 441;
Whitmarsh v. Conway F. Ins. Co., 16 Gray (Mass.) 359;
Niagara F. Ins. Co. v. De Graff, 12 Mich. 124; 4 Bennett 707.

"Stone dwelling house" will include a frame kitchen attached; it will include the building and such attachments as are usually occupied and used by the family for the ordinary purposes of a house. A dwelling house is an entire thing.

Chase v. Hamilton Ins. Co., 20 N. Y. 52; 4 Bennett 416.

"Store fixtures" in a policy of fire insurance are applied to all furniture and other articles in a shop or warehouse. Evidence is admissible of a well settled custom to that effect.

Whitmarsh v. Conway F. Ins. Co., 16 Gray (Mass.) 359; 4 Bennett 485.

"Change of title." Partition between co-tenants is an alienation or change of title within the meaning of a fire insurance policy.

Barnes v. Union M. F. Ins. Co., 51 Me. 110; 4 Bennett 728.

CHAPTER XVII.

EXPERT ACCOUNTING IN ITS RELATION TO THE ADJUSTMENT OF LOSSES.

I will now take up the method of making up a statement of loss from the books, and will show the wrong and right way to treat that question, and first, will show a statement of loss as actually adjusted by the adjusters (see Exhibit "A"). In order to arrive at a basis of settlement, they first ascertained the profits of the preceding year, including freights, but excluding cash discounts, to be 18.63 per cent., but stated they figured discounts on purchases and a 1 per cent. wastage in the statement of loss, because that was the only way they could get a depreciation which they were, in their judgment, entitled to; hence settled the loss as shown in Exhibit "A."

Exhibit "A."

Inventory of stock on hand Dec. 26, 1900		$42,189.71
Subsequent purchases to April 30, 1901	$80,436.17	
Less cash discounts	793.31	79,642.86
		$121,832.57
Deduct sales	$99,321.23	
Less profit per mdse. acc. 18.63 per cent. on cost, no items being debited or credited to mdse. other than mdse., except freights	15,597.69	$83,723.54
Stock on hand at time of fire		$38,109.03
Deduct 1 per cent. for wastage, etc.		381.09
Cash value at time of fire		$37,727.94
Agreed value of stock saved		8,889.35
Total loss		$28,838.59

The profits covered the 1 per cent. wastage, because the profit of 18.63 per cent. was made on top of wastage of all kinds. Hence the $381.09 wastage should not have been deducted from the statement.

The correct method of arriving at the loss is shown in Exhibit "B."

Exhibit "B."

Inventory, Dec. 26, 1900		$42,189.71
Add purchases, including freights		80,436.17
		$122,625.88
Sales	$99,321.23	
Less 18.63 per cent.	15,597.69	83,723.54
		$38,902.34
Value of Salvage		8,889.35
		$30,012.99
Less 00986 per cent. cash discount............		295.93
Assured should have collected.....................		$29,717.06
Assured did collect		28,838.59
Net loss to assured		$878.47

The reason for including freights with the purchases in the correct statement is that freights were considered in arriving at preceding year's profit, but discounts were not, and should therefore be applied to goods destroyed in the statement of loss.

The correct measure of damage is the market value not exceeding what it would cost the assured to replace the property destroyed with other of like kind and quality at the time immediately preceding the fire, which, in merchandise, means bill cost less rebates and discounts, if any, and plus freight and drayage, if any.

It is not always wrong to apply freights and discounts to purchases; its correctness depends on how you get at your ratio of profits. So also cross entries in merchandise account of return sales, return purchases, rebates, allowances, etc., are all important factors in getting at the profits, and, in figuring a statement of loss, the important question is in knowing how and when to apply them.

The whole question is one of bookkeeping. The following are some hypothetical statements of how profits are arrived at.

Showing Hypothetical Book Statements of Loss, and Methods of Showing Profits.

I will now not only prove the correctness of the statement as shown in Exhibit "B" by giving some hypothetical statements of the method of correctly figuring profits of the preceding year's business and how to apply those profits in arriving at the amount of stock on hand at the time of the fire, showing the correct method (see Exhibit "D") and the method adopted by the adjusters in arriving at the profit (see Exhibit "C") and the wrong manner in which they applied the discounts (see Exhibit "E").

To make the statement perfectly clear I will treat it as though the entire stock dealt in consisted of one kind of merchandise and will have to assume that each article weighed the same, cost the same, was sold for the same and did not fluctuate in price. I will, therefore, call the articles sacks of coffee which cost $12.50 per sack or bag, less 4 per cent. cash discounts if paid in 10 days and 5 per cent. freight drayage on the net cash price, making the net cash cost of each bag $12.60. In the course of a year's business 1 per cent. of the amount of the coffee handled is lost through wastage and other ways of handling, resacking, etc., hence

Exhibit "C."

Profit statement for year 1904. (In this statement freights are included but not discounts.)

Stock on hand January 1, 1904, 10,000 bags coffee
at $13.10 ....$131,000.00
Purchased during the year, including freights, 20,000
bags at $13.10 .... 262,000.00
Goods to be accounted for January 1, 1905, not forgetting that 1 per cent., or 300 bags, were lost in
wastage, rehandling, etc. $393,000.00
The inventory of January 1, 1905, accounts for 8,700
bags at $13.10 .... 113,970.00
The difference shows the cost of all goods that were
sold, wasted, stolen or given away to have been..$279,030.00
We also know that this $279,030.00 represents 21,300
bags of coffee; we also know that 300 bags went
to wastage in some shape or other as the books
show that 21,000 bags of coffee were sold for....$330,102.00
These 21,000 bags having cost, as shown above...... 279,030.00
The profit exclusive of discounts is the difference.... $51,072.00

The ratio of profit on cost is 18.3034 per cent., but as before explained this profit excludes cash discounts, but includes freight as part of the cost of the goods, hence our statement of loss must be treated in same manner and made up exclusive of discounts until the amount of the goods burned is ascertained and then the ratio of cash discounts must be deducted as shown in Exhibit "D," which follows:

Exhibit "D."

(Same method as Exhibit "B," and proves correctness of Exhibit "B.")

Stock on hand January 1, 1905, 8,700 bags coffee at
$13.10 ....$113,970.00
Subsequent purchases, 17,400 bags at $13.10......... 227,940.00

	$341,910.00

Sales (18,270 bags) $287,204.00
Less 18.3034 per cent. profit............ 44,435.04   242,769.36

	$99,140.64

Cash discounts 4 per cent. on bill cost, but only 3.8168
per cent. on bill and freight cost................   3,784.00

Net loss $95,356.64

Exhibit "E."

(Same method as used in Exhibit "A.")

Stock on hand January 1, 1905.....................$113,970.00
Subsequent purchases and freights......$227,940.00
Less 3.8168 per cent. discount..........   8,700.00   219,240.00

	$333,210.00

Sales $287,204.00
Less 18.3034 per cent. profit............ 44,435.04   242,769.36

	$90,440.64

Wastage 1 per cent. 904.40

Net loss $89,536.24
Now we know we have 7,569 bags coffee on hand,
worth $12.60 each $95,369.40

Hence the assured would be a loser by this method to
the tune of $5,833.16

Exhibit "F."

(Profit statement, all articles figured net.)

1904 inventory, 10,000 bags at $12.60.................$126,000.00
Purchases, 20,000 bags at $12.60.................... 252,000.00

30,000 bags of coffee to be accounted for Jan. 1,
    1905 ....$378,000.00

1905 inventory accounts for 8,700 bags at $12.60......$109,620.00

Leaving 21,300 bags coffee that went out of the
    house that cost $268,380.00
Sold 21,000 bags and 300 bags went to waste, sales.. 330,102.00

Profit ....: $61,722.00
        Ratio of profits 22.998 per cent.

Exhibit "G."

Statement of loss:

Inventory 1905 ....$109,620.00
Purchases 219,240.00

                                         $328,860.00
Sales $287,204.40
Less 22.998 per cent. 53,701.09 233,503.40

On hand at time of fire............ $95,356.60

Exhibit "H."

Statement of loss by quantities:

1905 inventory and purchases.......26,100 bags
    Sold 18,270 bags
Wasted   261 bags ....18,531 bags

Leaving on hand at time of fire.... 7,569 bags
    At $12.60 .... $95,369.40

Note the small difference of 4 cents in statements of loss in Exhibits "D" and "G" from the actual loss as shown in Exhibit "H," which is due, no doubt, to the ratio of profits, but a 4-cent error in a loss of $95,000 is of no importance.

Before giving any more hypothetical statements of loss and methods of arriving at profits it may be worth while to make a few statements concerning the treatment of inventories, discounts, freights, etc.

The inventory should be closely scrutinized and the prices carefully compared with the bills of purchases made prior to the date of the inventory. Of course, it is out of the question to compare every item or even half of them, but enough comparisons may be made to convince you either of its correctness or of its having been loaded. I remember settling a loss in one of the Southern States (and by the way Southern merchants have quite a proneness for loading their inventories from 5 per cent. to 20 per cent. to cover cost and carriage, but making no deductions whatever for cash discount) where the adjusters offered assured a sum that I thought should settle the loss, but I could not induce the assured to settle. Finally I went through their books again. Beginning with the inventory, I found that the price of each article would divide by 6. I then taxed them with having loaded their inventory 20 per cent. They never did admit it, but the loss was adjusted upon the figures offered by the adjusters. Draw your own conclusions as to whether I was right or wrong.

If the prices in an inventory have been loaded 5 per cent. each price per article can be divided by 1.05, if loaded 10 per cent. then by 11, if loaded 20 per cent. then by 6, and if loaded 33 1/3 per cent., each price can be divided by 4.

In taking their inventories very few if any merchants ever deduct anything from the cost of the goods for cash discounts, and I have never known any of them to do so, but quite a number do add a percentage to cover cost of freight and drayage.

If the loss requires you to go into the books, commence with the inventory and get it down to a cost basis, not by depreciation (I will treat of depreciation later) but by deducting cash discounts and adding the freights, then go back to the next preceding inventory and treat it in the same manner. Remember both inventories must always be treated alike, add to the last preceding inventory the purchases less the cash discounts the assured could have gotten if he had discounted all bills, then add freight and drayage on purchases only, being careful to eliminate freight and drayage on goods sold or on goods sold and returned. Get the net purchases, deducting goods purchased and returned to seller, and allowances made on purchases. The inventory and purchases of, I will say year 1904, gotten at in this manner, show the cost of the goods to be accounted for on January 1, 1905. The January 1, 1905, inventory deducted from the sum of 1904 inventory and purchases, shows the cost of the goods that went out of the house. (See Exhibit "C.") This amount deducted from the net amount of sales shows the profit.

To arrive at the percentage of profit on cost divide the cost of goods sold into the profit. In getting the sales take the gross sales, less goods sold and returned, also deduct from the sales allowances and rebates made on same, but never deduct cash discounts allowed assured's customers, the reason being if 1904 was a good year, with money plentiful, a larger proportion of his customers would discount their bills than in 1905 if business was dull and money tight, as in that case assured would be a considerable loser by the operation. If, on the other hand, conditions were reversed and a greater proportion of bills were discounted in 1905 than in 1904, your company would be the loser. If the profits arrived at in the methods shown be abnormally large, unless the assured can give you some satisfactory reason therefor, you may rest assured the last inventory has been loaded. Then you had better go back two or three years and ascertain what profits he had been in the habit of making.

And don't go off half cocked and offer to settle your loss arrived at by the ratio of profits made last year until your investigation is complete, suppose, for instance, his business last year was entirely retail, on which his profits were 37½ and this year he had branched out into the jobbing business as well as retail and is making only 20 per cent., or he may be handling an article this year on which he makes a small profit, but which swells his sales very materially, and you are liable to do your company out of quite a neat little sum of money. Better make a thorough inquiry into the class of goods handled as compared with last year. And as to making up statement of loss don't you think the safer plan is first to draw the other fellow's fire? Let him make up his claim against you, see what he wants, it's easier to criticise and, maybe he won't ask you to pay as much as you contemplated paying. The assured, better than any one else, knows what his loss actually is if everything is burned. You are in the dark and had better find out, if you can, all he knows about it before expressing your own opinion. If he is honest you can get him to present an honest claim; if he's not, you are no worse off.

DISCUSSION OF DEPRECIATION AND ITS RELATION TO PROFITS.

As to the question of profits, it is not only not always right to base your profits in the statement of loss on the result of the preceding year's business on account of the harm it may do your company, but sometimes it may harm the assured just as much, as he may have made a much larger profit during the current year than he did during the year preceding.

Almost every adjuster has met with losses where the assured kept a daily record of his profits by putting the cost price of the articles sold in one column, and the selling price in another, the difference being the profit. This method is not satisfactory and is never correct, notwithstanding the assured's statement that it is infallible. Nothing will prove its mistakes until the year's business is wound up, when the inventory will be found to be far short of what the system would show the stock on hand ought to be, and the reason is this: such a system deals merely with the goods actually sold and in so far as they are concerned it might be correct provided the profits were figured accurately in every instance, which is almost impossible, but in every business, small or large, there is more or less stealage and mistakes, not only by employes, but by shoplifters and non-employes, there is more or less wastage and leakage from causes too numerous to mention, and if you don't believe it, just interview the proprietors of some of the large department stores. All these leaks and wastage from different causes amount to a very large sum in the course of the year, and are not provided for by the system of figuring profits daily. This system, however, is a very good one and enables merchants to locate the leaks as far as it is possible to do so, at the end of the year when the inventory is taken, as the inventory will show the amount of stock actually on hand in each line, whereas the daily profit system will show how much ought to be on hand in each line or department.

There is no method of figuring profits which will always pan out exactly correct. I suggest as the one which I have found most satisfactory, that shown in Exhibit "F," i. e.: where both inventories are figured on a cash cost basis as well as the purchases. Though the method used in Exhibit "C" is just as correct. You will note the profits in one are shown to be 18.3034 per cent., in the other 22.998 per cent., and yet in applying these different ratios to the two statements of loss as shown in Exhibits "D" and "G," both dealing in the same quantities of goods as to inventories, purchases, wastage and sales, that there is only 4 cents difference in the final result. The reason the methods pointed out in Exhibits "C" and "F" will not always pan out exactly right, is that the wastage is figured on the total goods handled—that is, inventory and purchases; now then your profits of 18.3034 per cent. in "C" and 22.998 per cent. in "F" were figured on sales of $330,102.00. If these sales had been larger, the wastage would not have interfered with the profits in the same ratio and consequently the profit ratio would have been increased. And you will notice the ratios are the same in the loss statements as those in the profit statement, i. e., the purchases are double the amount of the inventory, the sales are 70 per cent. of the sums of the inventory and purchases combined. Had this not been the case I could not have made the statements figured in dollars and cents agree so closely with that figured in quantities. (See Exhibits "D," "G" and "H" for the reasons already explained, i. e., the wastage interfering with the profits.) But the difference is not great and the methods used in arriving at profits shown in Exhibits "C" and "F" are more accurate than any other known method, but as I have already observed, I consider that shown in "F" the most satisfactory.

As an evidence of the importance in knowing how and where to apply freight, discounts and rebates, and how to figure profits, I remember in one of the suits of the famous Kahnweiler v. one of the Companies, in the statement of loss the adjusters had applied the discounts to the purchases, assured's lawyer, in cross questioning the company's adjuster, put this hypothetical question to him: "Suppose I buy 10 pianos at $100 each, on which the discounts for cash payment are 10 per cent., and I sell 9 for $100 each, according to your method of figuring losses I am entirely sold out and have none on hand, whereas, you and I know that I still have one and that it is worth $90. Is this not so?" And Mr. Adjuster was so confused he could not explain it. He should have answered, "No." And if the lawyer demanded an explanation he could have "sewed him up" by saying 10 pianos bought at $100, less 10 per cent. off for cash, equals $900. Nine pianos sold at $100, less 10 per cent. profit would make the sales $810, leaving the stock on hand $90, and that's the method I used in figuring that statement.

If the assured depreciates his stock 10 per cent. each year you have no right to take off a further depreciation of 10 per

cent. unless you think you are entitled to a depreciation on top
of a depreciation, because the books will show a stock on hand
amounting to 10 per cent. less than an inventory would amount
to if it were taken at time fire occurred—that is, unless the purchases during the current year were out of proportion with
former years. You don't believe this, you say; well, I'll prove
it, and to do so will take statements shown in Exhibits "F"
and "G" and depreciate both inventories 10 per cent. (See
Exhibits "I" and "J" following.)

Exhibit "I."—Profit Statement.

Inventory stock on hand Jan. 1, 1904		$126,000
Deduct 10 per cent. depreciation		12,600
		$113,400
Purchases		252,000
Goods to be accounted for Jan. 1, 1905		$365,400
Inventory of Jan. 1, 1905, accounts for	$109,620	
Deduct 10 per cent. depreciation	10,962	98,658
Cost of goods that went out of store		$266,742
These goods were sold for		330,102
Profit		$ 63,360

Ratio of profit to cost, 23.754 per cent.

Exhibit "J"—Statement of Loss.

Inventory of stock on hand Jan. 1, 1905		$109,620.00
Deduct 10 per cent. depreciation		10,962.00
		$98,658.00
Subsequent purchases		219,240.00
		$317,898.00
Sales	$287,204.40	
Less 23.754 per cent. profit	55,127.54	232,076.86
Stock on hand at time of fire		$85,821.14
Stock on hand at time of fire as shown by Exhibit "H"	$ 95,386.60	
Less 10 per cent. depreciation	9,538.66	85,849.94
Difference		$ 26.80

If the current year's inventory be depreciated 10 per cent., but no depreciation whatever be taken off the 1904 inventory, it will show a reduction of over 20 per cent. in the amount of stock on hand at time of fire as shown by the books—that is, of course, taking a reasonable length of time after the last inventory when the sales have reached the proportion shown in Exhibit "G." This may be easily proven by depreciating the 1905 inventory as shown in Exhibit "F," 10 per cent., which will show a profit of $50,760, which is 18.171 per cent. on the cost, then use same statement as shown in Exhibit "G," except depreciate the inventory 10 per cent. and use 18.171 per cent. profit on cost instead of 22.998 per cent. and the statement will show a stock on hand at time of fire of $74,856.64 instead of $95,356.60, as shown in Exhibit "G" The better way to treat the loss would be to restore the depreciation on both inventories for the purpose of arriving at the profit, then restore depreciation on the last inventory in making up statement of loss and then depreciate only the goods burned.

I very well remember a loss that occurred in one of the Western cities some years ago, where the assured had deducted 10 per cent. from his last inventory and it was plainly evident that he had done so, but he had not taken his former inventories in that way. After the fire he claimed that he had arbitrarily marked off 10 per cent., not as a depreciation, but merely to be on the safe side. Some of the adjusters were for standing pat on the value he had placed on his goods, some were in favor of restoring the depreciation on his inventory, and that was what was finally done. I favored restoring the depreciation for the purpose, merely, of arriving at the true ratio of profits, then taking the depreciated inventory as a basis to start our statement of loss. If a merchant is not bound by the value he places on his own goods, what value is binding? Can he say to himself and his stockholders, we will depreciate these goods 10 per cent. and enter them in their books at the depreciated value, then in case of fire say to the insurance companies, it was all a mistake, the goods were worth 100 cents on the dollar and not 90 cents, as shown by the books?

Of course, with up-to-date merchants the custom is to keep the price of goods down to real value in taking inventories. Most of them ignore both freight and cash discounts, and the insurance company is in such cases entitled to whatever per cent. the discounts exceed freights. But the great majority of merchants do not take off enough depreciation; they tell you they have marked everything way down, but make them show you what goods were marked down and how much. Study the inventory and study the purchases and sales, and where there is any part of the stock left, study its character and suitableness for the market in which it was to have been sold. Sometimes a day or so spent in this sort of work and posting yourself as to conditions, will repay your company for the cost of your time and expenses.

Unquestionably your company is a subscriber to one of the mercantile agencies. If not, they should be, and you should be furnished with a full and complete report on every mercantile loss you are called upon to adjust. I remember a few years ago at a Hannabal (Mo.) fire, the assured either added a flat $50,000 to their last inventory or else lied to their creditors, because after the fire they issued a circular letter to their creditors, giving a copy of their statement of loss as adjusted with the insurance companies, the amount of the inventory showed $50,000 in excess of what they had stated it amounted to in their statement to Dun and Bradstreet. Their explanation to their creditors was, they had concealed $50,000 they had owed, and had reduced their inventory that amount in their statement to mercantile agencies to make things even. If they would lie once they would lie twice, maybe they lied about owing that $50,000 which they concealed from their creditors, and maybe they lied to the insurance companies when they handed in the amount of their inventory as being $50,000 in excess of the amount they had stated it to be to their creditors. At any rate the truth would have been known and possibly the companies would have been saved $50,000 if the adjusters had taken the precaution to have gotten a special report from Bradstreet or Dun.

How many independent adjusters representing a long list of companies in every large fire are subscribers to a mercantile agency? I dare say not half a dozen in the whole country, and yet it is information they should not be without. Every one of them should be a subscriber to Dun or Bradstreet. If not, they are just as certain to overpay some loss as that daylight follows night.

Sample Page Merchandise Account on Ledger and Statement of Loss Therefrom—Profits in Manufacturing Plant.

The following is a fair sample of a merchandise account as it appears in the ledger of a merchant's book:

1904.						1904.					
Jan.	2	To	Inventory..		$26,000	Jan.	31	By	Mdse.	Sales....	$13,800
"	31	"	Mdse.	Pur......	10,800	"	31	"	"	Ret......	250
"	31	"	"	Ret. & A.	700	Feb.	28	"	"	Sales....	10,575
Feb.	28	"	"	Pur.....	8,600	"	28	"	"	Ret......	325
"	28	"	"	Ret. & A.	375	Mar.	31	"	"	Sales....	16,425
Mar.	31	"	"	Pur......	9,675	"	31	"	"	Ret......	435
"	31	"	"	Ret. & A.	567	Apr.	30	"	"	Sales....	12,150
Apr.	30	"	"	Pur.	6,756	"	30	"	"	Ret......	193
"	30	"	"	Ret. & A.	437	May	31	"	"	Sales....	14,236
May	31	"	"	Pur.	7,693	"	31	"	"	Ret......	178
"	31	"	"	Ret. & A.	842	June	30	"	"	Sales....	20,789
June	30	"	"	Pur......	6,957	"	30	"	"	Ret......	237
"	30	"	"	Ret. & A.	359	July	31	"	"	Sales....	15,283
July	31	"	"	Pur......	10,764	"	31	"	"	Ret......	364
"	31	"	"	Ret. & A.	653	Aug.	31	"	"	Sales....	19,476
Aug.	31	"	"	Pur......	12,786	"	31	"	"	Ret......	113
"	31	"	"	Ret. & A.	689	Sep.	30	"	"	Sales....	8,679
Sep.	30	"	"	Pur......	19,436	"	30	"	"	Ret......	147
"	30	"	"	Ret. & A.	347	Oct.	31	"	"	Sales....	17,124
Oct.	31	"	"	Pur.	10,798	"	31	"	"	Ret......	236
"	31	"	"	Ret. & A.	878	Nov.	30	"	"	Sales....	22,187
Nov.	30	"	"	Pur......	11,745	"	30	"	"	Ret......	475
"	30	"	"	Ret. & A.	1,087	Dec.	31	"	"	Sales....	4,851
Dec.	31	"	"	Pur......	8,649	"	31	"	"	Ret......	122
"	31	"	"	Ret. & A.	983	"	31	"	Inventory.......		32,232
"	31	"	P. & L...		51,306						
					$210,882						$210,882
1905.						1905.					
Jan.	1	To	Inventory.......$32,232			Jan.	31	By	Mdse.	Pur......$14,287	
"	31	"	Mdse.	Pur......	9,786	"	31	"	"	Ret......	342
"	31	"	"	Ret. & A.	329	Feb.	28	"	"	Pur......	11,364
Feb.	28	"	"	Pur.....	9,873	"	28	"	"	Ret......	239
"	28	"	"	Ret. & A.	597	Mar.	31	"	"	Pur......	17,747
Mar.	31	"	"	Pur......	11,397	"	31	"	"	Ret......	539
"	31	"	"	Ret. & A.	324						

On the night of March 31, 1905, a fire occurs which destroys the greater portion of the stock. All bills were entered, plus freight, and minus cash discounts, so that merchandise account shows net cost of stock. But all cross entries should be deducted, as the sales that were returned are debited to merchandise, not at cost, but with the profit added and to add them to the purchases is unfair to the companies; also purchases that were returned to the seller and are credited to merchandise and should come out of the sales as it reduces the assured's profits. A great many adjusters are in the habit of taking the ledger footings as the purchase and sales and deducting the sum of the returns on both sides from the debit and credit side and while this method will bring the same results as getting at the exact purchases, yet it is not correct in this case to call the purchases for 1905 $32,306, because they were not that amount, being merely the debit side of the merchandise account, less the amount of the inventory, and if the statement be made up in that way it is confusing and is liable to cause you to make a mistake. I will give an example of both ways of figuring, which will show exactly the same result. (See Exhibits "K" and "L.")

Exhibit "K"—Correct Method.

PROFIT STATEMENT.

Inventory January 2, 1904......................		$26,000.00
Subsequent purchases $125,659.00		
Less purchases returned 3,075.00		
		122,584.00
Goods to be accounted for Jan. 1, 1905.....		$148,584.00
Inventory of January 1, 1905, accounts for.......		32,232.00
Showing that goods that went out of store cost		$116,352.00
Merchandise sales $175,575.00		
Less goods sold and returned................... 7,917.00		
		167,658.00
The difference is the profit, or..............		$51,306.00

A profit ratio of 30.60 per cent. on sales, or 44.09 per cent. on cost, hence following

STATEMENT OF LOSS.

Stock on hand Jan. 1, 1905, per inventory........		$32,232.00
Subsequent purchases ....$ 31,056.00		
Less purchases returned 1,120.00		
		29,936.00
		$62,168.00
Merchandise sold ....$ 43,398.00		
Less goods sold and returned................... 1,250.00		
Net sales ....$ 42,148.00		
Less 30.60 per cent. profit on sales.............. 12,897.29		
		29,250.71
Book value of stock on hand at time of fire		$32,917.?9

Exhibit "L."

PROFIT STATEMENT.

1904 inventory and purchases....................		$159,576.00
(It is not; it is debit side of Mdse. acct. for 1904.)		
Less cross entries, returns and allowances.......		10,992.00
Goods to be accounted for Jan. 1, 1905........		$148,584.00
Inventory Jan. 1, 1905, accounts for.............		32,232.00
Showing that goods that went out of store cost		$116,352.00
Merchandise sales in 1904....................$178,650.00		
(The sales were only $175,575.)		
Less cross entries 10,992.00		
		167,658.00
The difference is the profit, or..............		$51,306.00

Same as Exhibit "K," therefore same ratio, hence following

STATEMENT OF LOSS.

Stock on hand Jan. 1, 1905, per inventory........ $32,232.00
Subsequent purchases ....$ 32,306.00
    (The purchases were $31,056 and $32,306 is
    the debit side of Mdse. acct., less the inven-
    tory.)
Less cross entries, returns and allowances....... 2,370.00

                                                           29,936.00
                                                           $62,168.00

Merchandise sales ....$ 44,518.00
    (This is cr. side of Mdse. acct., and not sales.)
Less cross entries, returns and allowances....... 2,370.00

                                         $42,148.00
Less profit, 30.60 per cent. on sales............. 12,897.29

                                                           29,250.71

Book value stock on hand at time of the
    fire $32,917.29

If the loss be on the stock of a manufacturer, the profit is arrived at in the same manner except that pay-roll is added to the cost of the goods the same as purchases; also, fuel, water, heat and power, but if labor and fuel costs about the same per centage of amount of purchases of raw material during the current year that it did during the preceding year, it makes very little difference in the general result whether cognizance be taken of these items or not, it merely decreases the profit (see Exhibit "M"), which is same statement as Exhibit "K," except 20 per cent. is added to purchases for labor in manufacturing.

Exhibit "M."

Inventory Jan. 2, 1904............................. $26,000.00
Subsequent net purchases.......................$122,584.00
Labor, fuel, etc., in manufacturing............... 24,516.80

                                                           147,100.80

Goods to be accounted for Jan. 1, 1905...... $173,100.80
Inventory of Jan. 1, 1905, accounts for.......... 32,232.00

Showing that goods sold cost................. $140,868.80
The net sales amounted to....................... 167,658.00

The difference is the profit.................. $26,789.20

A profit ratio of 15.98 per cent. on sales, hence the following

STATEMENT OF LOSS.

Jan. 1, 1905, inventory............................. $32,232.00
Subsequent purchases net 29,936.00
Labor, fuel, etc., in manufacturing............... 5,987.20

                                                           $68,155.20

```
Net sales ........................................$ 42,148.00
Less 15.98 per cent. profit on sales...............   6,735.25
                                                     _____
                                                       35,412.75

    Book value of stock at time of fire...........     $32,742.45
```

Or $174.84 less than statement of loss as shown in Exhibits "K" and "L."

If the amount paid for labor during current year be a greater per centage of the purchases of raw material than preceding year the advantage is with the insured, if the proportion was larger the preceding year, the advantage is with the company.

Why is it that insurance companies and adjusters lay so much stress on figuring on cost, rather than on sales as the merchants and manufacturers do? A merchant marks his goods to sell for what they will bring, and at the end of the day if his sales have been $1,500 on goods that cost him $1,000, he calls his profits 33 1/3 per cent.—that is, on sales. The insurance adjuster calls it 50 per cent.—that is, on cost. What is the difference, pray? The bookkeeper, at the end of the year, figures his profit ratio on sales. Why stand for an old fogy way of doing things when it is entirely different from the methods in general use by merchants and manufacturers throughout the country? It is just as easy to determine the ratio of profit on sales as it is on cost, and a great deal easier to figure loss by multiplying the amount of the sales by the profit ratio as was done in Statement of Loss in Exhibit "K," than it would be to divide the profit ratio on cost—i. e., 44.09 per cent. plus $1.00, into the amount of the sales when both methods give practically the same results or should do so within a dollar or so, owing entirely to the accuracy of your figures. In this particular case the difference is but .24 cents.

I have known adjusters to ascertain a merchant's profits from his books to be 33 1/3 per cent. of the sales and in making up his statement of loss apply that ratio of profit to the cost, and I am firmly of the opinion they did it because they did not know any better and not through any desire to harm the assured.

I know one adjuster who was selected by a committee of adjusters because of his supposed ability as an expert accountant to go through a set of books and draw off a statement of the loss. He worked on these books for more than a month, the adjusters who employed him had to raise his figures on the book statement alone $22,000 because he had reduced the preceding year's sales by deducting the rebates and allowances on sales, thereby reducing the profit ratio, and refusing to treat the current year's sales in the same manner.

Another adjuster in adjusting a loss wanted to deduct from the purchases (the debit side of merchandise account) the returned sales charged to merchandise without deducting them from the sales or credit side of merchandise. A man who would make a mistake of that kind against the insured is just as apt to make one against his company. And this happened only a short time ago and the adjuster referred to is looked on as a leader in his territory. But an older and more experienced adjuster happened to be on the loss and finally convinced him of his mistake.

Accurate Method of Apportionment—Treatment of Fraud Losses, and Losses Where Books Should Be Ignored.

As to certain criticism of my statements of loss I will say I attempted to make it clear that all of them were supposed to be computed in dollars from the books. The statement by count was given merely as an illustration to prove the correctness of the book statement. If a count might be had of the goods on hand at the time of the fire, there would be no use in trying to determine the ratio of profits, or making a long drawn out statement concerning them. It would be necessary only to apply the market price to each article, making it short and to the point as was shown in Exhibit "H."

The following is a very good rule for the apportionment of the loss to the policies, and is as nearly perfect as it is possible for human rules to be. The loss is $71,836.93, the insurance $87,593.78, consisting of one policy of $60,000, one of $8,625, one of $7,031.42 and one of $11,937.36. We first find the loss ratio to each $1,000 of insurance which is $820.1145.

Therefore, $2,000	pays	$ 820.1145	plus	$820.1145	equals	$1,640.2290
" 3,000	"	1,640.2290	"	820.1145	"	2,460.3435
" 4,000	"	2,460.3435	"	820.1145	"	3,280.4580
" 5,000	"	3,280.4580	"	820.1145	"	4,100.5725
" 6,000	"	4,100.5725	"	820.1145	"	4,920.6870
" 7,000	"	4,920.6870	"	820.1145	"	5,740.8015
" 8,000	"	5,740.8015	"	820.1145	"	6,560.9160
" 9,000	"	6,560.9160	"	820.1145	"	7,381.0305
" 10,000	"	7,381.0305	"	820.1145	"	8,201.1450

Hence following apportionment, a $60,000 policy will pay 10 times as much as $6,000, or $49,206.87.

We divide the $11,937.36 policy as follows:	$10,000.00	pays	$8,201.14
	1,000.00	"	820.11
	900.00	"	738.10
	30.00	"	24.60
	7.00	"	' 5.74
	30	"	25
	.06	"	.05
The $7,031.42 policy is divided as follows:	7,000.00	"	5,740.80
	30.00	"	24.60
	1.00	"	82
	40	"	33
	.02	"	.02
The $8,625 policy is divided as follows:	8,000.00	"	6,560.92
	600.00	"	492.08
	20.00	"	16.40
	5.00	"	4.10
Total paid by all the policies,			$71,836.93

All done by changing the decimal in the table from right to left or vice versa as the case may be. I never use but one column of figures shown in the table and that is the last or right hand column. The figures prove themselves, as when you have added what $1,000 pays to the amount paid by $9,000, the result will be ten times the sum that $1,000 pays, otherwise you will have made a mistake. The other figures in the table are given to make the method perfectly clear.

Having given a number of book statements in my former letters and I hope having made them clear to the mind of the average man, I will take up the adjustment of some losses where the books ought to be left out of the adjustment or method of arriving at the loss.

Some years ago, I was appointed by the companies as appraiser on a fraud loss in an Illinois town. We found on arriving at the place that all of the goods had been removed from the building where the loss occurred, to a building some distance away, the goods all straightened out and inventoried. The insurance was about $10,000 or $12,000. The saved goods inventoried about $1,800 or $2,000. The adjusters claimed assured's stock never was over $3,500, and I think they were right. I found assured had shipped a lot of old goods that he had collected together in St. Louis, that he bought a few goods subsequently and I believe obtained a lot of fraudulent bills for a great deal more than he bought, judging from the class of people he bought of. I obtained from other merchants information to the effect that their purchases from St. Louis amounted to so many dollars and that the freight paid on same was a certain per cent.

Taking the assured's freight bills and giving him credit for the same ratio of purchases to the amount of freight paid by him, it would have given him a stock of about $3,500. And that would have been a perfectly fair method of settling his loss, because his were the commonest kind of goods, whereas the several merchants from whom I obtained the information dealt in a much better grade or class of goods. Therefore, it is plain that if goods costing 25c to 50c per yard, and boots and shoes costing $25.00 to $36.00 per dozen, can be shipped from St. Louis to the town where the fire was for one-half per cent. of their value the same kind of goods costing only half as much would cost one per cent. of their value for transportation. So that a $25.00 freight bill paid on the better class of goods would mean the bill of goods amounted to $5,000, whereas on the poorer quality it would mean but $2,500. But my co-appraiser wouldn't stand for that way of figuring at all, and the umpire stood with him. And as the adjusters had ordered the assured to remove his stock to another building, the damaged goods separated from the undamaged and an inventory made of the stock, the assured forthwith complied with their requirements, thereby destroying all evidence of the total loss or rather placing the claim in such condition that they were not in position to disprove his claim for a large amount of totally destroyed goods. Just think of them placing themselves at the mercy of that rascal, with over $10,000 insurance involved, for the sake of preserving the salvage on a stock that was not worth $2,000! Had they insisted on the stock remaining where it was, they would have shown to the appraisers the impossibility of assured's claim for total loss by the space the saved stock occupied and the conditions and appearances of the store. The other appraiser and umpire salted the companies for about $8,000, and would have given assured about $1,700 more, only the other appraiser got too smart and I tripped him on some figures.

Suppose on arriving at the scene of the loss you find the fire has caused practically a total loss in so far as the value is concerned, but the greater part of the property can be identified for the purpose of taking an inventory, and from its condition and relative position it then occupies, it gives you a pretty fair idea of what the total loss is as well as the character and amount of the entire stock on hand immediately before the fire. In such cases don't permit the goods to be removed or put in order until you have some good evidence by other merchants of the condition of affairs, or until your loss is adjusted. If an appraisal has to be had, let the appraisers see it as you saw it. Don't look at the books, bring into play all the good "horse" sense at your command. If the goods have been knocked off the shelves or have been thrown on the floor, sometimes, but not always, get the insured to replace them on the shelves in as near the same order as they were before the fire. When this is done it will refresh his memory as to what he had there that was totally obliterated· by the fire, and will help you to judge as to the truth or falsity of the claim.

How many times has the friction of a $3,000 stock, rubbing against $10,000 insurance, caused a fire? How many times in such cases, where the fire caused a 50 per cent. to 75 per cent. damage to such a stock, has all evidence of the value been destroyed by removing and conditioning the stock. To save $750 to $1,500 from the salvage, many young and inexperienced adjusters have destroyed all évidence their companies had to establish the value of the stock. If they had insisted on the stock being kept intact until they could have called in two or three responsible people to take an inventory, cautioning them to look carefully into conditions and circumstances of the stock, noting the class of goods and what proportion if any of it, could have been or was actually burned beyond identification, thus making of them good witnesses for you, should you be forced into court. It might also be a good idea to photograph the stock before allowing it to be handled even for the purpose of inventorying it.

Remember it is hard to burn the heels of boots and shoes. It is hard to burn a book. A fire that will burn a full bolt of cloth is very apt to entirely destroy the shelving which held it, and while the remnants of such articles may not be a correct basis on which to fix the value of the thing destroyed it will at least serve you in forming a fair estimate as to quantities destroyed.

I very well remember that when I first commenced adjusting losses I was called to San Antonio, Texas, on a wholesale and retail grocery loss. It was badly damaged by a flash fire. There were two or three other youngsters who had fully as much experience as I did, so we appointed our committees, I being in charge of the one on the books. We had assured send their books to us at the Menger Hotel and we proceeded to·wade through them, they showed a hopelessly total loss. We could see everyone looking at us as we supposed wondering how such young men secured such important positions.

Every adjuster has no doubt at some time or other, felt his importance and knows, therefore, how we felt. Well, as I say, we had figured out a total loss, we hadn't asked the assured if they would accept a total as we were waiting—merely out of courtesy though, for the arrival of another adjuster, one of the older ones—(Mr. J. R. Polak) (now of Atlanta, Georgia). When he came he looked over our statement, took our word that the schedule of insurance was correct, examined his own policy and then asked us to show him the loss. We introduced him to the assured, he asked for a small blank book and commenced taking down the various items, he and the assured agreeing on damages and the amount of goods totally destroyed as they went along. In about two and a half hours the loss was adjusted at about 65 cents on the dollar and then I began wondering how in the world I secured my job and how I was going to hold it, but did not look quite so important about the hotel as I had for several days previous thereto. This merely shows that we either had no brains, or that we were acting like machines following a beaten path and forgetting to bring into play what common sense we had. It shows, too, that an adjuster wants to consider carefully what is the best method for handling the particular loss he is called upon to adjust and that no fixed rule will govern all cases.

I also had a loss where nearly if not quite all of a stock of nearly $100,000 that was badly damaged by fire could be inventoried. Assured claimed to have taken an inventory which was completed twenty-four hours before the fire, but the extensions and additions were not complete. The adjusters did not like the looks of things and had another inventory made, which was $9,000 less than the one assured made before the fire. Then recourse was had to the books, which showed the inventory made by the adjusters was about correct. So you see the books sometimes play an important part and sometimes they don't.

As to buildings, if you don't know how to make an estimate of the cost to rebuild, learn. Get a carpenter, a brick mason, a plasterer and a painter to show you how to make an estimate, then when you are sent to adjust a loss, tell the assured to hire a builder to represent him, let assured sit down with you and his builder and give you a description of his building, then you and his builder make your estimate agreeing on each item as you go along. This method will save money for your company, and will post you so that in a very short time you will know all about it, and nearly always get your loss adjusted.

Don't take any stock in estimates of so much per cubic foot. If you get within 500 cubic feet of the right measure you will still have to guess at the price per cubic foot, for if 7½ cents per cubic foot don't land you where you wish it to, maybe 9 cents will and there you are, it's a guess from start to finish. You would not dare agree with assured on the price per cubic foot unless you first knew the number of cubic feet, which is proof enough the rule won't work.

The estimate in detail, is the most accurate method known and is easily mastered in a few months' time.

POINTS RAISED ON A LOSS IN ACTUAL PROCESS OF ADJUSTMENT.

There is now in process of adjustment a loss involving the rules or principles laid down in Exhibits "I" and "J" in my third letter, but the adjusters refuse to see it that way. They insist on figuring it the wrong way, claiming 2½ per cent. depreciation on top of a depreciation of over 6 per cent., which will not be conceded by the assured, as it would be manifestly unfair to do so.

The figures which are shown in the profit Statement No. 1 and Statement No. 2 are agreed to by both sides. The only question left open for adjustment being the one of depreciation, if any. Before taking up the statements, I will say assured charged their purchases less all discounts to merchandise account, hence all bills are entered net, exclusive of freights. The inventory was taken each year net, i. e., bill cost, less discounts, and plus actual freights except such items as were reduced for depreciation, the inventory plainly showing which goods were depreciated. After the inventory taken at cost and value was completed, a flat $2,500 was deducted each year. Statements of profits and the loss follow:

(Profit) Statement No. 1.

Total debit side of merchandise account year 1904....$286,892.05
From which deduct inventory of Jan. 1, 1904, entered
    in ledger at 50,646.52

                                              $236,245.53

Also deduct returns and allowances on
    sales debited to merchandise account.$1,156.58
And items that should have been charged
    to Profit and Loss................... 70.98   1,227.56

    Making the gross sales $235,017.97

Less reclamations on purchases credited to merchandise account 21.95

Net purchases for year 1904 ....$234,996.02
Freight paid on purchases for 1904................. 16,172.54
Inventory January 1, 1904...............$53,146.52
Less depreciation 2,500.00   50,646.52

Stock to be accounted for Jan. 1, 1905.............$301,815.08
Of which the inventory of Jan. 1, 1905, accounts for $48,342.63
Less depreciation 2,500.00   45,842.63

Showing the goods that went out of the store cost $255,972.45

Credit side of merchandise account year 1904....$325,812.82
Less reclamations on purchases credited to merchandise $21.95
And amounts which should have been credited to profit and loss.....................188.47   210.42

Making the gross sales.......................$325,602.40
Deduct returned sales and allowances debited to merchandise account 1,156.58

Thus showing net sales for 1904 to be..........$324,445.82
As shown above these goods cost assured......... 255,972.45

Making the gross profit for year 1904...........$68,473.37

The ratio of profit on sales being 21.105 per cent. and on cost 26¾ per cent., hence following book statement agreed to between assured and adjusters. The only question left to be determined is that of depreciation, or sound cash value at time of fire, hence

(Loss) Statement No. 2

Debit side of merchandise account year 1905.......$246,459.74
Less inventory of Jan. 1, 1905, as entered in ledger... 45,842.63

$200,617.11

Deduct returned sales and allowances on
   sales $1,042.45
And items not merchandise 55.75   1,098.20

Making gross purchases for 1905..............$199,518.91
Deduct reclamations on purchases 108.10

Net purchases year 1905 ....$199,410.81
Net freight on purchases of 1905.................   13,521.65

Credit side merchandise account 1905.........$237,381.29
Less reclamations on purchases $108.10
And items not merchandise.................   166.21   274.31

Gross sales for year 1905 ....$237,106.98
Less returned sales and allowances................   1,042.45

Net 1905 sales $236,064.53
Inventory stock on hand Jan. 1, 1905..............$ 48,342.63
Less depreciation 2,500.00

Value of stock Jan. 1, 1905, as entered in ledger.$ 45,842.63
Net purchases as previously shown.................   199,410.81
Net freight on purchases........................   13,521.65

                                             $258,775.09
Net sales as shown above.............$236,064.53
Less profit on cost, 26¾ per cent.......   49,820.33   186,244.20

Stock on hand at time of fire...................$ 72,530.89
Agreed value of stock in annex building not covered..   2,414.00

Book value of stock insured as agreed..............$ 70,116.89
   Which adjusters want to depreciate 2½ per cent.   1,752.92

   Company adjusters want to adjust loss at........$ 68,363.97
   My claim is that the profit takes care of the depreciation.
(See my third letter, Exhibits "I" and "J") and that if an inventory could have been taken of the stock on hand at time of fire it would have amounted to $75,030.89, from which the companies would be entitled to $2,500 depreciation following assured's usual custom of depreciating the stock $2,500 each year. In this the adjusters say I am wrong. To prove the correct-

ness of my position, I will make up a statement for the year 1904 treating it precisely as the adjusters want to treat the assured's loss.

Statement No. 3.

Inventory stock on hand Jan. 1, 1904		$ 53,146.52
Less depreciation		2,500.00
Value of stock as entered in ledger		$ 50,646.52
Net purchases for 1904 as heretofore shown		234,996.02
Net freight on 1904 purchases		16,172.54
		$301,815.08
Net sales 1904 as heretofore shown	$324,445.82	
Less 26¾ per cent. profit on cost or 21.105 on sales	68,473.37	255,972.45
Stock on hand at time of fire book value		$ 45,842.62
Deduct 2½ per cent. depreciation		1,146.06
Net value on basis adjusters want to adjust assured's loss		$ 44,696.57

Now we know that statement No. 3 is not correct, because that statement only shows a stock on hand of $44,696.57, and we know that assured did at that time take an inventory of their stock then on hand, and that it amounted to $48,342.63, that after they had depreciated all articles that ought to be depreciated, they arbitrarily deducted $2,500 more depreciation.

This proves that the profits take care of the depreciation. It proves that the insurance companies get the benefit of the depreciation in a book statement. It proves that assured, if he could have taken an inventory of the stock he had on hand at the time of fire, would have had a larger amount to depreciate than his books will show, and it proves the correctness of the position taken in Exhibits "I" and "J."

To further substantiate the correctness of my position, I will suppose that each article of merchandise dealt in is a suite of furniture and that its net cost is $10.00 each, and apply those prices, as nearly as possible, to the foregoing statement. See (Hypothetical) Statement No. 4, following:

(Hypothetical) Statement No. 4.

January, 1904, inventory, 5,314 suites at $10.00........$ 53,140.00
Net purchases 1904, 25,117 suites at $10.00.......... 251,170.00

To be accounted for Jan. 1, 1905, 30,431 suites
    at $10.00 ....$304,310.00
Inventory Jan. 1, 1905, accounts for 4,834 suites at
    $10.00 .... 48,340.00

Making the sales for 1904, 25,597 suites at $10.00.$255,970.00
These goods were sold for 319,962.50

Gross profit is the difference, or...............$ 63,992.50
Which is 25 per cent. on cost or 20 per cent. on sales.
Jan. 1, 1904, stock on hand, 4,834 suites at $10.00....$ 48,340.00
Net purchases 1905, 21,293 suites at $10.00........ 212,930.00

Total inventory and purchases, 26,127 suites at
    $10.00 ....$261,270.00
Sold 18,624 suites at $12.50.............$232,800.00
Less 25 per cent. profit................. 46,560.00 186,240.00

Stock on hand at time of fire...................$ 75,030.00
Foregoing statement shows that:
Inventory and purchases were ....26,127 suites
That sales were ....18,624 suites
Necessarily there were left 7,503 suites at $10.00..$ 75,030.00

On the $75,030, the companies would be entitled to a depreciation of $2,500 because the assured had been in the habit of taking that amount off each year.

As was noted in Letter No. 3, Exhibits "I" and "J," the only fair way to treat a loss where assured has arbitrarily taken off a percentage of flat depreciation, is to restore it in the beginning of the statement and take off the depreciation that assured has been in the habit of taking off, and more besides if you are entitled to it.

The loss referred to in this letter is on a wholesale furniture stock, common and medium priced stuff. You will note from the statements that assured's sales are six times greater than the inventories, that the sales less the profits show that assured turned the stock five times in a year. To do this they could not have had a very heavy depreciation. An old or out of date stock won't sell that fast, but when a wholesale furniture merchant can get rid of his stock five times in one year, he is going some. This particular merchant is ordering the same kind of goods as were destroyed by the fire and is paying about 5 per cent. more for about half of them than he paid before the fire and none are any cheaper. Why should his stock be depreciated under these circumstances? If you owned it would you stand for depreciation? Yet one of the adjusters on this loss insists that assured is unfair and unreasonable because he will not submit to a further depreciation than he himself deducted in January. I esteem him as a level-headed adjuster and among the top-notchers in the profession. I am sure he wants to be fair, but in this case it seems to me he is biased. All of us are human and sometimes even an adjuster errs, or as David Harum expresses it, "There's as much human nature in some folks as th' is in others, if not more."

The foregoing described loss was finally adjusted, the basis of settlement being as follows: The depreciation of $2,500 deducted from the inventory in January, 1905, was restored, and then 5 per cent. depreciation deducted from the total stock on hand at time of fire, which makes the loss to the insurance companies $68,986.05, a fair and square deal for both sides.

CHAPTER XVIII.

FORM OF PROOF AND STATEMENT OF LOSS ACTUALLY ADJUSTED—IRON SAFE CLAUSE—APPRECIATION.

The following is a model form of proof of loss, which may look simple enough, but at the time worried the adjusters not a little, as at least seven different sets of proofs could have been made, but all were embraced in the one form set out as follows·

CLAIM FOR LOSS

Under policy No. .... of the...........................
Insurance Company of ....

By your policy of insurance, issued at your Podunk, Texas, agency, the number, date, expiration, amount of policy and the amount claimed thereunder being shown in "Schedule of Insurance and Apportionment of Claim" here to attached, you insured Richard Roe Company, the party herein and therein named, against loss or damage by fire in the amount shown in said "Schedule of Insurance and Apportionment of Claim" on the following described property:

$.......... On stock in trade in building No. 232 W. Commerce street, $150,000. Total concurrent insurance permitted.

$.......... On stock in trade in building Nos. 234 and 236 W. Commerce street, $250,000. Total concurrent insurance permitted.

$.......... On stock in trade in building Nos. 238 and 240 W. Commerce street, $150,000. Total concurrent insurance permitted. All in the city of Podunk, Texas.

(Iron-safe clause attached to policy. Exact wording of policy is not given on account of its length.)

A fire occurred at about 2 o'clock a. m., November 19, 1900, and originated in building Nos. 238 and 240 W. Commerce street, occupied by us as a wholesale grocery, from cause unknown to assured or his affiant, which damaged and destroyed assured's property insured by you under said policy, as shown in "Statement of Loss" hereto attached.

219

There was no other insurance except such as is shown in "Schedule of Insurance and Apportionment of Claim" hereto attached. All of the insurance on each stock is concurrent in form. Note—Those policies dated prior to July 3, 1900, only permitted $220,000 total insurance on stock in building Nos. 234 and 236 W. Commerce street and were changed by endorsement to permit $250,000 total insurance, and those which permitted but $100,000 total insurance on stock in building Nos. 238 and 240 W. Commerce street were, by endorsement, changed to permit $150,000 total insurance. The "Schedule of Insurance and Apportionment of Claim" shows which stock and how much each policy covered at the time of fire, if any of them did not insure the property in that manner when first written, they were subsequently made to do so by endorsement.

At the time your policy was issued and at the time of the fire, the said property insured by you was owned by Richard Roe Company and there has been no change in the title, use, occupation, location, possession or exposure of said property since the issuance of your policy.

There was no mortgage or other encumbrance on any part of said property.

The actual cash value of the property insured by you and the amount of loss claimed thereon is shown in "Statement of Loss" hereto attached.

The assured occupied all of the following buildings on W. Commerce street for wholesale purposes as follows: No. 232 as boot, shoe, hat, cap and clothing store; Nos. 234 and 236 as dry goods and notion store; Nos. 238 and 240 as a grocery store, and for no other purpose.

Richard Roe Company's claim against your company or association, by reason of said loss, damage and policy of insurance, is shown in "Schedule of Insurance and Apportionment of Claim" hereto attached.

All statements and schedules hereto attached are hereby sworn to and made part of these proofs.

Podunk, Texas, December 21, 1900.

RICHARD ROE COMPANY,
(By John Doe, President.)

(Usual form of oath before notary, and certificate of notary follows.)

STATEMENT OF LOSS.

Richard Roe Company—(Exhibit "A.")

Statement of loss in building No. 232 W. Commerce street:

Stock on hand at time of fire per inventory taken after fire	$108,092.82
Freight and marine insurance in excess of cash discounts	2,215.90
Agreed book value of stock	$110,308.72
Add 5 per cent. appreciation per agreement	5,515.44
Agreed cash market value	$115,824.16
Salvage apportioned to this stock	85,726.47
Net loss and damage	$ 30,097.69

Note.—As to disposition and apportionment of salvage see Exhibit "B."

Exhibit "B."

Statement of loss in Building Nos. 234 and 236 W. Commerce street:

Inventory stock on hand January 1, 1900	$285,531.10
Add subsequent purchases	616,203.01
And purchases received in stock subsequent to January 1, but paid for and charged to merchandise prior thereto	2,364.75
	$904,098.86

Contra.

Returns and allowances on sales charged to merchandise		$ 11,040.74
Merchandise in transit		6,766.10
Received prior to January 1, 1900, but paid for and charged subsequent thereto		53,066.91
Cash charged to merchandise by defaulting clerk		2,000.00
Sales since Jan. 1, 1900	$684,842.64	
Less credited to merchandise a/c to entry of defaulting clerk	$2,000.00	

Returns and allow-
   ances on sales...11,040.74
Sold, not removed.... 1,044.76 14,085.50

Net sales $670,757.14
Less 28.88 per cent.
   profit 150,306.02
                             520,451.12

Stock in warehouse at 508-10 Market
   street 10,220.63
Stock in building 238 and 240 W. Com
   merce street .... 2,682.26 ·606,227.76

                                 $297,871.76

Freights and marine insurance exceed cash discounts
   2.05 per cent. 6,106.35

                                 $303,977.45
Deduct in compromise to agree with adjusters...... 236.95

Book value of stock in buildings 232, 234 and 236....$303,740.50
Agreed appreciation 5 per cent................... 15,187.02

   Agreed cash market value....................$318,927.52
Deduct cash market value of stock in building No.
   232 W. Commerce street 115,824.16

Cash market value stock in 234 and 236 W. Commerce street $203,103.36
Salvage apportioned to this stock................. 81,136.83

   Agreed loss and damage $121,966.53
   Note.—The Notion stock in second story of Nos. 234 and 236 W. Commerce street was damaged to such an extent that it was found impossible to inventory it correctly; but the first story and basement stock was saved in a damaged condition and inventoried (cost price), $96,782.24. The companies took the stock in both buildings at its agreed value, invited merchants and wreckers from Chicago, Kansas City, San Antonio, Waco, Galveston, Dallas and Houston to bid for the stock at open sale December 19, 1900. After deducting all expenses, the salvage netted $166,863.30, of which $81,136.83 was apportioned to the stock in building Nos. 234 and 236 W. Commerce street and $85,726.47 to stock in No. 232 W. Commerce street.

Statement of loss in building Nos. 238 and 240 W. Commerce street:

Grocery department. Assured took an inventory every Saturday evening as to quantities, but did not place the prices on the articles; hence, having taken an inventory on Saturday evening, November 17, 1900, and the fire having occurred early the following Monday morning, no sales or purchases having in the meanwhile been made, all that was necessary was to price the goods, make the extensions and additions, which when completed amounted to... ....$ 87,328.59

Add for merchandise from dry goods department, as shown in Exhibit "B.".................... 2,682.26

Goods on consignment 1,586.23

$ 91,597.08

Inventory of stock saved $31,433.04

Less agreed damage 15,751.99   15,681.05

Agreed loss and damage.....................$ 75,916.03

SCHEDULE OF INSURANCE AND APPORTIONMENT OF CLAIM.

Company	Stock in Bldg. 232 W. Commerce		Stock in Bldg. 234-36 W. Com'erce		Stock in Bldg. 238-40 W. Com'ce		Grand Total	
	Ins.	Claimed	Ins.	Claimed	Ins.	Claimed	Ins.	Claimed
A...	$62,250	$16,521.88	....	....	....	....	$62,250	$16,521.88
B...	....	....	$116,250	$67,573.50	....	....	116,250	67,573.50
C...	....	....	....	....	$34,000	$33,402.07	34,000	33,402.07
D...	15,000	3,981.18	17,500	10,172.35	....	....	32,500	14,153.53
E...	....	....	11,250	6,539.37	4,750	4,666.46	16,000	11,205.83
F...	5,500	1,459.76	....	....	7,000	6,876.90	12,500	8,336.66
G...	30,650	8,134.87	64,825	37,681.31	31,525	30,970.60	127,000	76,786.78
	$113,400	$30,097.69	$209,825	$121,966.53	$77,275	$75,916.03	$400,500	$227,980.25

The dates and numbers are not given on account of space it would require.

There are ninety-seven policies. I have consolidated them into seven.

THE EFFECT OF THE IRON-SAFE CLAUSE.

It will be seen from the foregoing statements, that assured's books for their grocery stock were kept separate from the others, and consequently they complied with the iron-safe clause in so far as that stock was concerned. But there was a technical, if not a flagrant, violation of the iron-safe clause on the other two stocks, because both were kept track of by one set of books, and had both buildings been wholly destroyed the assured could have shown by their books the sum total of both stocks, but it would have been impossible to have shown the value of either one separately. But the fact that the contents of one store was saved intact, no goods being destroyed therein, enabled the assured to show the value of the stock in each building. (See Exhibits "B" and "A.")

While a great many of the adjusters took non-waiver agreements, yet there was no attempt made by them to penalize the assured for a violation of the iron-safe clause. As we all know, the clause is a warranty. The Missouri Court of Appeals holds that a warranty is in the nature of a condition precedent in the contract and no inquiry is allowed as to the materiality of the fact warranted. Brooks v. Standard Ins. Co., 11 Mo. App. 349. 1st Phillips, Sec. 755, gives practically the same definition.

I am not ready to admit that this is so, in so far as the definition of a warranty relates to the iron-safe clause, for where is the insurer harmed by reason of a breach of such warranty, if the loss be only a damage to the goods in sight or if a partial loss and some of the goods be wholly destroyed and the assured abandons claim for such goods and only claims a damage on those that can be identified? Yet, on the other hand, the insurance companies might claim, and with some reason, they would not have been on the risk at all had they known the facts in the case.

However, for the sake of argument, let us concede the Missouri doctrine as to the meaning of a warranty does apply to the iron-safe clause and that assured in this particular case did not so keep their books as to show a true record of sales and purchases in each store, but that they were so kept as to show the aggregate in both stores, then those policies of companies "A" and 'B" would be void entirely, "E" void as to the amount covered in building Nos. 234 and 236, "F" void as to the amount covered in building No. 232. Those of companies "D" and "G" would be valid. The reason being the iron-safe clause does not require the assured, who has one set of policies which insures two or more stores, to keep a record of purchases and sales in each store, and this, too, even when such policies insure a specific amount on each store. If, however, under a statement of facts he should have two other sets of policies, one set covering entirely in one store, the other covering entirely in the other store, both sets of such policies would be void by reason of breach of the iron-safe clause.

The iron-safe clause is unlike lines 7 and 11 of the standard policy, in that it does not render the entire policy void by reason of breach of its conditions, but merely renders void that portion insuring the property to which the clause itself refers.

Most of the courts hold that the clause is a warranty and that it must be strictly complied with. Tennessee holds that a substantial compliance is all that is necessary. (See McNutt v. Va. F. and M. Ins. Co.), and so too do some of the United States Courts (see L. and L. and G. Ins. Co. v. Kearney et al. U. S. C. C. A. 8th District, 94 Fed. Rep. 314), Kentucky holds that its violation does not work a forfeiture, it not being competent to contract with the insured for the preservation of testimony in behalf of either party. Phenix Ins. Co. v. Angel et al., Ky. C. A., 38 S. W. Rep. 1067

Where a promise in a policy of insurance is declared to be a warranty, the only concern of the courts, in the absence of a contract statutory enactment, is to ascertain whether or not it has been complied with.

Where a policy is issued for a gross amount in consideration of a single premium, paid or to be paid, for the whole, though part of the amount is placed on a building and part on a stock of merchandise therein contained, and by its terms becomes void, whether by reason of a breach of the promise to make, preserve and produce an inventory of the merchandise or by reason of a breach of the condition as to the ownership of the ground upon which the insured building stands, the contract is indivisible, and, though there be but one such breach, there can be no recovery.

St. Landry Wholesale Mercantile Co. (Ltd.) v. New Hampshire Fire Ins. Co., 113 La. 1053, 38 Southern Reporter (April 8, 1905) 87.

I apprehend, however, that in case part of the assured's stock be burned beyond identification and the remainder be not so badly damaged but what it can be identified, that most, if not all, of the courts would hold the contract valid if the insured should abandon all claim for loss on those goods wholly destroyed, and try to enforce collection of claim on only such goods as could be identified.

One Set of Books for Two Stores.

Where the assured has two or more stores, with one set of policies covering the stocks in such stores and one set of books which merely shows the aggregate sales and purchases of all, but not that of each and such stores be separate and distinct risks, being divided by fire walls, all openings protected by fire doors, there is but one safe rule to follow for both the insurance company and the insured, and that is to write a blanket form covering all of the stock under one amount in all the locations which might, by any possible chance, be destroyed by one fire, with an average clause making the insurance attach in each location as the value in each bears to the aggregate value in all. If you do not do this, Mr. Agent and Mr. Daily Report Examiner, you are liable to cause all kinds of trouble for both your adjuster and the assured. If the risks be remote from each other so that in no possible contingency will more than one of them be destroyed by one fire, then it is all right to write each for a specific amount, but not otherwise, unless assured's books be so kept that they keep track of what goes in and out of each building. Remember, too, that if the risks be located in a territory where the iron-safe clause is required, that such clause does not apply separately to each stock insured, but to the aggregate business of all the stocks insured and this, too, whether such stocks be insured under one policy or a specific amount on each or under a blanket policy of one amount on all. It seems most, if not all, the courts hold, that compliance with the iron-safe clause is a condition precedent to recovery.

Appreciation.

There is one point I wish to refer to—the item of 5 per cent. appreciation which the adjusters agreed to. The insured had been engaged in business for a great many years and, while the average rate of advance in prices had been even greater than 5 per cent., yet I very seriously question the wisdom of allowing appreciation, as I believe the depreciation in this case should have offset any advance in the price it cost to buy a new stock.

The assured is entitled, though, to whatever it would cost him in cash to replace his property, less whatever depreciation from any cause there may have been to the property.

In this particular case, however, the adjusters were confronted with either a law suit or allowing the claim for appreciation, after selecting appraisers and they, being unable to agree on an umpire, adjuster finally decided to allow the claim, rather than be annoyed by a long legal fight, especially one involving no law point, but entirely on a question of fact for the jury, for we all know in advance what the decision will be.

CHAPTER XIX.

FACTS WORTH KNOWING.

WEIGHTS AND MEASURES.

MEASURES OF LENGTHS.

```
   12 inches ..................................... 1 foot
    3 feet ....................................... 1 yard
 16½ feet ....................................... 1 rod
  5½ yards ....................................... 1 rod
1,760 yards—5,280 feet .......................... 1 mile
  320 rods ....................................... 1 mile
   40 rods ....................................... 1 furlong
    8 furlongs ................................... 1 sta. mile
    3 miles ...................................... 1 league
```

LAND—SURVEYOR'S MEASURE.

```
 7.92 inches ..................................... 1 link
  100 links—66 ft. 4 rods........................ 1 chain
   10 chains—220 yards .......................... 1 furlong
    8 furlongs ................................... 1 mile
   10 sq. chains—160 sq. rods................... 1 acre
   25 links ...................................... 1 rod
   80 chains ..................................... 1 mile
  640 acres ...................................... 1 sq. mile
   36 sq. miles .................................. 1 township
```

MISCELLANEOUS.

```
1,000 mils ....................................... 1 inch
    4 inches ..................................... 1 hand
    6 inches ..................................... 1 span
    3 inches ..................................... 1 palm
   18 inches ..................................... 1 cubit
 21.8 inches ..................................... 1 Bible cubit
  2½ feet ....................................... 1 military pace
    2 yards ...................................... 1 fathom
```

SQUARE MEASURE.

```
  144 sq. inches or 183.3 circular inches............. 1 sq. foot
    9 sq. feet.................................... 1 sq. yard
 30¼ sq. yards or 272¼ sq. feet................. 1 sq. rod
   10 sq. chains or 160 sq. rods or 4,840 sq. yards
        or 43,560 sq. feet.......................... 1 acre
  640 acres ...................................... 1 sq. mile
```
An acre equals a square whose side is 208.71 feet.

SOLID OR CUBIC MEASURE.

```
1,728 cubic inches............................. 1 cubic foot
   27 cubic feet ............................... 1 cubic yard
    1 cord wood a pile 4x4x8.................. 128 cubic feet
    1 perch of masonry 16½x1½x1 ft......... 24¾ cubic feet
   40 cubic feet............................... 1 ton (shipping)
2,150.42 cubic inches.......................... 1 standard bushel
  268.8 cubic inches........................... 1 standard gallon
```
1 cubic foot equals about 4/5 of a bushel.

LIQUID MEASURE.

```
    4 gills ........................................ 1 pint
    2 pints ....................................... 1 quart
    4 quarts ...................................... 1 gallon
31½ gallons ..................................... 1 barrel
 42 gallons ..................................... 1 tierce
    2 barrels or 63 gallons...................... 1 hogshead
 84 gallons or 2 tierces.....................: 1 puncheon
    2 hogsheads or 126 gallons.................. 1 pipe or butt
    2 pipes or 3 puncheons..................... 1 tun
```
A gallon of water at 62° F. weighs 8.3356 lbs.
The U. S. gallon contains 231 cu. ins., 7.4805 gal., 1 cu. ft.

APOTHECARIES' FLUID MEASURE.

```
60 minums ....................................... 1 fluid drachm
 8 drachms ..................................... 1 fluid ounce
```

DRY MEASURE, U. S.

```
2 pints............................................. 1 quart
8 quarts........................................... 1 peck
4 pecks............................................ 1 bushel
```
A bushel contains 2,150.42 cubic inches.
A bushel contains 1.2445 cubic feet.
36 bushels equal 1 chaldron.

MEASURES OF WEIGHT—AVOIRDUPOIS OR COMMERCIAL WEIGHT

```
    16 drachms or 437.5 grains...........1 ounce
    16 ounces or 7,000 grains............1 pound
    28 pounds ..........................1 quarter
     4 quarters ........................1 hundredweight 112 lbs.
    20 hundredweight ...................1 ton of 2,240 lbs. or long ton
 2,000 pounds ..........................1 metric ton
 2,240.6 pounds ........................1 net or short ton
    14 pounds iron, lead, etc............1 stone
21½ stone iron, lead, etc................1 pig
     8 pigs ............................1 fother
   100 pounds grain or flour.............1 cental
   100 pounds, raisins ..................1 cask
   100 pounds dry fish ..................1 quintal
   100 pounds nails ....................1 keg
   196 pounds flour ....................1 barrel
   200 pounds pork, beef or fish........:1 barrel
   240 pounds lime .....................1 cask
   280 pounds salt .....................1 barrel
```

TROY WEIGHT.

```
24 grains ......................................1 pennyweight
20 pennyweights ...............................1 ounce—480 grains
12 ounces .....................................1 pound—5,760 grains
```

APOTHECARY'S WEIGHT.

```
20 grains .....................................1 scruple
 3 scruples ...................................1 drachm—60 grains
 8 drachms ...................................1 ounce—480 grains
12 ounces ....................................1 pound—5,760 grains
```
The ounce and pound in this case are the same as in Troy Weight.

CIRCULAR MEASURE.

```
 60 seconds.................................... 1 minute
 60 minutes.................................... 1 degree
 90 degrees................................... 1 quadrant
360 degrees................................... 1 circle
 30 degrees................................... 1 sign
```
4 quadrants equal 12 signs or 360 degrees or circumference.

TIME MEASURE.

```
60 seconds.....................................................1 minute
60 minutes.....................................................1 hour
24 hours.......................................................1 day
 7 days........................................................1 week
365 days—5 hours, 48 minutes, 48 seconds.....................1 year
        30 days equal 1 month in computing interest.
        366 days in leap year.
```

CLOTH MEASURE.

```
2¼ inches........................................... 1 nail
 4 nails............................................ 1 quarter
 4 quarters......................................... 1 yard
```

MARINER'S MEASURE.

```
  6 feet ........................................... 1 fathom
120 fathoms ........................................1 cable length
 7½ cable lengths .................................. 1 mile or knot
5,280 feet ......................................... 1 stat. mile
6,085 feet ......................................... 1 naut. mile
  9 inches ......................................... 1 span
  3 miles .......................................... 1 league
```

LINEAR MEASURE—METRIC EQUIVALENTS.

```
1 centimeter ................................... 0.3937 in.
1 decimeter .................................... 3.937 in. 0.328 feet
1 meter ........................................ 39.37 in. 1.0936 yards
1 dekameter .................................... 1.9884 rods
1 kilometer .................................... 0.62136 mile
1 inch ......................................... 2.54 centimeters
1 foot ......................................... 3.048 decimeters
1 yard ......................................... 0.9144 meter
1 rod .......................................... 0.5029 dekameter
1 mile ......................................... 1,6098 kilometer
```

SQUARE MEASURE.

```
1 sq. centimeter ............................... 0.1550 sq. inch
1 sq. decimeter ................................ 0.1076 sq. foot
1 sq. meter .................................... 1.96 sq. yards
1 are equals ................................... 3,954 sq. rods
1 hektar ....................................... 2.47 acres
1 sq. kilometer ................................ 0.386 sq. mile
1 sq. inch ..................................... 6.452 sq. centimeters
1 sq. foot ..................................... 9.2903 sq. decimeters
1 sq. yard ..................................... 0.8361 sq. meter
1 sq. rod ...................................... 0.2529 are
1 acre ......................................... 0.4047 hektar
1 sq. mile ..................................... 2.59 sq. kilometer
```

WEIGHTS.

```
1 gram ......................................... 0.0527 ounce
1 kilogram ..................................... 2.2046 pounds
1 metric ton ................................... 1.1023 English tons
1 ounce ........................................ 28.85 grams
1 pound ........................................ 0 4536 kilogram
1 English ton .................................. 0.9074 metric ton
```

APPROXIMATE METRIC EQUIVALENTS.

```
1 decimeter .................................... 4 inches
1 meter ........................................ 1.1 yards
1 kilometer .................................... ⅝ mile
1 hektar ....................................... 2½ acre
1 stere or cubic meter.......................... ¼ cord
1 liter ........................................ 1.06 quarts liquid
                                                 0.9 quart dry
1 hektoliter ................................... 2⅝ bushels
1 kilogram ..................................... 2 1/5 pounds
1 metric ton ................................... 2,200 pounds
```

TO FIND CAPACITY OF TANKS AND BINS.

TO FIND CAPACITY OF TANKS AND BINS.

To find number of cubic feet in four-sided tank or bin, multiply width by length by height.

To find number of cubic feet in round tank or bin, multiply the square of diameter by .7854 by height.

To find number of bushels in tank or bin, multiply the number of cubic feet in same by .8035.

To find number of gallons in tank or bin, multiply the number of cubic feet in same by 7.4805.

CAPACITY OF CIRCULAR TANKS.

(For each ten inches in depth.)

2 feet in diameter holds..	19 gals.
2½ feet in diameter holds.........................	30 gals.
3 feet in diameter holds..	44 gals.
4 feet in diameter holds..	78 gals.
4½ feet in diameter holds...	99 gals.
6 feet in diameter holds..	122 gals.
6½ feet in diameter holds...	176 gals.
7 feet in diameter holds..	206 gals.
8 feet in diameter holds..	239 gals.
9 feet in diameter holds..	313 gals.
10 feet in diameter holds..	396 gals.
11 feet in diameter holds..	489 gals.
12 feet in diameter holds	592 gals.
13 feet in diameter holds..	705 gals.
14 feet in diameter holds..	820 gals.
15 feet in diameter holds..	959 gals.
20 feet in diameter holds..	1101 gals.
25 feet in diameter holds..	3059 gals.

Tabular view of the number of barrels contained between the walls for each foot in depth.

SQUARE TANKS.

5 feet by 5 feet holds.....................................	5.92 barrels
6 feet by 6 feet holds.....................................	8.54 barrels
7 feet by 7 feet holds.....................................	11.63 barrels
8 feet by 8 feet holds.....................................	15.19 barrels
9 feet by 9 feet holds.....................................	19.39 barrels
10 feet by 10 feet holds.....................................	23.74 barrels

MEASUREMENTS AND WEIGHTS.

Five stricken measures are equal to four heaped measures.

The standard bushel of the United States contains 2,150.42 cubic inches, and the imperial bushel of Great Britain, 2,216.192 cubic inches.

BUSHELS AND BINS.

To find the number of bushels in a bin, divide the contents in cubic inches by the number of cubic inches in a bushel, or in the United States, for all practical purposes, diminish the number of cubic feet by one-fifth.

And to find the number of cubic feet in a given number of bushels, multiply the number of bushels by the number of cubic inches in a bushel, and divide the product by 1,728, or in the United States, for all practical purposes, increase the number of bushels by one-fourth.

To find the number of bushels of apples or potatoes in a bin (in the United States), multiply the number of cubic feet by 4-5 or by .8.

A ton of coal contains 36½ cubic feet, and a box 4 feet long, 3 feet wide and 3 feet deep contains 36 cubic feet.

TO MEASURE CORN IN CRIB.

Find the length, breadth and depth of the body of corn, in feet, and multiply these three dimensions together; then multiply this product by .63. This will give the heaped bushels of corn. Sometimes 1½ bushels of ear corn are allowed for a bushel of shelled corn, and sometimes two bushels, the amount depending upon the shape of the ear, the size of the cob, etc.

THE WEIGHT OF HAY.

In estimating the weight of hay, allow 540 cubic feet for a ton, if on the wagon or newly stored; but if well settled in mow or stack, allow 512 cubic feet. Two hundred and seventy cubic feet of baled hay will weigh a ton.

NOTE—To find the number of cubic feet in a circular stack, multiply the average circumference in yards by itself, and this product by four times the height in yards;·then divide this product by 100 and multiply the quotient by 27.

To find diameter of a circle, multiply circumference by .31831.
To find circumference of a circle, multiply diameter by 3.1416.
To find area of a circle, multiply square of diameter by .7854.
To find surface of a ball, multiply square of diameter by 3.1416.
To find side of an equal square, multiply diameter by .8862.
To find cubic inches in a ball, multiply cube of diameter by .5236.

CONTENTS IN FEET OF JOISTS, SCANTLING, AND TIMBER.

LENGTH IN FEET

SIZE	12	14	16	18	20	22	24	26	28	30
	FEET BOARD MEASURE									
2 x 4	8	9	11	12	13	15	16	17	19	20
2 x 6	12	14	16	18	20	22	24	26	28	30
2 x 8	16	19	21	24	27	29	32	35	37	40
2 x 10	20	23	27	30	33	37	40	43	47	50
2 x 12	24	23	32	36	40	44	48	52	56	60
2 x 14	28	33	37	42	47	51	56	61	65	70
3 x 8	24	28	32	36	40	44	48	52	56	60
3 x 10	30	35	40	45	50	55	60	65	70	75
3 x 12	36	42	48	54	60	66	72	78	84	90
3 x 14	42	49	56	63	70	77	84	91	98	105
4 x 14	56	65	75	84	93	103	112	121	131	140
6 x 6	36	42	48	54	60	66	72	78	84	90
6 x 8	48	56	64	72	80	88	96	104	112	120
6 x 10	60	70	80	90	100	110	120	130	140	150
6 x 12	72	84	96	108	120	132	144	156	168	180
6 x 14	84	98	112	126	140	154	168	182	196	210
8 x 8	64	75	85	96	107	117	128	139	149	160
8 x 10	80	93	107	120	133	147	160	173	187	200
8 x 12	96	112	128	144	160	176	192	208	224	240
8 x 14	112	131	149	168	187	205	224	243	261	280
10 x 10	100	117	133	150	167	183	200	217	233	250
10 x 12	120	140	160	180	200	220	240	260	280	300
10 x 14	140	163	187	210	233	257	280	303	327	350
12 x 12	144	168	192	216	240	264	288	312	336	360
12 x 14	168	196	224	252	280	308	336	364	392	420
14 x 14	196	229	261	294	327	359	392	425	457	490

TABLE OF WEIGHTS.

	Avg. Wt. of a Cub. ft. lbs.
Air, atmospheric; at 60° Fah. and under the pressure of one atmosphere or 14.7 lb. per sq. inch, weighs 1/815 part as much as water at 60°	.0765
Alcohol,, pure	49.43
" of commerce	52.1
" proof spirit	57.2
Ash, perfectly dry ....average..	47.
1,000 feet, board measure, weighs 1.748 tons.	
Ash, American white, dry	38.
1,000 feet, board measure, weighs 1.414 tons.	
Alabaster, falsely so called, but really marbles	168.
" real; a compact white plaster of Paris	144.
Aluminum	162.
Antimony, cast, 6.66 to 6.74 ....average..	418.
" native "	416.
Asphaltum, 1 to 1.8 "	87.3
Basalt "	181.
Bath Stone, Oolite	131.
Bismuth, cast. Also native	607.
Bitumen, solid. See Asphaltum	
Brass, (Copper and Zinc) cast, 7.8 to 8.4 ..	504.
" rolled	524.
Bronze, Copper 8 parts; Tin 1 (Gun Metal) "	529.
Brick, best pressed	150.
" common hard	125.
" soft inferior	100.
Boxwood, Dry ....average..	.60
Calcite, transparent "	169.9
Charcoal, of pines and oaks. ....average..15 to	30.
Chalk, 2.2 to 2.8 ....average..	156.
Clay, potters' dry, 1.8 to 2.1 "	119.
" dry, in lump, loose.... " ..	63.
Coke, loose, of good coal ....average..23 to	32.
Coke, a heaped bushel, loose 35 to 42 lbs.	
Cherry, perfectly dry ....average..	42.
1,000 feet, board measure weighs 1.562 tons.	
Coal, anthracite, 1.3 to 1.84 of Penn. 1.3 to 1.7 usual	93.5
" " broken, any size, loose ....average..52 to	56.
" " " moderately shaken ... " ..56 to	60.
A cubic yard, solid, averages about 1.75 cubic yards when broken to any market size, and loose.	
A ton loose, averages from 40 to 43 cubic feet.	
At 54 lbs. per cubic foot, a cubic yard weighs 1,458 pounds =0.651 ton.	
Coal, bituminous, 1.2 to 1.5 ....=0.651 ton	84.
" " broken, any size, loose " .....47 to	52.
" " moderately shaken " .....51 to	56.
A cubic yard, solid, averages about 1.75 yards when broken to any market size, and loose.	
Chestnut, perfectly dry ....average..	41.
1,000 feet, board measure, weighs 1.525 tons.	
Cement, hydraulic, American, Rosendale; ground, loose " ..	56.
" " " Louisville, struck bush. 62 lbs...	49.6
" " " Copley, struck bush. 67 lbs.......	53.6
" " English Portland, U. S. struck bush., by Gilmore, 100 to 128 ....81 to	102.
" hydraulic, English Portland, various, weighed by writer 95 to 102 ....76 to	81.6
" hydraulic, English Portland, a barrel 400 to 430 lb.	
" " French Boulogne Portland, struck bush., 95 to 110 ....76 to	88.
Cork	15.6
Elm, perfectly dry ....average..	35.

Glass, 2.5 to 3.45.. 186.
" common, window .... -- 157.
" Millville, N. J., thick flooring glass............ 158.
Hemlock, perfectly dry .... 25.
    1,000 feet, board measure, weighs 1.971 tons.
India Rubber .... 58.
Lard 59.3
Mahogany, Spanish, dry .... 53.
" Honduras, dry .... " 35.
Maple, dry .... 49.
Mica, 2.75 to 3.1..................................... 183.
Naphtha 52.9
Oak, live, perfectly dry, .88 to 1.02...........average.. 59.3
" white, " " 66 to .88.................... .. 48.
" red, black, etc. ....average..32 to 43.
Oils, whale, olive ....average.. 57.3
" of turpentine .... " .. 54.3
Petroleum 54.8
Peat, dry, unpressed ....20 to 30.
Pine, white, perfectly dry, .35 to .45................ 25.
    1,000 feet, board measure, weighs .930 ton.
" yellow, Northern, .48 to .62.................... 34.3
    1,000 feet, board measure, weighs 1,276 tons.
" yellow, Southern, .64 to .80.................... 45.
    1,000 feet, board measure, weighs 1.674 tons.
" Heart of long-leafed Southern yellow, unseasoned....... 65.
    1,000 feet, board measure, weighs 2.418 tons.
Pitch 71.7
Powder, slightly shaken 62.3
Salt, coarse, per struck bushel; Syracuse, N. Y.....56 lbs..... 45.
" " " " " Turk's Island, Cadiz..76 to 80 62.
" " " " " St. Barts ....84 to 90 70.
" " " " " West India ....90 to 96 74.
" " " " " Liverpool ....50 to 55 42.
" Liverpool, fine, for table use....................60 to 62 49.
Tallow ....average.. 58.6
Tar .... " 62.4
Wines, .993 to 1.04.................................. " 62.3
Walnut, black, perfectly dry.......................... 38.
Wax, bees 60.5

MATERIAL	MEASUREMENTS			WEIGHTS	
WOOL	Floor Space	Cubic feet	Gross	Per sq. ft.	Per cubic foot
Bale East India.............	3.0	12.	340	113	28
" Australia	5.8	26.	385	66	15
" South America.........	7.0	34.	1000	143	29
" Oregon	6.9	33.	482	70	15
" California	7.5	33.	550	73	17
Bag Wool	5.0	30.	200	40	7
Stack of Scoured Wool......	...	...	....	...	5

WOOLEN GOODS

MATERIAL	Floor Space	Cubic feet	Gross	Per sq. ft.	Per cubic foot
Case Flannels	5.5	12.7	220	40	17
" " heavy	7.1	15.2	330	46	22
" Dress Goods	5.5	22.0	460	84	21
" Cassimeres	10.5	28.0	550	52	20
" Underwear	7.3	21.0	350	48	16
" Blankets	10.3	35.0	450	44	13
Horse Blankets	4.0	14.0	250	63	18

COTTON, ETC.

Bale	8.1	44.2	515	64	12
" Compressed	4.1	21.6	550	134	25
" Dederick Compressed...	1.25	3.13	125	100	40
" Jute	2.4	9.9	300	125	30
" Jute Lashings	2.6	10.5	450	172	43
" Manilla	3.2	10.9	280	88	26
' Hemp	8.7	34.7	700	81	20
' Sisal	5.3	17.0	400	75	24

COTTON GOODS

Bale Unbleached Jeans	4.0	12.5	300	72	24
Piece Duck	1.1	2.3	75	68	33
Bale Brown Sheetings	3.6	10.1	235	65	23
Case Bleached Sheetings	4.8	11.4	330	69	30
Case Quilts	7.2	19.0	295	41	16
Bale Print Cloth	4.0	9.3	175	44	19
Case Prints	4.5	13.4	420	93	31
Bale Tickings	3.3	8.8	325	99	37
Skeins Cotton Yarn	...	...	...		11
Burlaps	...	...	130		30
Jute Bagging	1.4	5.3	100	70	24

RAGS IN BALES

White Linen	8.5	39.5	910	107	23
White Cotton	9.2	40.0	715	78	18
Brown Cotton	7.6	30.0	442	59	15
Paper Shavings	7.5	34.0	507	68	15
Sacking	16.0	65.0	450	28	7
Woolen	7.5	30.0	600	80	20
Jute Butts	2.8	11.1	400	143	36

PAPER

Calendered Book	...	...	...	...	50
Super-calendered Book	...	...	...	...	69
Newspaper	...	...	...	...	38
Straw Board	...	...	...	...	33
Leather Board	...	...	...	...	59
Writing	...	...	...	...	64
Wrapping	...	...	...	...	10
Manilla	...	...	...	...	37

GRAIN

Wheat in Bags	4.2	4.2	165	39	39
" " Bulk	...	...	...	...	44
" " "	...	...	...	...	39
" " " mean		...	...		41
Barrels Flour on side	4.1	5.4	218	53	40
" " on end	3.1	7.1	218	70	31
Corn in Bags	3.6	3.6	112	31	31
Cornmeal in Barrels	3.7	5.9	218	59	37
Oats in bags	3.3	3.6	96	29	27
Bale of Hay	5.0	20.0	284	57	14
Hay, Dederick Compressed...	1.75	5.2	125	72	24
Straw "	1.75	5.2	100	57	19
Tow "	1.75	5.2	150	86	29
Excelsior "	1.75	5.25	100	57	19

DYE STUFFS

Hogsheads Bleaching Powder	11.8	39.2	1200	102	31
" Soda Ash	10.8	29.2	1800	167	62
Box Indigo	3.0	9.0	385	128	43
" Cutch	4.0	3.3	150	38	45
" Sumac	1.6	4.1	160	100	39

Caustic Soda in iron drum...	4.3	6.8	600	140	80
Barrel Starch	3.0	10.5	250	83	23
" Pearl Alum	3.0	10.5	350	117	33
Box Extract Logwood.......	1.06	.8	55	52	70
Barrel Lime	3.6	4.5	225	63	50
" Cement, American ...	3.8	5.5	325	86	59
" English	3.3	5.5	400	105	73
" Plaster	3.7	6.1	325	88	53
" Rosin	3.0	9.0	430	143	48
" Lard Oil..............	4.3	12.3	422	98	34
Rope	.....	.....	....	...	42

MISCELLANEOUS.

Box Tin	2.7	0.5	139	99	278
" Glass	....	.....	....	...	60
Crate Crockery	9.9	39.6	1600	162	40
Cask Crockery	13.4	42.5	600	52	14
Bale Leather	7.3	12.2	190	26	16
" Goatskins	11.2	16.7	300	27	18
" Raw Hides	6.0	30.0	400	67	13
" " Compressed	6.0	30.0	700	117	23
" Sole Leather	12.6	8.9	200	22	16
Pile Sole Leather...........	....	....	....	..	17
Barrel Granulated Sugar....	3.0	7.5	317	106	42
" Brown Sugar.........	3.0	7.5	340	113	45
Cheese	.....	.....	....		30

MEASURES AND WEIGHTS OF VARIOUS MATERIALS.

(Approximate)

Brickwork:—Brickwork is estimated by the thousand, and for various thickneses of wall runs as follows:

8¼ in. wall, or 1   brick in thickness, 14 bricks per superficial foot.
12¾ in. wall, or 1½ brick in thickness, 21 bricks per superficial foot.
17 in. wall, or 2   brick in thickness, 28 bricks per superficial foot.
21½ in. wall, or 2½ brick in thickness, 35 bricks per superficial foot.

An ordinary brick measures about 8¼x4x2 inches, which is equal to 66 cubic inches, or 26.2 bricks to a cubic foot. The average weight is 4½ pounds.

Fuel:—A bushel of bituminous coal weighs 76 pounds and contains 2685 cubic inches = 1.554 cubic feet. 29.47 bushels = 1 gross ton.

A bushel of coke weighs 40 lbs. (35 to 42 lbs.)

One acre of bituminous coal contains 1600 tons of 2240 lbs. per foot of thickness of coal worked. 15 to 25 per cent. must be deducted for waste in mining.

41 to 45 cu. ft. bituminous coal when broken down = 1 ton, 2240 lbs.
31 to 41 "   " anthracite, prepared for market = 1 ton, 2240 lbs.
123   "   " of charcoal = 1 ton, 2240 lbs.
70.9   "   " of coke = 1 ton, 2240 lbs.
1 cubic foot of anthracite coal = 55 to 66 lbs.
1   "   "   " bituminous coal = 50 to 55 lbs.
1   "   "   " Cumberland coal = 53 lbs.
1   "   "   " Cannel coal = 50.3 lbs.
1   "   "   " Charcoal (hardwood) = 18.5 lbs.
1   "   "   " Charcoal (pine) = 18 lbs.

A bushel of charcoal.—In 1881 the American Charcoal-Iron Workers' Association adopted for use in its official publications for the standard bushel of charcoal 2748 cubic inches, or 20 pounds. A ton of charcoal to be taken at 2000 pounds. This figure of 20 pounds to the bushel was taken as a fair average of different bushels used throughout the country, and it has since been established by law in some states.

ORES, EARTHS, ETC.

```
13 cubic feet of ordinary gold or silver ore, in mine = 1 ton = 2000 lbs.
20   "    "    "    broken quartz                      = 1 ton = 2000 lbs
18 feet of gravel in bank                             = 1 ton.
27 cubic feet of gravel when dry                      = 1 ton.
25   "    "    "    sand                              = 1 ton.
18   "    "    "    earth in bank                     = 1 ton.
27   "    "    "    earth when dry                    = 1 ton.
17   "    "    "    clay                             = 1 ton.
```

Cement.—English Portland, sp. gr. 1.25 to 1.51 per bbl.   400 to .430 lbs.
           Rosendale, U. S., a struck bushel   .62 to .70 lbs.
Lime.—A struck bushel   .72 to .75 lbs.
Grain.—A struck bu. of wheat=60 lbs.; corn=56 lbs.; of oats=30 lbs.
Salt.—A struck bushel of salt, coarse, Syracuse, N. Y.........=56 lbs.

WEIGHT OF EARTH FILLING.

	Average Weight in Pounds Per Cubic Foot	
Earth, common loam, loose.....................	72 to	80
" " " shaken	82 to	92
" " " rammed moderately	90 to	100
Gravel	90 to	106
Sand	90 to	106
Soft flowing mud	104 to	120
Sand, perfectly wet	118 to	129

WEIGHTS OF LOGS, LUMBER, ETC.

WEIGHT OF GREEN LOGS TO SCALE 1000 FEET, BOARD MEAS.

```
Yellow Pine (Southern) ........................8000 to 10000 pounds
White Pine (Michigan) off stump.................6000 to  7000    "
  "      "       "    out of water..............7000 to  8000    "
Norway Pine (Michigan) .........................7000 to  8000    "
White Pine (Pennsylvania) bark off..............5000 to  6000    "
Hemlock (Pennsylvania) bark off.................6000 to  7000    "
```
    Four acres of water are required to store 1,000,000 feet of logs.

WEIGHT OF 1000 FEET OF LUMBER, BOARD MEASURE.

Yellow or Norway Pine.......... Dry, 3000 pounds Green, 5000 pounds
White Pine..................... Dry, 2500 pounds Green, 4000 pounds
    Weight of One Cord of Seasoned Wood—128 Cubic Feet Per Cord.

```
Hickory or Sugar Maple...................................4500 pounds
White Oak ..............................................3850    "
Beech, Red Oak or Black Oak.............................3250    "
Poplar, Chestnut or Elm.................................2350    "
Pine (white or Norway)..................................2000    "
Hemlock bark, dry.......................................2200    "
```
    One cubic foot of anthracite coal weighs about 53 pounds.
    One cubic foot of bituminous coal weighs from 47 to 50 pounds.
    A gallon of water (United States standard) weighs 8 1/3 pounds and contains 231 cubic inches.

AMOUNT OF PAPER REQUIRED FOR A ROOM.
HEIGHT OF WALL TO CEILING.

No. ft. around room	8 ft.	9 ft.	10 ft.	11 ft.	12 ft.	13 ft.	14 ft.
28	7	8	9	10	11	11	12
32	8	9	10	11	12	13	14
36	9	10	11	12	13	14	16
40	10	11	12	14	15	16	17
44	11	12	14	15	16	18	19
48	12	13	15	16	18	19	21
52	13	15	16	18	19	21	22
56	14	16	17	19	21	22	24
60	15	17	19	20	22	24	26
64	16	18	20	22	24	26	28
68	17	19	21	23	25	27	29
72	18	20	22	24	27	29	31
76	19	21	23	26	28	30	33
80	20	22	25	27	30	32	34
84	21	23	26	28	31	33	36
88	22	24	27	30	32	35	38
92	23	26	28	31	34	37	39
96	24	27	30	32	35	38	41
100	25	28	31	34	37	40	43
104	26	29	32	35	38	41	44
108	27	30	33	36	40	43	46
112	28	31	34	38	42	44	48
116	29	32	36	39	43	46	50
120	30	33	37	40	45	48	51

EXPLANATION.

Look for height of ceiling at top of column, number of feet of wall around the room in the left-hand column; in angle will be found the number of single rolls required.

EXAMPLE.

Number of feet around the room, 36; height of wall of ceiling, 11 feet; in the angle will be found twelve rolls. Subtract one roll for each opening.

FOR CEILING.

Multiply the length of room by the breadth, divided by 30, and the result will be the number of rolls required.

FOR BORDER.

Divide the number of feet around the room by 3, and it gives you the number of yards of border required.

There are 8 yards in a roll of 18-inch border, and — yards in a roll of 9-inch border.

Table showing number of square feet in veneered doors upon which prices are based.

HEIGHT.

Width	6.8	6.10	7	7.2	7.4	7.6	7.8	7.10	8	8.2	8.4	8.6	8.8	8.10	9
2.2	17.6	17.6	17.6	17.6	17.6	17.6	17.6	17.6	17.6	18.	18.	18.6	19.	19.	19.6
2.4	17.6	17.6	17.6	17.6	17.6	17.6	18.	18.6	19.	19.	19.6	20.	20.6	20.6	21.
2.6	17.6	17.6	17.6	18.	18.6	19.	10.	19.6	20.	20.6	21.	21.6	22.	22.	22.6
2.8	18.	18.6	19.	19.	19.6	20.	20.6	21.	21.6	22.	22.6	23.	23.6	23.6	24.
2.10	19.	19.6	20.	20.	21.	21.6	22.	22.	23.	23.	23.6	24.	24.6	25.	25.6
3.	20.	20.6	21.	21.6	22.	22.6	23.	23.6	24.	24.6	25.	25.6	26.	26.6	27.
3.2	21.	22.	22.	23.	23.	24.	24.6	25.	25.6	26.	26.6	27.	27.6	28.	28.6
3.4	22.6	23.	23.6	24.	24.6	25.	25.6	26.	27.	27.6	28.	28.6	29.	29.6	30.
3.6	23.6	24.	24.6	25.	26.6	26.6	27.	27.6	28.	29.	29.	30.	30.6	31.	31.6
3.8	24.6	25.	26.	26.6	27.	27.6	28.	29.	29.6	30.	30.6	31.	32.	32.6	33.
3.10	25.6	26.	27.	27.6	28.	29.	29.6	30.	31.	31.6	32.	32.6	33.6	34.	34.6
4	27.	27.6	28.	29.	29.6	30.	31.	31.6	32.	33.	33.6	34.	35.	35.6	36.
4.2	28.	28.6	29.	30.	30.6	31.6	32.	33.	33.6	34.	35.	35.6	36.	37.	37.6
4.4	29.	29.6	30.6	31.	32.	32.6	33.6	34.	35.	35.6	36.	37.	37.6	38.6	39.
4.6	30.	31.	31.6	32.6	33.	34.	34.6	35.6	36.	37.	37.6	38.6	39.	40.	40.6
4.8	31.6	32.	33.	33.6	34.6	35.	36.	36.6	37.6	38.	39.	40.	40.6	41.6	42.
4.10	32.6	33.	34.	35.	35.6	36.6	37.	38.	39.	39.6	40.6	41.	42.	43.	43.6
5.	33.6	34.	35.	36.	37.	37.6	38.6	39.	40.	41.	42.	42.6	43.6	44.	45.
5.2	34.6	35.6	36.	37.	38.	39.	39.6	40.6	41.6	42.	43.	44.	45.	46.	46.6
5.4	35.6	36.6	37.	38.6	39.	40.	41.	42.	43.	43.6	44.6	45.6	46.6	47.6	48.
5.6	37.	37.6	38.6	39.6	40.6	41.6	42.	43.	44.	45.	46.	47.	48.	48.6	49.6
5.8	38.	39.	40.	40.6	41.6	42.6	43.6	44.6	45.6	46.6	47.6	48.	49.	50.	51.
5.10	39.	40.	41.	42.	43.	44.	45.	46.	47.	48.	48.	49.6	50.6	51.6	52.6
6.	40.	41.	42.	43.	44.	45.	46.	47.	48.	49.	50.	51.	52.	53.	54.
6.2	41.	42.	43.	44.	45.6	46.6	47.6	48.6	49.6	50.6	51.6	52.6	53.6	54.6	55.6
6.4	42.6	43.6	44.6	45.6	46.6	47.6	48.6	50.	51.	52.	53.	54.	55.	56.	58.
6.6	43.6	44.6	45.6	46.6	48.	49.	50.	51.	52.	53.	54.	55.6	56.6	57.6	58.6
6.8	44.6	45.6	47.	48.	49.	50.	51.	52.6	53.6	54.6	55.6	57.	58.	59.	60.
6.10	45.6	47.	48.	49.	50.	51.6	52.6	53.6	55.	56.	57.	58.	59.6	60.6	61.6
7.	47.	48.	49.	50.	51.6	52.6	54.	55.	56.	57.	58.6	59.6	61.	62.	63.
7.2	48.	49.	50.	51.6	52.6	54.	55.	56.	57.6	58.6	60.	61.	62.	63.6	64.6
7.4	49.	50.	51.6	52.6	54.	55.	56.6	57.6	59.	59.6	61.	62.6	63.6	65.	66.
7.6	50.	51.6	52.6	54.	55.	56.6	57.6	59.	60.	61.6	62.6	64.	65.	66.6	67.6
7.8	51.	52.6	54.	55.	56.6	57.6	59.	60.	61.6	62.6	64.	65.	66.6	68.	69.
7.10	52.6	53.6	55.	56.	57.6	59.	60.	61.6	63.	64.	65.6	66.6	68.	69.	70.6
8.	53.6	55.	56.	57.6	59.	60.	61.6	63.	64.	65.6	67.	68.	69.6	71.	72.

As labor is the principal item in cost of doors, we figure no door less than 17.6 square feet.

NUMBER OF BRICK REQUIRED TO CONSTRUCT ANY BUILDING.

(Reckoning 7 Brick to Each Superficial Foot.)

Superficial Feet of Wall.	NUMBER OF BRICKS TO THICKNESS OF					
	4 in.	8 in.	12 in.	16 in.	20 in.	24 in.
1	7	15	23	30	38	45
2	15	30	45	60	75	90
3	23	45	68	90	113	135
4	30	60	90	120	150	180
5	38	75	113	150	188	225
6	45	90	135	180	225	270
7	53	105	158	210	263	315
8	60	120	180	240	300	360
9	68	135	203	270	338	405
10	75	150	225	300	375	450
20	150	300	450	600	750	900
30	225	450	675	900	1125	1350
40	300	600	900	1200	1500	1800
50	375	750	1125	1500	1875	2250
60	450	900	1350	1800	2250	2700
70	525	1000	1575	2100	2625	3150
80	600	1200	1800	2400	3000	3600
90	675	1350	2025	2700	3375	4050
100	750	1500	2250	3000	3750	4500
200	1500	3000	4500	6000	7500	9000
300	2250	4500	6750	9000	11250	13500
400	3000	6000	9000	12000	15000	18000
500	3750	7500	11250	15000	18750	22400
600	4500	9000	13500	18000	22500	27000
700	5250	10500	15750	21000	26250	31500
800	6000	12000	18600	24000	30000	36000
900	6750	13500	20250	27000	33750	40500
1000	7500	15000	22500	30000	37500	45000

In brick work, corners are not measured twice as in stone work. Openings over two feet square are deducted. Arches are counted from spring. Fancy work counted one and one-half bricks for one. Pillars are measured on their face only.

THE WEAR AND TEAR OF BUILDING MATERIALS.

MATERIAL IN BUILDING	Frame Dwlg.		Brick Dwg. Shingle Roof		Frame Store		Brick Store Shingle Roof	
	Average Life Years	Per cent of Depreciation Per annum	Average Life Years	Per Cent of Depreciation Per Annum	Average Life Years	Per Cent. of Depreciation Per Annum	Average Life Years	Per Cent. of Depreciation Per Annum
Brick	…	…	75	1⅛	…	…	66	1½
Plastering	20	5	30	3⅓	16	6	30	3⅓
Painting, outside	5	20	7	14	5	20	6	16
Painting, inside	7	14	7	14	5	20	6	16
Shingles	16	6	16	6	16	6	16	6
Cornice	40	2½	40	2½	30	3⅓	40	2½
Weather-boarding	30	3⅓	…	…	30	3⅓	…	…
Sheathing	50	2	50	2	40	2½	50	2
Flooring	20	5	20	5	13	8	13	8
Doors, complete	30	3⅓	30	3⅓	25	4	30	3⅓
Windows, complete	30	3⅓	30	3⅓	25	4	30	3⅓
Stairs and Newel	30	3⅓	30	3⅓	20	5	20	5
Base	40	2½	40	2½	30	3½	30	3⅓
Inside Blinds	30	3⅓	30	3⅓	30	3⅓	30	3⅓
Building Hardware	20	5	20	5	13	8	13	8
Piazzas and Porches	20	5	20	5	20	5	20	5
Outside Blinds	16	6	16	6	16	6	16	6
Sills and First Floor Joints	25	4	40	2½	25	4	30	3⅓
Dimension Lumber	50	2	75	1⅓	40	2½	66	1½

MADE TO ORDER SHADES.

List price of shades made to order of Victor cloth, mounted on Hartshorn rollers, ready to hang.

PRICE PER SHADE, YEAR 1913.

Width in Inches.	38	42	45	48	54	63	72	81	90	102	114	120	150
4 feet....	$.88	$1.32	$1.38	$1.56	$1.82	$2.38	$3.18	$3.80	$4.32	$5.36	$8.82	$10.30	$17.40
5 "	1.00	1.50	1.56	1.78	2.08	2.70	3.56	4.26	4.86	6.08	9.76	11.62	10.60
6 " ..	1.10	1.66	1.74	2.00	2.34	3.02	3.96	4.72	5.40	6.78	10.70	12.90	21.78
7 "	1.24	1.84	1.94	2.22	2.60	3.34	4.36	5.20	5.94	7.52	11.64	14.22	23.98
8 "	1.34	2.00	2.12	2.44	2.82	3.68	4.76	5.66	6.48	8.24	12.58	15.54	26.16
9 "	1.46	2.30	2.44	2.78	3.30	4.18	5.40	6.38	7.34	9.32	13.90	17.20	28.36
10 "	1.76	2.48	2.62	2.98	3.56	4.50	5.80	6.86	7.88	10.06	14.84	18.52	30.54
11 "	1.88	2.66	2.82	3.20	3.80	4.84	6.20	7.32	8.42	12.90	15.78	19.84	38.98
12 "	1.98	2.94	3.12	3.56	4.24	5.34	6.82	8.02	9.26	13.98	17.08	21.48	41.16
13 "	2.54	3.28	3.48	3.84	4.92	5.88	7.46	8.50	9.80	14.72	18.02	22.80	43.36
14 "	2.64	3.46	3.68	4.06	5.20	6.20	7.84	8.96	10.34	15.44	18.96	24.12	45.54
15 "	2.88	3.74	3.96	4.52	5.62	6.70	8.46	9.68	11.20	16.50	20.28	25.78	47.74

All shades under 38 inches, charged at 38-inch price. When shades are longer than even feet, take next length price.

DUPLEX OR DOUBLE FACED OIL OPAQUE SHADE.

List price of Duplex shades made to order, mounted on Hartshorn rollers, ready to hang.

PRICE PER SHADE.

Width in Inches.	38	42	45	48	54	63	72	81	90	102	114	120	150
4 feet....	$1.18	$1.74	$1.84	$2.06	$2.40	$3.10	$4.12	$4.94	$5.62	$6.96	$11.58	$13.56	$23.06
5 " ...	1.36	1.98	2.06	2.34	2.74	3.50	4.60	5.52	6.32	7.88	12.78	15.26	25.96
6 "	1.50	2.18	2.30	2.62	3.08	3.92	5.10	6.10	7.00	8.87	14.00	16.94	28.84
7 "	1.68	2.42	2.56	2.92	3.42	4.32	5.60	6.70	7.68	9.72	15.20	18.64	31.74
8 "	1.80	2.64	2.80	3.20	3.74	4.76	6.12	7.28	8.38	10.62	16.42	20.36	34.62
9 "	1.98	3.02	3.22	3.64	4.34	5.42	6.94	8.20	9.48	12.02	18.14	22.54	37.52
10 "	2.38	3.26	3.44	3.90	4.68	5.82	7.44	8.82	10.18	12.96	19.34	24.24	40.38
11 "	2.56	3.50	3.70	4.20	5.00	6.26	7.94	9.40	10.86	16.70	20.54	25.96	51.60
12 "	2.70	3.86	4.10	4.66	5.58	6.90	8.74	10.30	11.94	18.10	22.24	28.10	54.48
13 "	3.44	4.32	4.58	5.04	6.50	7.60	9.56	10.90	12.64	19.04	23.44	29.83	57.38
14 "	3.58	4.54	4.84	5.32	6.84	8.02	10.04	11.48	13.32	19.96	24.66	31.54	60.26

Duplex combination, with colors, shown in this book, will be furnished at above prices.

VICTOR HAND MADE OIL OPAQUE SHADE CLOTH.

Made from the finest grade of shade muslin and painted with best oil paint. Will not crack or face. About 50 yards to piece.

PRICE PER YARD.

Width in Inches.	38	42	45	48	54	63	72	81	90	102	114	120	150
Full piece per yard......	$0.44	$0.60	$0.64	$0.72	$0.84	$1.20	$1.40	$1.60	$1.80	$2.20	$2.80	$3.80	$6.00
Less per yard..	.48	.64	.68	.78	.92	1.30	1.50	1.76	2.00	2.50	3.20	4.50	6.00

BUILDING HINTS.

One thousand shingles laid four inches to the weather will cover 100 square feet of surface, and five pounds of shingle nails will fasten them on.

One-fifth more siding and flooring is needed than the number of square feet of surface to be covered, because of the lap in the siding and matching.

One thousand lath will cover 70 yards of surface, and 11 pounds of lath nails will fasten them on. Eight bushels of good lime, 16 bushels of sand and 1 bushel of hair will make enough good mortar to plaster 100 square yards.

A cord of stone, three bushels of lime, and a cubic yard of sand will lay 100 cubic feet of wall.

Five courses of brick will lay 1 foot in height on a chimney; 16 bricks in a course will make a flue 8 inches wide and 16 inches long.

Cement 1 bushel and sand 2 bushels will cover 3½ square yards 1 inch thick, 4½ square yards ½ inch thick, and 6¾ square yards ¼ inch thick. One bushel of cement and one of sand will cover 2¼ square yards 1 inch thick.

Stone walls are measured by the perch (24¾ cubic feet). Openings less than 3 feet wide are counted solid; over 3 feet, deducted; but 18 inches are added to the running measure for each jamb built. Arches are counted solid from the spring; corners of buildings are measured twice; pillars less than 3 feet are counted on three sides as lineal, multiplied by fourth side and depth.

It is customary to measure all foundations and dimensions of stone by the cubic foot; water table and base courses by lineal feet; all sills and lintels or ashler by superficial feet, and no wall less than 18 inches thick.

PRICES QUOTED THE WM. WINDHORST DRY GOODS CO. BY RELIANCE TEXTILE AND DYE WORKS CO., BOTH OF CINCINNATI, OHIO, FOR CONDITIONING SALVAGE, DEC. 4TH, 1907.

Linens	2c	Linings	2c
Toweings	¾c	Dress goods	3c
Buntings	¾c	Outing flannel	1¼c
Crash	¾c	Blankets, cotton	15c
Danish cloth	1¼c	Blankets, wool	25c
Poplar cloth	1¾c	Quilts	12½c
Woolen serge	3c	Comforts	12½c
Canton flannel	1¾c	Cashmeres	1½c
Cotton domestic	1¼c	Mor. sateens	2½c
Wool flannel	2¼c	Sheetings	¾c
Bleached sheeting	1¼c	Ticking	1c
Unbleached sheeting	¾c	Ginghams	1c
Prints	¾c		

Doubling 1c per yard extra.

This stock was conditioned as per the above bid. The author never saw a damaged fire stock put into better condition. Captain Conway and his salvage corps put part of the stock in condition and did grand work.

When iron or machinery has been damaged, dip in the following solution, or apply solution with a brush.

1 part muriatic acid
20 parts kerosene oil
40 parts paraffine oil.

Then when you want to clean them off (this solution will protect from further rust), redip them in paraffine oil and rub off with waste.

A good wash, but expensive, is water with oxalic acid. This is good for knives and saw blades. Let lay in solution about ten minutes, then take out and dip in paraffine oil and rub off.

Black goods, such as hangers, etc. Iron filler thinned with turpentine. This gives a bluish tint. If you want a jet black color, mix in some lampblack ground in oil.

To clean brass goods, dip in oil of vitriol.

RECEIPT FOR LAUNDERING CLOTHES SMOKED BY FIRE.

This receipt by a colored woman, a former slave, owned by the author's father:

"Fust Ah puts the smoked and soiled clothes into a tub of cold watah, into which Ah has already put a handful of common bakin' soda. Then Ah lets 'em soak all night. Next mornin' Ah puts on a boiler of watah, into which Ah poah's a cup of kerosene oil, two-thirds of a bar of soap and a handful of washing powder. Ah lets them clothes boil in that watah a while, then Ah takes 'em out and washes 'em. They come out clean, too."

WHAT CHICAGO BUILDING COST.

COMPILED BY HARRY FOX,

Cook Co. Manager, Milwaukee Mechanics Ins. Co.

Up-to-date table for estimating the approximate value of buildings at present 1915 prices for labor and materials.

Good judgment must be exercised in estimating values by taking into consideration the manner of construction and the quality of materials put into the building.

Cost of buildings new at price in cents per cu. ft. in structure. To obtain cu. ft. multiply length of building by the width and then by the average height, measuring from the bottom of basement to square of roof.

DWELLINGS.

FRAME.—Shingle roof, pine floors and trim, two coats of paint inside and outside, no bath room or furnace, plain finish........8c to 10c

BRICK.—Same class ....10c to 12c

FRAME.—Shingle roof, hardwood floor in hall and parlor, bath, furnace, fair plumbing..9c to 11c

BRICK.—Same class, composition roof...................11c to 13c

FRAME.—Shingle roof, hardwood floor and trim on first floor, pine floor and Georgia pine trim on second floor, good plumbing, furnace, artistic design, some interior ornamentation, well painted..13c to 15c

HANDSOME BRICK.—Pressed brick and stone trim front, artistic design, hardwood floors and trim throughout, good plumbing, furnace, tasty interior ornamentation, very desirable residence......14c to 17c

FIRST-CLASS BRICK.—The kind you find on the boulevards, pressed brick and stone trimmed front, hot water or steam heat, elaborate design and interior ornamentation, hardwood floors and trim throughout, best of plumbing.................................17c to 22c

PALATIAL STONE FRONT.—Quarter-sawed oak or mahogany trim, hardwood floors, steam heat, extra plumbing, very artistic design, every modern convenience.............................25c to 35c

BARNS.

PRIVATE BARNS—FRAME—Shingle roof, painted, good foundations, stall and bins complete....................................5c to 10c

PRIVATE BARNS—BRICK.—Composition roof, stalls and bins complete ....10c to 12c

FLATS.

(Complying with City Ordinance.)

FRAME.—Shingle or composition roof, hardwood floors and trim, good plumbing, furnace, artistic design, well painted........10c to 12c

BRICK.—Pressed brick front, composition roof, good plumbing, furnace, bath, Georgia pine or oak trim, hardwood floors....12c to 15c

FIRST-CLASS BRICK.—Pressed brick and stone front, hot water or steam heat, elaborate design, interior ornamentation, hardwood throughout, best of plumbing.................................15c to 18c

PALATIAL STONE FRONT.—Quarter-sawed oak or mahogany trim and hardwood floors, steam heat, extra plumbing, artistic design, every modern convenience, marble entrance..........20c to 30c

CHURCHES AND SCHOOLS.

FRAME ....10c to 12c
BRICK ....12c to 14c
STONE ....15c to 25c
        If slate or metal roof, add ¼c per foot to above.

STORES AND FLATS.

        (Stores 1st floor and flats above, 2 to 3 stories in height.)
        FRAME.—Composition roof, pine floors and trim, bath, furnace, fair plumbing ....10c to 12c
        BRICK.—Pressed brick, stone trimmings, hardwood floors and trim, good plumbing, hot water or steam heat...............12c to 15c

STORE BUILDINGS.

        (Stores and Lofts, 2 to 3 stories in height.)
        FRAME.—Ordinary construction, gravel or metal roof, hydraulic elevator ....6c to 8c
        BRICK.—Same construction ....7c to 10c
        REINFORCED CONCRETE ....12c to 15c
        REINFORCED CONRETE.—Above 3 story, heavy carrying capacity ....17c to 20c

BUILDINGS OF LARGE AREA.

        (Mill Construction)
        BRICK AND STONE.—For factories and warehouses....7c to 9c
Smaller area ....10c to 12c

FIREPROOF OFFICE BUILDINGS.

        BRICK AND STONE.—Steel construction, every modern convenience, measuring from floor to basement to top of roof, omitting courts ....35c to 55c

FIREPROOF STORES, FACTORIES AND WAREHOUSES.

        BRICK, STONE AND STEEL CONSTRUCTION—Modern Equipment ....18c to 22c

FIREPROOF APARTMENT BUILDINGS.

        BRICK, STEEL AND CONCRETE CONSTRUCTION.—Modern conveniences ....20c to 25c

ESTIMATES OF DEPRECIATION.

        The figures given above are for new buildings. To ascertain the present value, a discount between old and new buildings should be made as follows:
        BRICK, occupied by owner, ½ to 1 per cent. per year.
        FRAME, occupied by owner, 1 to 2 per cent. per year.
        BRICK, occupied by tenant, 1¼ to 1½ per cent. per year.
        FRAME, occupied by tenant, 1½ to 2½ per cent. per year.
        These figures for depreciation are to include buildings where ordinary repairs have been made. If extraordinary repairs have been made the discount should not be so heavy. Exercise good judgment as to depreciation, as no accurate rule can be established, and when you have determined what the present worth of the building is, insure it for about 80 per cent. of same in the old reliable.

COST OF LABOR AND MATERIAL

For Estimating Repairs to Buildings.

        NOTE.—The following prices for lumber and material are the retail prices, labor being figured at Contractor's prices for repair work. A space 10x10 feet constitutes one square.

WALL PAPER.

Cost of hanging, 15c to 30c per single roll for ordinary work, according to quality of paper.

Three and one-half rolls will cover one square.

PLASTERING.

Two coats of plastering repair work cost 50c per sq. yd.

Three-coat work costs 60c per sq. yd.

For cement plaster add 10c per sq. yd. extra.

Small jobs add for cartage.

Plaster labor costs 75c per hour, plus contractor's profit.

Plasters' helper costs 45c per hour.

Lathers' labor $6.00 per day of 8 hours.

NOTE.—To ascertain the number of yards of plaster, multiply the length of ceiling by the width. Do the same with each side wall and add all together, divide by nine and the result will be the number of yards. Make no deductions for openings unless very large.

PLUMBING.

30 gal. iron boiler, connected	$20.00 each
Enameled sinks, 18x24 in., connected	15.00 each
5 foot enameled bathtub, connected	35.00 each
Porcelain washout closet with tank, connected	30.00 each
Hopper closet, connected	20.00 each
Laundry tubs, 2 divisions, cement, connected	35.00 each
Wash bowls, plain marble slabs, connected	25.00 each
Brass faucets, put on	2.00 each
Plated faucets, put on	2.25 each

6 in iron soil pipe, put in, $1.00 per running foot.

4 in iron soil pipe, put in, 60c per running foot.

Plumbing labor costs $6.40 per day of eight hours, plus contractor's profit.

SEWERS.

6 in. sewer, ordinary digging, laid with proper drain, well cemented, 50c per lineal foot.

Traps, $1.50 each.

Elbows, $1.25 each.

Catch basins, 5x6, stone cover, $15.00.

ELECTRIC WIRING.

To estimate the cost of electric wiring in ordinary buildings ascertain the number of lights and multiply same by $3.00; conduit, $5.00.

GAS PIPING.

To estimate cost of gas piping in ordinary buildings, ascertain the number of lights and multiply by $2.50.

Gas pipe put in, connected, 20c per running foot.

Gas fitters' labor costs $6.50 per day of eight hours.

ROOFING.

Gravel roof, 3-ply, $3.50 per square.

Gravel roof, 4-ply, $4.00 per square.

Gravel roof, 5-ply, $4.25 per square.

Slate roof, ordinary black slate, $10.00 to $12.00 per square.

Slate roof, fancy green and red, $15.00 to $30.00 per square.

Best galvanized iron roofing, standing seams, $9.00 to $12.00 per square, painted.

Best tin roofing, standing seams, $8.00 to $11.00 per square, painted.

Tile roofing, $12.00 to $15.00 per square, according to design.

METAL CEILINGS.

Fancy metal ceilings with cornice cost $8.00 to $12.00 per square.

Corrugated iron ceiling, $6 00 to $7.00 per square.

CARPENTRY.

Carpenter labor costs 70c per hour, plus contractor's profit. Eight hours constitute one day.

13/16x5¼ in. common yellow pine flooring costs $25.00 per M., 13/16x3¼—$23.00 per M.

1x4 or 1x6 in. white Norway C. pine flooring costs $40.00 per M. Labor for laying 6 in. pine flooring, $2.00 per square; 4 in., $2.50 per square.

13/16x2¼ in. face clear maple flooring costs $47.00 per M. Labor for laying 2¼ in. face maple flooring, smooth for oil finish, $3.50 to $4.50 per square.

13/16x2¼ in. plain white oak flooring costs $60.00 per M.

13/16x2¼ in. faced quarter-sawed white oak flooring costs $94.00 per M.

Labor for laying and scraping oak floor, 2¼ in. face, for wax or varnish, $7.00 to $8.00 per square.

Smoothing and scraping oak floors alone costs $2.50 to $3.50 per square.

Base, pine, 2 member moulded, put down, 8c per running foot; 3 member, 12c.

4 and 6 in. clear Northern pine beveled siding costs $32.00 per M.

4 and 6 in. clear Washington redwood beveled siding costs $33.00 per M.

4 and 6 in. clear Washington spruce beveled siding costs $26.00 per M.

Labor for putting on siding, $2.75 per square for 4 to 6 in. siding; for narrow mitred siding, $3.75 per square.

Labor for putting on shingles, $2.50 to $3.00 per thousand shingles.

Best grades of clear red cedar shingles cost $4.00 per thousand.

Common No. 2 pine doors, complete with frames, placed in position, with hardware, not painted, cost $8.00 to $12.00 each.

Fancy oak front doors complete, placed in position, with hardware, cost $15.000 to $25.00 each, according to style.

Oak veneered doors, 1¾ in. pine core, 20c to 35c per square foot for door only. Labor and hardware extra.

Oak veneered doors, as above, complete with frame, placed in position, with hardware, $14.00 to $18.00 each.

Mantles—Hardwood, artistic design, complete with mirror and grate, set $45.00 to $65.00 each.

Grilles—Fancy oak, $1.25 to $1.75 per lineal foot set.

Windows—With sash, frame, casing, cords, weights complete, put in, $9.00 to $12.00 each. If hardwood frame and trim, with sash, $12.00 to $14.00.

Stairs—Common oak, for dwellings, without rail, $2.50 per riser, labor included.

Stair Rail—Oak, moulded design, 30c to 35c per running foot, labor included.

Stair Rail—Pine moulded design, 15c to 25c per running foot, labor included.

Balusters—Pine, fancy turned 12c to 15c each; oak 15c to 30c each, labor included.

Newels—5 in. quarter-sawed oak, moulded cap $6.00 to $9.00; plain oak $5.00 to $7.00; pine $4.00 to $6.00 each, labor included.

Porches—Front, frame, ordinary construction, 6 to 7 feet wide, shingle roof, ceiled, square or turned columns, frieze and cornice, balusters at floor, complete, $8.00 to $10.00 per front foot measure, 12x12 in. stone pillars under porches, $1.00 per lineal foot.

PAINTING AND GLAZING.

Painting, two-coat work, costs 20c per sq. yd.

Painting, three-coat work, costs 25c per sq. yd.

Painters' labor cost 70c per hour, plus contractor's profit.

Calcimining costs $3.00 to $5.00 per room for small rooms and 80c per square for large rooms.

NOTE.—To ascertain the number of yards painted surface, multiply the length by the width, in feet, and divide by nine, and the result will be the number of yards.

Lattice work and stair balusters are counted double.

For reglazing old work, add 20 to 50 per cent. to cost of glass, according to quantity set.

STONE WORK.

Common rubble stone, 100 cu. ft. to the cord, costs, laid in wall, $20.00 to $25.00 per cord, according to location and necessary hauling.

Rock face, 4 in. Bedford stone for facing, furnished and set in wall, costs $1.75 to $2.25 per square foot face measurement.

Mason labor costs $6.00 per day, plus contractor's profit.

Mason helper costs 40c per hour, plus contractor's profit.

BRICK WORK.

Common brick, furnished and laid in 12 in. wall, costs $14.00 per M. wall count.

Pressed brick, for facing, laid in wall, colored mortar, rodded joints, add to cost of brick $10.00 to $20.00 per thousand for laying, according to character and design of front.

CEMENT BLOCK WALLS.

12 in. block walls cost about the same as 12 in. common brick wall, laid, less 25 per cent. of the cost of brick for similar wall.

Concrete basement walls cost 28c per cubic foot, wall measurement.

Cement sidewalk costs 12c to 15c per square foot.

Cement basement floors cost 10c per square foot.

CHIMNEYS.

Ordinary single flue chimneys cost $1.00 per lineal foot. For double flue $1.75 per lineal foot.

INTERIOR MARBLE WORK.

(For Wainscoting and Floors in Apartment Houses and Office Buildings.)

Wainscoting, Italian, white, $1.00 per sq. ft. set.

Wainscoting, English Vein Italian, white, $1.05 per sq. ft. set.

Wainscoting, Tennessee Marble, 80c per sq. ft. set.

Wainscoting, Vermont white marble, 95c per sq. ft. set.

Wainscoting, Vermont green marble, $1.60 per sq. ft. set.

Floors—Marble tile, 80c per sq. ft. laid; mosaic, 75c per sq. ft. laid.

TO ESTIMATE COST OF RADIATION PER CUBIC FOOT.
(Direct Radiation.)

Steam Heat—Allow 1 foot radiation for each 50 cu. ft. of space. Figure radiation at 72c per radiation foot.

Hot Water Heat—Allow 1 foot radiation for each 30 cu. ft. of space. Figure radiation at 75c per radiation foot.

The above is for average rooms. If rooms have extraordinary large window exposure, increase radiation. If smaller window space than average, decrease radiation.

Be careful in the distribution of radiation, as the success of a heating plant depends largely upon arrangement and location of radiators.

FROM REPORT OF NATIONAL BOARD OF FIRE UNDERWRITERS.

Some Important Losses on Fire Proof Buildings.

	Value	Damage Per Ct.
Pittsburg, Pa.—Holmes estate, owners six story department store building, exposure fire, May 3, 1897	$386,980	57

Pittsburg, Pa.—Holmes Estate, owners 4-story building, mercantile purposes, 1st and 2d, offices above. Exposure fire May 3, 1897 120,322   **49**

New York City—Home Life Ins. Co., owners 15 story building, mercantile purposes, 1st, offices above. Exposure fire, Dec. 4, 1898. 900,000   **22**

Pittsburg, Pa.—Holmes Estate, owners, 6-story Department Store building. Internal fire, April 7, 1900 475,000   **32**

New York City—American Fine Arts Society, 4-story Art School building. Internal fire, May 8, 1901 185,000   **11**

Chicago, Ill.—Iroquois Theatre. Internal fire, Dec. 30, 1903.

    Building 311,114   **18**

    Scenery **100**

    Other contents **70**

Patterson, N. J.—City Hall, 4-story detached office occupancy. Conflagration Feb. 9, 1902 310,183   **58**

New York City—Broadway Improvement Co., owners, 8-story mercantile building. Internal fire, Feb. 26, 1903................. 300,000   **23**

Rochester, N. Y.—Granite Building Co., owners, 12-story department store, 1st and 2d, offices above. Exposure fire, Feb. 29, 1904.. 600,000   **41**

Rochester, N. Y.—Granite Building Co., owners, 7-story stable and storage, unprotected iron. Exposure fire, Feb. 29, 1904.

Rochester, N. Y.—Granite Building Co., owners, 7-story wholesale dry goods and department store, unprotected iron. Exposure fire, Feb. 20, 1904 247,360   **92**

Baltimore Conflagration, February 7, 1904—

    Calvert Building Co., owners, 12-story office building 634,075   **57**

    National Bank of Commerce, owners, 1-story bank building 92,000   **50**

    Union Trust Co., owners, 11-story bank and office building 348,795   **61**

    International Trust Co., owners, 1-story bank building 120,364   **70**

Herald, owners, 6-story newspaper and printing office building 217,131   59

Chesapeake and Potomac Telephone Co., owners, 7-story office and telephone building 115,000   39

National Mechanics Bank, owners, 4-story and attic office building................. 156,854   95

National Union Bank, owners, 1-story bank building 119,744   54

Merchants National Bank, owners, 7-story bank and office building................. 405,000   54

Continental Trust Co., owners, 16-story office building 1,028,461   65

Calvert Building Co., owners, "Equitable Building," 10-story office building........1,037,965   74

Baltimore Trust Co., owners, Maryland Trust Co., building 10-story bank and offices 404,000   60

Firemen's Ins. Co., owners, 6-story office building 106,000   52

The insurance loss ratio to values insured on all classes of property in the Baltimore conflagration was 90 per cent.—that is, the total value of all classes of property involved in the conflagration was $37,382,426.49, covered by $32,245,273.39 insurance, on which the losses paid amounted to $29,074,358.51.

Excluding seven of the largest and best fire-proof buildings involved, the loss ratio to insurance involved, was 90.4 per cent.

The insurance loss on these seven buildings was 88.4 per cent. The loss ratio to insurance involved on these seven fire-proof buildings and sixteen other so-called fire-proof buildings, was 76.3 per cent. Loss ratio to insurance involved, excluding these seven fire-proof buildings, and the sixteen so-called fire-proof buildings, was 92 per cent. Loss ratio to value of the twenty-three fire-proof and so-called fire-proof buildings referred to, was 56.4 per cent.

WHAT SOME FIREPROOF BUILDINGS COST PER CUBIC FOOT.

City	Building	Date Built	Cost per Cubic Foot
Memphis	Memphis Trust Bldg.	1905	$0.349
Cincinnati	Traction Bldg.	1903	3906
Cincinnati	First National Bank	1904	31779
Boston	Chamber of Commerce	1892	32
Boston	Exchange Bldg.	1891	32
Chicago	Borden Block	1891	15
Chicago	Stock Exchange	1893	33
Chicago	Rookery	1893	32
Chicago	Masonic Temple		58
New York	Herald Bldg.	1893	46
Cincinnati	Chamber of Commerce		26
San Francisco	Croker Bldg.		63
Chicago	Auditorium		36

The following shows the itemized construction cost of a fireproof office building in the insurance district of New York City, built in the panic year 1893, when both labor and material were to be had at low cost—at least forty per cent. lower than at this time, December, 1904. The cost per cubic foot (from the bottom of the concrete foundation to the top of the roof) was 40 cents.

Mason's work	$ 80,000.00
Granite	4,588.00
Terra Cotta	8,185.00
Steam heating	23,278.00
Carpenter work	40,041.00
Iron work	89,340.00
Exterior marble	43,325.00
Interior marble	39,112.00
Plumbing	16,535.00
Elevators	21,000.00
Electric lighting, etc.	22,311.50
Plastering	9,596.00
	$397,311.50

Table No. 2.— PROPORTION OF VALUE AND FIRE DAMAGE IN THE VARIOUS ITEMS OF CONSTRUCTION FOR EIGHT FIREPROOF OFFICE BUILDINGS IN THE BALTIMORE CONFLAGRATION.

OLA	Union Trust A%	Union Trust B%	Cert. A%	Cert. B%	M. A%	M. B%	Continental A%	Continental B%	Equitable A%	Equitable B%	Mer. Nat. Bank A%	Mer. Nat. Bank B%	Maryland Trust A%	Maryland Trust B%	C. & P. Tel. Co. A%	C. & P. Tel. Co. B%	Average A%	Average B%
Foundations																		
Excavations and bank filling	5.62	1.4	4.37	.3	7.25	4.6									4.3	3.9	5.5	2.5
Shoring banks and holding adjacent property	1.22		1.25		2.07										4.3	3.9	2.21	.97
Foundations, footing and concrete or caps	4.4	3.2	1.6		5	3.8											1.6	
The Stone and granite or caps			.74														3.88	2.38
Sidewalks and curbs	.13		.13	10.06	.18	37.3											.156	23.68
Steel Frame	13.6	1.03	14.54	1.2	19.52	30.67	9.9	9.4	9.00	42.5	10.1	11.6	11.4	6.3	17.5		13.195	12.93
Material	11.79		11.79	.5													11.79	.5
Erection	1.7		1.7	.68													1.7	.68
shop drawings	.49		.49	3.57													.49	3.57
Painting	.24		.24														.24	
reaming	.32		.32														.32	
Mason Work	23.76	57.2	28.50	45.6	34.15	58	30.15	42.5	31.31	69	37.2	50	29.94	66	35.5	36.7	31.31	53.125
Brick—common	0.1	31.8	6.59	5.6	11.21	28.75							8.98	55.6	13.5	33.4	8.25	81.05
" face or pressed			1.82	48.6	1.26	100											1.54	74.8
" enameled			.86	7.1													.86	7.1
" cleaning and pointing			.21	65.9													.21	65.9
Terra cotta	4.34	1.00	7.61	73.6	5.07	100	3.9	72.2	2.5	68.8			3.5	75.4			4.48	81.6
Stone	2.55	95	4.22	47.5	9.34	40.81	4.05	58.4	7.4	61.5	27.3	52.4	8.7	100	9.4	61.4	9.12	64.5
Marble									.83	63.8							.88	63.8
Mill lining or furring	.77	50							1.8	00							1.28	75
Floor arches roof, etc	3.87	40	4.73	7.5	3.68	50	6.8	55	6.6	94.2	3.4	69.7	3.6	70.5	6.6	27.6	4.91	51.7
concrete filling for floor arches	.67	80	.58	66.66	.49	100									6.0	14.5	1.91	65.3
Partitions	1.56	80	1.88	89.2	3.1	98.5											2.18	89.2
" cleaning and wrecking	1.88	80																
Safety deposit vaults													5.16	.461			6.38	0.88
Miscellaneous scaffolding, shoring and wrecking					7.6		7.6	1.3	.48	100	6.5	86.5					.48	100
this masonry					7.8	48.4	7.8	48.4	11.70	51.8							8.66	45.4

Item	19.18	56.7	24.54	82	15.96	82.5	18.69	78.5	26.71	52	15.23	45.5	21.23	55	12.69	53	19.27	62.52
Equipment	19.18	56.7	24.54	82	15.96	82.5	18.69	78.5	26.71	52	15.23	45.5	21.23	55	12.69	53	19.27	62.52
Elevator plant	7.6	83.3	7.08	61.6	8.16	77.4	5	61.01	5.2	67.4	3.8	50.2	7.7	86.9	4.02	44.3	6.15	54.01
Plumbing	3.26	96.4	3.55	88.9	2.61	91.2	4.13	75.9	8.5	92.9	3.7	60.3	8.4	63.3	3.36	71.9	8.48	80.1
Heating system	4.6	89	7.06	91	3.54	80	4.2	73.9	8.8	89.6	2.2	49.9	6.7	89.7	4.15	85.8	4.5	62.8
Boiler plant										29.7							1.9	29.7
Lighting, wiring and fixtures	2.54	80.8	5.05	98.4	1.38	100	2.03	98.08	1.9	100	1.6	59.3			1.16	90.6	2.38	90.9
Dynamos, switchboards, etc.									2.18	35.2							2.18	85.2
Fixtures	.7	100	.49	100			1.05	75.9	.65	78.7			3	100			.72	88.65
Mail chute	.48	98	.27	88.3	.28	91.7	.18	100			.33						.82	88
Filter plant			.44	9.								100	.43	100			.44	9
Refrigerating plant																	.93	70.8
...es																	1.9	72.4
fit and safe drs							.98	70.09	1.9	72.4	3.6	20.2					2.11	57.1
Flash signals and ...s																	.54	100
Turkish baths							.63	93.9	.68	100							.68	100
Furniture							.54	100	5.4	73.5							5.4	73.5
Piping high pressure									.70	43.4							.70	43.4
Trim and Finish	36.06	98	27.56	84	22.83	85.5	36.20	94	28.78	89.5	36.63	68	26.89	82	25.04	72.5	29.99	84.18
Carpentry—Rough	2.03	100	2.59	98.1	.22	100	10.9	99.6	9.8	99.4	5.4	72.7	7.9	100	1.6	94.7	5.05	96.1
" Finish	5.27	99.2	4.31	98.4	.51	100									5.7	96.9	8.94	97.3
Hardware—Rough	.74	90.7	.29	72.5	1.7	100	.88	100	.64	98.5	.9	81.1	1.16	94.5	1.95	87.2	.99	89.2
" Finish		99.5	.88	98.2	5.1	100											1.88	99.4
Marble	6.74	97.8	7.11	97.6	1.42	100	10.5	94.5	5.4	90.2	10.1	75.8	6.2	100	2.8	96.9	6.28	98.2
Mic	.14	100			1.90	97.7					1.2	77.4					1.11	91.7
...lass	1.44	100	.9	99.1	1.18	100					1.4	895			.39	100	1.23	98.3
Slate							1.4	100	7.5	100								
Plastering	2.94	98.6	3.05	97.4	2.96	100	2.9	100	4.21	100	3.7	69.2	2.7	100	1.4	100	2.98	95.65
Fresco	.88	100															.88	100
Paint and Varnish	2.00	99.4	1.34	100	1.45	100	2.9	100	1.6	100	1.4	00	2.9	100	1.5	100	1.88	99.9
Office partitions (wood and glass)	2.65	97.5															2.65	97.5
Ornamental iron	9.70	94.5	5.87	37.1	4.62	36.1	6.4	76.6	5.0	63.8	10.5	51.3	5.5	21.7	6.8	25.9	6.79	60.8
Skylights and sheet metal	.71	70	1.22	40.4	1.54	95.8	.37	57.7	.63	61.3	.88	21.6	.53	100	2.4	87.7	1.02	66.75
Office grill	.5	100			.19	100					1.2	34.8					.68	78.1
General Expenses	1.83	70	1.92	5.42			5.17	42	4.31	77	.36	73.97	11.2	100	6.94	14	4.53	61.59
Miscellaneous	1.88	70	1.92	5.42			.27	82.2	.67	100	.36	73.97	10	60	1.94	49.3	2.43	62.56
Architects' fees, etc							4.9	89.07	1.82	45.6			1	100	5.0		3.31	28.22
Permits, out survey, or fire													.2	100			1.2	100
charging out this or fire									1.82	100							1.82	100

A = Ratio of and value of each item to the total sound value of building.
B = Ratio of fire damage on each item to the sound value of same ... nt.

TOPICAL INDEX

TABLE OF CASES

Lightning Source UK Ltd.
Milton Keynes UK
UKHW02f0749141117
312715UK00013B/1272/P